ORGANIZING FOR RESILIENCE

Organizing for Resilience provides a fresh and novel insight into research on how leaders can prepare their organizations to face up to shocks and disruptions in a turbulent and unpredictable world. It provides an analysis of the topic of organizational resilience in a comprehensive and integrative way, with fresh theoretical and research implications as well as important implications for leaders.

The first book to synthesize themes from across a spectrum of resilience using the metaphor of a 'resilience landscape', chapters in Part I are devoted to five analytical levels: individual level resilience; small firms in which major disruption can threaten survival; large firms with disruptions in one part of the organization; large firms facing enterprise-wide disruption; and disruption to a complete community or economic ecosystem of individuals and organizations. Cases and practice insights are presented to bring the topics to life, allowing reflection and debate at each level. In Part II, the construct of the 'resilience landscape' is developed, along with a discussion on leadership for resilience by instilling a resilience mind-set and developing capabilities in relational resilience.

The book is ideally suited to bachelor's and master's degree courses on strategy, organizational behaviour and leadership. PhD and DBA researchers in the field of resilience and strategy will also find the book useful, as will practising consultants and business leaders.

Christopher Williams is Professor in the Strategy and Entrepreneurship Department at NEOMA Business School in France. His research interests include international strategy, innovation in international firms and contexts, and organizational resilience. Before entering academia in 2007, Dr Williams spent two decades in industry, mostly in innovative and international environments. His research appears in journals such as *Asia*

Pacific Journal of Management, International Business Review, Journal of Business Research, Journal of Management, Journal of Management Studies, Journal of World Business and *Research Policy*. He has also published a range of teaching cases on strategy and innovative issues in international contexts with Ivey Publishing and is author of *Venturing in International Firms: Contexts and Cases in a High-Tech World* (Routledge, 2018) and *Management Consultancy for Innovation* (Routledge, 2019).

Jacqueline Jing You is a doctoral graduate from Durham University Business School in the UK. Her research interests include organizational resilience and disruption, inter-organizational relationships and organizational ecosystems. She worked in industry with international companies and as an entrepreneur before her doctoral studies. Jacqueline has published in the *Journal of Sustainable Tourism* and *The Palgrave Handbook of Corporate Sustainability in the Digital Era*. She holds degrees from the University of Shanghai Science and Technology and the University of St Andrews.

ORGANIZING FOR RESILIENCE

Leading and Managing Risk in a Disruptive World

Christopher Williams and Jacqueline Jing You

Routledge
Taylor & Francis Group
LONDON AND NEW YORK

First published 2022
by Routledge
2 Park Square, Milton Park, Abingdon, Oxon OX14 4RN

and by Routledge
52 Vanderbilt Avenue, New York, NY 10017

Routledge is an imprint of the Taylor & Francis Group, an informa business

British Library Cataloguing-in-Publication Data
A catalogue record for this book is available from the British Library

Library of Congress Cataloging-in-Publication Data
A catalog record for this book has been requested

ISBN: 9780367279684 (hbk)
ISBN: 9780367680459 (pbk)
ISBN: 9780429298974 (ebk)

Typeset in Joanna
by Apex CoVantage, LLC

For our families

CONTENTS

PREFACE

At the time of writing, a cursory Google search on the word 'resilience' came up with 191 million hits, while a similar search on the word 'strategy' yielded nearly seven billion hits. It seems the world has been more concerned with "overall plans of action" (i.e. strategy, see Hambrick and Fredrickson (2005)) than it has with "the capacity to recover from adversity" (i.e. resilience, see Fiksel (2006)). There are more sources of information out there shedding light on how to understand our environments, position ourselves appropriately, understand and develop our internal resources and capabilities and combine this knowledge together in a way that will lead to sustainable competitive advantage than there are on what to do when things go wrong.

Unfortunately for strategists, things do go wrong. And they go wrong with alarming frequency and intensity and in spite of the best intentions from the world of top-level plans and grand ideas. To list the number of private sector firms that have failed to survive would be an impossible task and fill up all the pages of this book and countless more. Check out any business news website on any day of the week and you will find stories of firms fighting for their lives. And public sector organizations fail too, although they are sometimes bailed out by their governments using taxpayers' money or merged into other forms and structures. Non-governmental not-for-profit organizations and charities also sometimes completely fail and disappear off the face of the Earth. In all these types of situations, the strategic intent of the organization was ultimately not realized. People ended up losing money, jobs, reputations and worse.

This book is motivated in large part by what we perceive as an imbalance between strategic thinking on the one hand and resilience thinking on the other. If resilience is about coping with shocks and difficulties once a strategy has been established, why is there not more in strategic thinking about how capabilities for resilience come about and how they are deployed? Perhaps resilience has been thought of as a rather boring topic in comparison to the seductive world of setting visions and plotting a path to future glory. Perhaps resilience has been seen as an operational, psychological or even engineering type of issue that doesn't merit the same strategic limelight. Perhaps it has always been part of strategic analysis but somewhat hidden underneath and among other constructs.[1]

Resilience is not a word that strategists should be frightened of. It should be front and foremost in the minds of those who set strategy for an organization. During our own work in international and entrepreneurial firms we experienced countless situations in which our company's strategy was challenged by disruptions and disturbances. Some of these shocks were external, but some originated internally. What they had in common was that they adversely affected the company's ability to execute its strategy and perform. Examples include a new professional services team that failed to win any new clients and was disbanded after two years; the effects of competitors' technologies that took market share; allegations of cooking the books that distracted employees from their work and undermined trust in leaders; mergers and acquisitions that culminated in culture clashes that precipitated an exodus of employees; poor product development choices that led to financial losses; economic downturns that led to financial losses; outsourcing decisions that delayed product development; and,

1 Some have made clear connections between strategy and resilience. Carmeli and Markman (2011), for instance, examined 1,000 years of data on the history of Rome, linking resilience and strategy explicitly. There are generic strategies (capturing new segments and governing them effectively) that underpin organizational resilience.

more recently, a global pandemic that caused a lockdown-induced panic and strategic U-turn by a university's leadership team.[2] Any CEO, practising manager or consultant could undoubtedly give you countless examples of disruptions and traumas faced by their organizations. If you have experience of organizational life you will be able to recall many examples yourself.

Most of these experiences do not make headline news. Most are relatively small scale. However, some cases do become newsworthy and make the headlines very quickly: think of British Airways' IT problems on one day in 2019 that caused over a hundred flights to be cancelled and another two hundred to be delayed, or drones flying over Gatwick Airport in the UK in 2018 that led to the closure of the airport. Others can cost firms billions of dollars (or equivalent): think of BP's Deepwater Horizon catastrophe in 2010, the Olympus Corporation fraud scandal in Japan in 2011, or the failure of the Euro Disney venture outside Paris in the early 1990s. And yet others still can cost the organization its existence: think of rogue traders like Nick Leeson who brought down Barings Bank in 1995, the collapse of Enron in 2001, the closure of airline and travel companies such as Monarch Airlines (2017) and Thomas Cook (2019), or the bankruptcy of Kodak (2012). Still other cases can result in irreparable damage to a complete industry or economy: think of the Austrian wine scandal in 1985 when it was discovered (in Germany) that certain Austrian sweet wine companies were illegally adding diethylene glycol (an antifreeze ingredient) to make their wines appear sweeter. The Austrian wine industry has not yet fully recovered. Or the COVID-19 coronavirus outbreak that resulted in whole countries being put in lockdown and a complete halt to normal economic activity across the world. None of the internal and external disruptions that led to these outcomes were anticipated in the *initial* strategy of the organizations involved. If they had been anticipated, one would hope that the leaders of the organization would have taken steps to prevent them having an impact.

2 "Durham University rethinks virus teaching plan", BBC News Online, 22 April 2020, www.bbc.co.uk/news/uk-england-tyne-52387360, accessed 13 May 2020

Sadly, many of these stories have profound implications for humans, society and the environment. The COVID-19 outbreak killed millions of people. The Deepwater Horizon explosion resulted in the deaths of 11 workers and the worst environmental disaster in US history. The collapse of Monarch Airlines led to the largest peacetime repatriation of UK citizens in history: over 110,000 people were left stranded abroad. Diethylene glycol was detected in amounts that could have been lethal to humans. While Nick Leeson spent time in prison his wife divorced him. It is not just entrepreneurs, shareholders and owners that suffer as a result of these disruptions. The suffering extends to a wide array of human and social stakeholders as well as the natural world.

Some argue that the world has become more disruptive than ever, that we live in an increasingly 'shocking' context.[3] People refer to disruptive technology, disruptive innovation, new political forces, intensifying terrorist and cyber-threats, the threat (and opportunity) of emerging markets and even a 'new world order'. Such trends shape our world. On the upside, while the world is more populous than ever we live in an era of longer life expectancy. There are more opportunities for people to travel and learn from each other. More now gets invested globally in R&D. At the time of writing, stock markets are at an all-time high. On the flipside, global warming and the adverse effects of climate change are at a peak. There is more plastic in the oceans and pollution in our cities than ever before. Inequality is greater than ever, with wealth concentration at a peak. There are problems with poor quality water, access to sanitation, poverty and child mortality in certain parts of the world. Many have become dissatisfied with the ruling elites. Given this mixed, uncertain and disruptive context, it is extremely difficult for organizations to predict where the next shock will come from.

As the world grows more disruptive, it becomes more vital for organizations to understand resilience. We believe that this understanding holds the key to organizations continuing to perform through adversity. This book is about nurturing and harnessing this understanding. To have a capability that can be described as resilient it is necessary to understand resilience, the different forms it may take, and how it can be used to offset the curse

3 Kimhi (2016), among others, uses the word "traumatic"

of disruptive forces for organizations. We believe that strategy and strategic thinking should have resilience as a core ingredient, as the backbone of the strategic management of the organization. In essence, understanding resilience is an imperative for any strategic leader, not least in order to avoid the suffering that unforeseen disruption can cause to a wide body of human, social and natural world stakeholders as a consequence of the organization's existence within a disruptive context.

This book aims to build on the extensive work of many other scholars from various sub-fields of the broader resilience literature, as well as related literature in strategy, organizational studies and leadership in order to provide a new and relatively easily accessible way of understanding resilience for students, established scholars and strategic managers. At the core of our line of thinking, first, is the notion that it is possible to organize for resilience; it is the way we organize that ultimately matters. And, second, we believe that we can gain the clearest and most relevant understanding of organizing for resilience by first understanding the nature of disruption in context.

We stand alongside many researchers and commentators in the field of resilience and we bring together in one place a reflection of the many studies (conceptual and empirical) that have contributed to this literature. We do this in a structured way by examining both literature and real-world cases in a framework that accounts for the fundamental nature of disruption. This structure has five main components, the first and last being resilience at an individual level and resilience at a collective level. In between these extremities we consider (1) resilience in small firms where the nature of shock can be threaten the survival of the organization, (2) resilience in parts of large firms where the nature of shock can be – to an extent – 'compartmentalized', and (3) shocks to whole large firms that have the potential to inflict fatal harm to the whole organization. These five components are described in more depth in the Introduction, as well as in the whole of Part 1 of the book. Five cases are reproduced in full to correspond to each of these lenses. In Part 2 of the book we reflect on this spectrum of scenarios and develop a new construct relating to the 'Resilience Landscape'. We also discuss broader leadership implications that arise from the model as well as implications for researchers and consultants.

We would like to acknowledge the help and support of numerous people and institutions who have provided support without which this book would not have been possible. To Ivey Publishing we are grateful for permission to publish in full four cases that illustrate the themes in four of the chapters in Part 1 of the book. These are the cases on Expatica Communications: Leading through tragedy; Tesco's Fresh & Easy: Learning from the U.S. exit; Philips NV: Dealing with a global financial crisis; and St Helena: Landing a future for a South Atlantic island. We are grateful to Kirsty Joshua for her insights into the economic development of St Helena and to Giselle Richards, founder of G-Unique Designs on St Helena, for her permission to use the previously unpublished case of her small business in this book. We thank Simon Haslam and the Institute of Consulting for permission to reproduce a segment of our 2018 article in Management Consulting Journal in chapter 8. Others who have inspired and provided insights into the theme of organizing for resilience throughout this project include Keith McCoy, Clare Agutter and Nick Waters, and we thank them for their practice insights.

We hope you enjoy reading this book as much as we enjoyed researching for it and writing it. Whether you are a student or scholar of organizations and their fortunes or a practising manager, leader or consultant living and breathing the day-to-day struggle for survival in an organization, we trust that the book will at least provide some new ideas and insights that will help in the understanding and enacting of 'organizing for resilience'.

Christopher Williams
Jacqueline Jing You
Rouen and Durham, Fall 2020

PART I

LOOKING BACK

RESEARCH AND CASES OF ADVERSITY AND RESILIENCE

1

INTRODUCTION

The suffering factor: why care about organizing for resilience?

Examples of disruptions that have caused tremendous damage and suffering to organizations and their stakeholders abound. Some of these disruptions originate externally to the organization while some spring up from within. Some disruptions are highly newsworthy and gain the attention of the world's press. Many go relatively unnoticed and knowledge about them is confined to people in and around a focal organization. Some disruptions come as a shock to the organization; there is a surprise factor that leaves managers scratching their heads. Others were anticipated: "We knew an earthquake was probable, we just didn't know when."

To think that an organization on this planet will never be confronted by disruption is a ludicrous suggestion. And not only is disruption ubiquitous, its effect can be felt in many different ways. Obrist et al. (2010: 285), citing Chambers (1989: 4), referred to this in terms of loss; this taking "many forms – becoming or being physically weaker, economically impoverished, socially dependent, humiliated or psychologically harmed". As noted by Quarantelli, Lagadec and Boin (2007), negative social phenomena such as natural disasters (e.g. earthquakes, floods, sudden epidemics, tsunamis) and man-made disasters (e.g. hostile inter- and intra-group relationships, conflicts, wars) can be traced back to the times when human beings started living in groups thousands of years ago.

Our working definition of disruption is consistent with the literature (e.g. Bhamra et al., 2011): *an event occurring externally or internally to the organization that has the potential to negatively impact the operating strategy and performance of the organization*. The word disruption has its roots in Latin: *disrumpere*, meaning to break apart, split, shatter, or break into pieces.[1] Organizations are confronted by disruptions all the time and at any time. Quite literally, they are in danger of breaking up and shattering! Each time an organization ignores a disruption it runs the risk of incurring damage, some kind of loss. Its costs are increased and/or its sales are reduced. Its suppliers, clients, staff and owners are harmed and may become less motivated to supply, buy, work for or own the organization. This progressive loss – if left unchecked – ultimately leads to the death of the organization (Hall, 1976).[2]

Organizations simply cannot afford to overlook disruptions and they cannot afford to ignore the need to organize themselves in ways that allow them to cope with disruptions. This coping with disruptions lies at the heart of the definition of resilience. The word also has Latin roots: *resilire*, to rebound or recoil.[3] Bhamra et al. (2011) noted how the concept of resilience across different fields (such as ecology, psychology, strategy, metallurgy and engineering) is more or less consistent; it is about returning a system to a stable state following a disruption. Importantly for our discussion, the concept relates to an organizational system as opposed to a mechanical system. While the emphasis on the outcome is one of stability and

1 Online Etymology Dictionary, www.etymonline.com/word/disruption, accessed 25 May 2020

2 As Lengnick-Hall and Beck (2005: 748) noted: "If a firm does not meet the needs of its environment, competitive performance suffers."

3 Online Etymology Dictionary, www.etymonline.com/word/resilience, accessed 25 May 2020

prevention of loss, the desirable outcome of a stable state does not have to be the same state that the system was in prior to the disruption. Resilience is just as much about moving from one equilibrium to another as it is about returning to the previous state. Linnenluecke's (2017) review of resilience in business and management made a similar observation. Resilience is a "desirable characteristic" (p. 4) that allows an organization to recover in the face of adversity. However, Linnenluecke (2017) showed that different fields have used slightly different conceptualizations and operationalizations over time. This is echoed by Thornley et al. (2015), who described it as a "contested term" (p. 23). Our working definition of resilience aligns with these review works, and is the one put forward by Fiksel in his (2006: 16) essay: resilience is "*the capacity for an enterprise to survive, adapt, and grow in the face of turbulent change*" (italics added).[4]

Organizations need resilience because the alternative is "absurd" (Fiksel, 2006: 16), undesirable (Linnenluecke, 2017) and potentially disastrous (Bhamra et al., 2011). They need the capacity to face up to turbulent change and the shocks that affect their attempts to realize their vision and perform for their stakeholders. Importantly, resilience does not come about by magic or luck. It is a property of the organizational system that needs careful thinking, preparation and execution. Nevertheless, we do not fully understand organizational resilience. There is no unified approach or single theory on how to build this capacity for dealing with turbulent change and disruption (Welsh, 2014). Meanwhile, the world continues to throw up many examples of organizations and economic systems negatively impacted by shocks. As Linnenluecke (2017: 24) noted: "existing theoretical

4 Numerous definitions of resilience exist. Review articles such as Bhamra et al. (2011) provide many examples. The definition we use is consistent with that used by the American Psychological Association: "the process of adapting well in the face of adversity, trauma, tragedy, threats or even significant sources of stress" (Southwick et al., 2014: 5). It is also consistent with recent work in organizational theory, e.g. Williams et al. (2017: 742): "the process by which an actor (i.e. individual, organization, or community) builds and uses its capability endowments to interact with the environment in a way that positively adjusts and maintains functioning prior to, during, and following adversity."

and empirical insights may have not yet uncovered the full range of factors leading to resilience, and . . . existing insights might not be directly applicable or transferable to different or future contexts."

Can we control resilience?

One reason for the lack of a unified approach for understanding how to organize for resilience is that organizations do not always need to internalize resilience. Maybe scholars have failed to fully appreciate this. In other words, one approach could be to outsource resilience and buy in the services of external organizations that are on hand to help out when things go wrong. This may extend to professional services firms such as management consultancy firms that are able to help clients become more resilient in both proactive and reactive ways (Williams and You, 2018). It may have been difficult for the scholarly community to unpick the intricacies of decisions that organizations make when contemplating the externalization of resilience capability. Nevertheless, scholars have acknowledged this aspect. Some have argued that at least part of the solution for how to build the capacity for coping with disruptions is to consider the interconnections an organization has with other stakeholders. Supply chains are highly interconnected and vulnerability in one part of the supply chain can impact organizations in other parts. This raises the question of interdependence in the literature (Linnenluecke, 2017: 25). In the words of Bhamra et al. (2011: 5376): "In an ever-more interconnected world (social, technological and environmental), no organisation can retain a competitive position and survive disruptions as an independent entity."

Williams, You and Joshua's (2020) study of resilience in small businesses on the remote South Atlantic island of St Helena shows how various aspects of relationships with stakeholders have an important role to play in reinforcing small firms' responses to adverse situations. We will refer to the case of St Helena throughout the book, but especially in chapter 2 on resilience at an individual level and chapter 6 on resilience at a collective level.

However, to 'outsource' resilience in the same way that firms may outsource specific capabilities such as back office operations, IT support and development, call centre and service operations could be a tall order. What happens when the external party on which we depend for our resilience is affected by their own set of disruptions? We could be jumping out of the frying pan and into the fire.

The quintessential 'make or buy' decision that organizations face with regards to any capability certainly applies to capabilities that offer the means to deal with disruptions. But the consequences of externalizing transactions can lead to a greater susceptibility to be affected by disruptions! This dilemma cannot be ignored by scholars and practitioners. The question of 'organizing for resilience' is not just an internal one; it extends to the organizational system around any focal organization and the decisions that organizations make to relate and transact with others.

Organizing for resilience as a contingency

Holling (1973) is widely recognized as a ground-breaking article in the field of resilience research. His work was based on ecological systems and how to model them. There was a prominent real-world element to the study, including his assertion that realism is needed to understand resilience in ecological systems. These systems are not deterministic but are affected by random events. He concluded that systems have both resilient and stability properties; these are not one and the same thing. While resilience is "a measure of the ability of . . . systems to absorb changes of state variables", stability is the "the ability of a system to return to an equilibrium state after a temporary disturbance" (Holling, 1973: 17). Systems can be high in resilience but low in stability. Decades later, Holling's ideas were to have an important influence beyond ecology and the natural world in a wide array of areas including rural studies, safety science, sustainable tourism and organization and management studies.

It is the latter that we are most interested in, the field of organization and management studies. Here we note how the literature has produced a multitude of insights into ways in which organizations deal with external disruptions and threats. The literature also provides insights into the situational context in which one type of response might be more useful than another. For instance, Staw et al. (1981) discussed the threat-rigidity thesis; under intense environmental pressure and threat, some organizations become more rigid, reducing their information processing and constricting their control. While this is often a result of prior learning (that the rigidity response worked in the face of earlier threats), when the threat involves a change that is radical in nature, it becomes a maladaptive response that can lead to failure. Staw et al. (1981) noted the example of the death of the *Saturday Evening Post* magazine in 1969 that was attributable in part to the response to a drop in circulation of raising its prices (Hall, 1976). However, for incremental environmental changes, rigidity can be useful. Meyer et al. (1990) noted the importance of adaptability under conditions of discontinuous changes in an industry. Their study stressed that when a whole industry order is overturned by radical change, there is no new equilibrium to be found. Incremental adaptation is not as important as is a need to experiment, including forming new exploratory inter-organizational relationships (sometimes across industry boundaries). Lengnick-Hall and Beck (2005) examined the differences between adaptive fit and robust transformation in an important review and reassessment of the literature on how organizations deal with uncertainty and surprise. Adaptive fit is the ability of an organization to survive in the face of a complex and threatening environment by choosing an organizational response that is suited (i.e. fits) with the nature of the environmental challenge (Chakravarthy, 1982). Chakravarthy (1982) identified three fit states: (1) an unstable one which is defensive in nature and tries merely to buffer the firm in the short term while not making any fundamental changes to its technology or methods – they tend to ignore the environment; (2) a stable state in which the firm is open to the environment and reacts to it through surveillance mechanisms; and (3) a neutral state in which the firm anticipates change before it occurs and invests proactively in an adaptive ability. According to Chakravarthy (1982), organizations need to choose the appropriate fit depending on the nature of material capacity (defensive, reactive, proactive) and organizational capacity (mechanistic, bureaucratic and organic). Lengnick-Hall and Beck (2005) took the concept of adaptive fit further by arguing that adaptive fit is appropriate in environmental situations that simply move from equilibrium to equilibrium. In situations of more widespread temporary and continuous change, it is robust transformation that is more likely to yield outperformance. Robust transformation is defined as "a deliberately transient, episodic response to a new, yet fluid, environmental condition" (Lengnick-Hall and Beck, 2005: 742). Robust transformation involves a constant reconfiguration of the organization and routines that absorb complexity rather than trying to reduce complexity.

Embedded in this literature is the idea that some organizations are more adept at coping with disruptions than others. Ultimately, this is why we see some fail and some succeed. An organization could be robust in the sense of not really making m(any) changes in response to a disruption (a rigid response in Staw et al.'s (1981) terms or pursuing an unstable state in Chakravarthy's (1982) terms) but its performance may slowly erode. On the other hand, an organization could continually seek to transform itself in a deliberate and routinized way (Lengnick-Hall and Beck, 2005), and this is most suitable in constantly changing and disruptive environments. The world is a pretty heterogeneous place when it comes to how organizations make sense of the environment and decide on a suitable response.

Also embedded in the resilience literature is the notion that threats and disruptions are not just forces that emanate external to the organization; they can also arise within. For example, Meyer's (1982) seminal work on resilience was based on striking hospital physicians. Other well-known examples such as Chernobyl, Exxon Valdez, Bhopal and the Space Shuttle Challenger (Linnenluecke, 2017) all have put a spotlight on internal sources of disruption. Environmental jolts can come from the internal environment as well as the external environment. These can even be encouraged by the organization's own culture, routines and decisions or by the unethical behaviour of leaders (we will refer to this theme in chapter 5). What they do have in common with externally emanating disruptions is that they too can occur in a highly sudden way, presenting a surprise to the organization's stakeholders and management. On some occasions disruptions from both external and internal sources confront management at more or less the same time, and they can be inter-linked. For instance the case of Tesco's Fresh & Easy supermarkets in the USA (Chandrasekhar and Williams, 2014) (one of the cases reproduced in this book) includes labour relations issues that spilled over into local community protests in the parking lots of the Fresh & Easy stores in California.[5] The case of the Fukushima nuclear reactor disaster included both external disruption (the earthquake and subsequent tsunami) as well as the inability of the site to withstand the tsunami in order to cool the reactors. Indeed, the failure

---

5 See www.youtube.com/watch?v=1DHhu37zzuM, accessed 25 February 2020

of backup generators led to the cooling problem and eventual meltdown. These examples illustrate the often complex and inter-dependent nature of external and internal disruption and the need for those who design and lead organization systems to be able to understand the complex nature of equilibrium and change in the specific situation in which its effects are most acutely felt.

Organizing for resilience across levels

With the growth of the academic field of resilience, literature review and summary articles have emerged highlighting various sub-fields as well as the multi-level nature of the phenomenon. Linnenluecke's (2017) review pointed to analysis at individual, group and organizational levels. Bhamra et al. (2011: 5375) opened with the line: "Countries, communities, organisations and individuals are all subject to a diverse and ever changing environment." These authors provided different definitions of resilience from individual, organizational and systems levels (see Table 1 in Bhamra et al. (2011) on page 5379). Southwick et al. (2014) recognized resilience at individual, family, community and cultural levels. According to Southwick et al. (2014), the higher-order non-individual levels matter because they provide contexts that can vary in the extent to which support is offered to an individual in times of crisis.

Literature on resilience at the *individual level* has emphasized the determinants of what makes some people more resilient than others, as well as the consequences for individuals of being able to 'bounce back' from adversity. Rachel Yehuda, quoted in Southwick et al. (2014), raised the possibility that resilience in individuals is a function of biological or genetic make-up. Ann Masten, in the same article, stressed the social systems around an individual as well as the ability to learn from others (or from elders). She also argued for the mastery perspective: individuals are motivated by interacting with the environment in ways that are perceived as successful. Catherine Panter-Brick, also in the same article, talked of the "meaning-making" aspect of broader culture in which an individual's resilience is derived. She put a spotlight on future-orientation – and having a sense of hope – in order for individuals to cope with prior disruptive events. While the purpose of this book is to discuss the challenge of resilience in organizations, clearly we cannot do this without understanding essential aspects of the construct at an individual level. The main reason for this is that people are employees and employees are people: each is a unique and distinct human being.

Literature also exists at a *team* – or *group* – *level*. Alliger et al.'s (2015) work with the NASA Long Duration Space Mission Teams stressed the importance of resilience in teams. It is not just individuals that face disruptions, setbacks and shocks: these can also be felt by a collection of individuals. Kahn et al. (2018), for instance, found that relations between teams fundamentally shape organizational resilience because the mounting strain on one team (e.g. front lines in a hospital) trigger the movement of the team towards other teams for extra resources and capabilities in order to manage adversity. Alliger et al. (2015) noted how teams are ubiquitous in the working world, and that team resources, cohesion and performance can all suffer as the team faces adversity. What is also different at a team level is that a resilient team is not necessarily one that is made up of resilient individuals. Key team processes, such as communication may suffer. Team members may disagree and become engaged in disputes about how to cope with disruption. Alliger et al. (2015) listed a wide range of challenges facing teams that can impact their performance (Table 1, page 177). These include time pressure, hazardous work, missing team members and even angry customers! The authors described a number of ways in which teams can boost their resilience as a team. These include having the right tools to deal with disruptions, having team resilience training, conducting post-challenge debriefs, and having a team culture conducive to resilience. The latter point incorporates a number of useful ideas including maintaining composure during a crisis, keeping an eye on one another in order to support one another, and thanking one another for helping out on challenging situations.

Moving up the spectrum, there is an impressive literature on resilience at an *organizational level* (Lengnick-Hall and Beck, 2005; Lengnick-Hall et al., 2011). Much of the earlier work on adaptive fit was set entirely at an organizational level, for instance examining how firms seek long term survival by finding ways to fit appropriately with a changing environment (Chakravarthy, 1982). Early work also examined evolution and responses of organizations in the context of changing environmental conditions (Meyer et al., 1990). Lengnick-Hall and Beck (2005) shone a spotlight on organizational routines for dealing with complexity and how these influence the response organizations make to disruptive shocks. Gilly et al. (2014) defined organizational resilience as a set of capacities, including a reactive capacity that resists an external event and an active capacity to anticipate events and thus open up towards new development pathways. Furthermore, they pointed out the importance of a 'pivot firm' in linking these two types of resilience, internal and external to the organization; the pivot firm possesses several essential skills needed in response to environmental disturbance. Herbane (2010) drew attention to the need for research on resilience in small businesses, an organization form that is critically important to the modern entrepreneurial economy but which is vulnerable to interruption from crisis. Chrisman et al. (2011) examined resilience in family firms in their Introduction to a Special Issue in *Entrepreneurship: Theory and Practice* on this topic. These types of studies all have in common a shared interest in understanding resilience at an organizational level. It is here we find the capabilities, knowledge and decisions of managers to be critical to the ability of the organization to withstand and cope with disruption and thereby extend the value of organizational membership to all employees and stakeholders.

A number of writers have examined resilience at a broader *systems level* (Fiksel, 2006; Welsh, 2014). It is here we find work that looks at the way complex communities respond to adversity. An example of this is Thornley et al. (2015) who examined resilience in communities in Canterbury, New Zealand, following the devastating earthquakes of 2010 and 2011. The study showed the importance of pre-existing community infrastructure, as well as post-disaster community infrastructure. We also see research on groups of interconnected firms, such as resilience across whole supply chains in an increasingly interconnected world (Christopher and Peck, 2004). Research also examines whole economies. Hill et al. (2008) is a noteworthy illustration of this, examining definitional, operationalization and methodological issues relating the concept of regional economic resilience. Garmestani et al. (2006) examined economic resilience in industries, showing how functional diversity in terms of the size of firms helps industries survive in the face of volatility in employment levels. Others look at whole industrial ecosystems. For instance, Zhu and Ruth (2013) explored the way industrial ecosystems maintain eco-efficient material and energy flows when placed under disruption. What these types of studies have in common is their interest in understanding how whole groups of networked and interconnected individuals and organizations pull through when confronted by existential threats.

Literature explicitly recognizing the *multi-level nature of resilience* has become prominent. Literature of this type emphasizes interactions and interdependencies across levels, a recognition of the complexity of the phenomenon (Bhamra et al., 2011). An example is Fleming and Ledogar's (2008) essay on resilience in aboriginal communities and the impact of culture in a whole community on the resilience of an individual within that community. Kimhi (2016) went further and examined associations between resilience at individual, community and national levels, noting how all levels contribute to well-being at the individual level. Obrist et al. (2010) developed a multi-level model of social resilience,[6] arguing that social fields that need competence to deal with threat exist at household, intermediate and national and international levels, with economic, social and cultural capitals existing at each level.

Our approach in this book

There are some clear messages emanating from this literature that will guide our journey in this book. First, there is a question of contingency and of needing to understand the nature of disruption in the literature. Obrist et al. (2010) made this point in their essay, posing the question: resilience to what? Disruptive events and disasters can come in all kinds of shapes and sizes. They constitute a wide variety of events that generate adversity while requiring organizations to make urgent decisions. These events include social-political changes, terrorist attacks, public crisis (e.g. pandemics), natural disasters, environmental threats, disruptive innovation, cyber-attacks, financial meltdowns and organizational decline, among others. The effects of disruption can also vary wildly (Obrist et al., 2010). Herbane (2010: 53), in a study of four cases of small

6 Defined as "the capacity of actors to access capitals in order to – not only cope with and adjust to adverse conditions (that is, reactive capacity) – but also search for and create options (that is, proactive capacity), and thus develop increased competence (that is, positive outcomes) in dealing with a threat" (Obrist et al., 2010: 289)

businesses in the UK, revealed three dimensions with which managers describe crisis: a lack of control, a lack of cash and a compressed time to respond. Herbane (2010) also highlighted the aspect of whether the crisis was foreseen, i.e. its degree of surprise. This leads to the point that some responses are planned, others need to be ad hoc. Williams, You and Joshua (2020) showed how small businesses on the remote island of St Helena experience a wide range of external shocks that affect their ability to function. This study revealed business owners' mental models of how local stakeholders bolster their resilience in times of need. This type of research illustrates the need to understand the unique conditions and properties of the context in which the affected entity is situated. Williams et al. (2017) discussed adversity in terms of different "situations that hold potential to jeopardize survival" (Williams et al., 2017: 751). These range from those that are ongoing, non-novel and non-surprising (i.e. 'routine' hardship) to those that are novel, temporary, surprising and broad in scope (i.e. discontinuous events). One important theme emerging from this literature is the question of *responding to disruption in ways that are proportionate to the nature of the disruption.*

Second, there is a theme that says 'organizing for resilience' is something that applies at various levels, from an individual person level to a whole economic systems level, and that it is important to examine effects and influences across and between the levels (Fleming and Ledogar, 2008; Kimhi, 2016). Our approach is to scrutinize resilience at different levels of analysis (i.e. a 'spectrum of resilience'). This spectrum ranges from individuals to small firms to large economic ecosystems of organizations and communities. We believe a narrow focus on only one part of the spectrum is problematic because it will exclude the influence that capabilities, knowledge and routines derived from other levels influence the resilient outcome. Hence, a second relevant theme in the literature is the need to *appreciate resilience at different levels of analysis.*

Third, the literature consistently emphasizes the importance of people and the management of people as a key organizing imperative in developing effective resilience (Lengnick-Hall et al., 2011). Herbane (2010) showed that there is an emotional side to crisis affecting a firm. Williams et al. (2017), citing various writers, noted the cognitive and behavioural aspects to resilience. Ultimately, it is people that will have the vision, resolve and knowledge to deal with a variety of different forms of disruption in ways that benefit – collectively – complete organizational units and systems of organizations. Research shows an important role for strategic human resource management in building and maintaining people's attitudes and behaviours that will underpin a capacity for resilience (Lengnick-Hall et al., 2011). Again, we build on this theme in the book: *effective organizing for resilience has people at its core.*

These themes and 'messages from the literature' are taken into consideration throughout the chapters that follow. We do this by considering the question of organizing for resilience at various points in the spectrum of resilience (Part 1 of the book), and then considering the imperative for synthesis and leadership (Part 2). We also draw from in-depth cases that tell the story of disruption, crisis and trauma over time as well as details of response, decision-making and knowledge.

A focus on the phenomenon: cases of resilience in context

While much of the work on resilience is conceptual in nature, we believe in the importance of learning about resilience through cases and examining the phenomenon. Conceptual work tends to review and discuss prior literature (both empirical and conceptual) and generate new insights in terms of models and frameworks for understanding resilience, criticisms of prior literature and suggestions for future work. Back et al. (2016), at an individual level, developed an approach to resilience in palliative care physicians based on prior literature review. Hedner et al. (2011) discussed properties of the resilient entrepreneur. At a firm level, Moore and Manring (2009) examined the literature on sustainability strategies in SMEs, putting a particular focus on networked SME strategies. There are also many conceptual studies that cut across levels. Liu et al. (2017), for instance, built a multi-level conceptual model of resilience involving an individual's core resilience (intra-individual factors), an individual's internal resilience (social and interpersonal skills) and external resilience (socio-economic factors). The latter set of factors include social groups and formal and informal institutions. And as noted above, seminal review works have highlighted interactions between the different levels (Linnenluecke, 2017; Southwick et al., 2014).

Aside from this conceptual format, a large amount of the literature on resilience uses a phenomenological case-based approach or a heavily contextualized approach, such as studying resilience in individuals and organizations in the aftermath of a natural disaster (Lowe et al., 2015), in front-line hospital services (Kahn et al., 2018), or adverse events such as power outages (Parker and Ameen, 2018). Much of this work fits with the call made by resilience researchers to conduct studies over time in order to unpack temporal processes and interactions across levels (King et al., 2016). Williams et al. (2017) emphasized how scholars have looked at crisis as 'process' rather than simply a discrete event. Lowe et al. (2015) examined individual-level resilience in households in New York City post-Hurricane Sandy, which occurred in October 2012. Furniss et al. (2011) used the context of nuclear power plant control room crews to develop insights into resilience at a small team level. At an organizational level, Biggs et al. (2012) used interviews and surveys to understand business enterprise responses to the 2004 tsunami and 2008 political crisis in Thailand. Williams, You and Joshua (2020) studied the resilience of small businesses on the remote island of St Helena to understand resilience from a stakeholder perspective. Botes et al. (2017) used a single case study within the petrochemicals industry to examine buyer–supplier interaction and its indirect effect on supply chain resilience. Dai et al. (2013) examined the survival of foreign multinational enterprise (MNE) subsidiaries in conflict zones around the world, showing how exposure to threats in host countries reduces the likelihood that the subsidiary will survive. At a higher order system level, Carmeli and Markman (2011) used historical data on the story of Rome in their work on resilient strategy. Although one can identify these types of studies examining resilience at different levels of analysis, the key point is they are highly contextualized.

While the review and conceptual articles on resilience are useful in this book, one cannot deny the benefit of studying specific examples of disruption and resilience in context. Our reading of the literature shows there to be a tendency to learn about resilience both directly from single cases as well as from larger sample sizes that were captured in the setting of a specific disruptive context.

The approach we adopt in this book is entirely in line with this tradition. We draw on five cases to aid our learning along the spectrum of resilience in the chapters in Part 1. These cases are reproduced in full. We also use a number of insights kindly provided by practising managers and professionals, as well reflections on other situations. In chapter 2 on resilience at an individual level, we use the case of a single entrepreneur, Giselle Richards, and her small business on the remote South Atlantic island of St Helena to illustrate some key themes in individual resilience. This case is previously unpublished. We also have a very insightful note from Keith McCoy, a mental health practitioner and author. In chapter 3 on resilience in the context of big shocks confronting small firms, we draw on the case of Expatica Communications in The Netherlands and the leadership challenge facing the company when one of the founding owners and managing partners of the company was tragically killed. The sudden event raised an existential question for the remaining partner. We also include an interesting practice insight from Claire Agutter, director of ITSM Zone, an online e-learning business. In chapter 4 on shocks confronting parts of bigger organizations, we examine the case of Tesco's Fresh & Easy investment in the grocery sector in the US. Tesco, a UK headquartered MNE, suffered a huge loss as a consequence of disruptions encountered in the US, resulting eventually in its complete exit from the US. Chapter 5, on shocks that confront entire large organizations, includes the case of Dutch electronics giant Philips and the strategic challenge it faced when dealing with the global financial crisis of 2008. We include here a fascinating practice insight from Nick Waters MBA, a pilot and aviation expert. He makes some telling comments about how airlines attempted to cope – in different ways – with the outbreak of the global pandemic and the global lockdown. And in chapter 6 on resilience at a collective level, we again return to the island of St Helena. Here we use an Ivey case to look at the shock facing the island when a newly built airport failed to produce the desired economic benefits. We also include a practice insight of a wonderful example of relational resilience on the island in response to the global lockdown and the risk of coronavirus and COVID-19 arriving on the island. Throughout Part 1 of the book we review key literature on each of the thematic areas of resilience, discuss these in light of the related case, and then reflect and draw conclusions and learning points.

Much of the literature we review and the cases we use are set in the private sector, in various countries and industries. However, we do recognize the vital importance of organizing for resilience in the public sector and in social enterprises. The pressures in these sectors may be quite different, but they are very real. There will, for instance, be greater dependence on government budgets, and focus on volunteering activities and fund-raising strategies. We believe much of the learning and understanding about organizing for resilience that we glean from studies and cases in the private sector are also transferable to the public sector and social enterprises.

In Part 2, we have three chapters that bring together the ideas from Part 1 in new ways. First, in chapter 7 we define and discuss the concept of a 'Resilience Landscape'. This concept is essential for anyone wanting to understand what it means to organize for resilience. It is a landscape view that covers detection of disruptive shocks across all levels and in both internal and external domains. But it is also a tool that analysts can use to find ways to cope with disruption. Without a picture of this landscape, leaders will be blind, deaf and dumb to the shocks and responses that can end up destroying their organizations and their careers. Second, in chapter 8 we delve more explicitly into leadership implications of the resilience landscape. If the Resilience Landscape is what leaders need to navigate, organizational mind-sets and mentalities will have an enormous bearing on how they do this. In chapter 8 we open up the leadership mind-set needed to navigate the Resilience Landscape. We place a strong emphasis here on the need to be continually analytical and mindful within a dynamic Resilience Landscape, discussing this with respect to relational resilience and the role of external sources of knowledge from consultants and scientists. In essence, we return to the individual level, but the individuals in question now being the ones who influence overall strategy of the organization. Finally, chapter 9 provides overall conclusions and thoughts for embracing a future in which strategy and resilience become inseparable in the eyes of leaders, analysts and researchers.

2

RESILIENCE AT AN INDIVIDUAL LEVEL

It starts with the person

It goes without saying that the basic element of any organizational system is the individual person. It is individuals that perform functions at a micro-level, work together in teams towards common goals, come up with new ideas and innovations, make decisions on how to allocate scarce resources, and inspire others and lead. Organizing for resilience, then, needs to appreciate how the concept of resilience at an individual level is understood, researched and debated. Reviews of the research field on resilience underline how individuals are at the hub of an organization's ability to cope (Van der Vegt et al., 2015). However, much of the literature on resilience at an individual level does not come from study of individuals as employees in a workforce in a traditional sense but rather from the wider world of trauma and stress. Each of us may find ourselves in such a situation at some point in our lifespan. There are insights from the field of social work on how poor and underprivileged children and youth bounce back from adversity in traumatic contexts (Ungar, 2008; Winfield, 1991). There is work that looks at resilience in professions where the stresses are extreme and the potential for burnout is high, such as with palliative care clinicians (Back et al., 2016) or members of the armed forces (Cornum et al., 2011). This stream of work highlights the internal psychological state of an individual, as well as the skills the individual has developed over time and the resources they have learnt to draw on through inter-personal connections (Liu et al., 2017).

We can draw from this body of research as we seek to understand resilience in individuals within a broader organizational context. Some studies do examine resilience amongst individuals in the workplace. For instance, scholars have looked at coping amongst team members who work on failed projects (Moenkemeyer et al., 2012), how an 'emotional carrying capacity' between individuals helps boost individual and team resilience in the workplace (Stephens et al., 2013), and how coaching can improve individuals' 'cognitive hardiness' – a measure of individual-level resilience (Grant et al., 2009). This literature is important; it not only acknowledges how some individuals are better able to cope with adversity than others, it also points to interventions and solutions that can be provided by an organization to help vulnerable employees. While organizing for resilience does start with the individual, it does not stop there. We cannot ignore how the organizational system and managerial actions around the individual influence the individual's coping ability.

Literature on resilience in individuals

Definitional considerations

What is resilience at an individual level?

It's about ways of protecting people. Rutter (1987) noted how people respond differently to stress and adversity. Some individuals are able to cope successfully with adverse events, whereas others react negatively. He argued that resilience is concerned with protective processes or mechanisms, rather than being about a fixed set of attributes or variables of individuals. Winfield (1991) also explained the notion of resilience at an individual level in terms of protective processes and mechanisms that minimize risk and enhance resilient capacity, as opposed to being about risk management that focuses on risk identification and categorization.

It's about people having the abilities and assets to recover. Van der Vegt et al. (2015) viewed resilience in terms of an ability to absorb and recover from shocks.

Ungar and colleagues (2007: 295) identified five internal aspects of resilience; these include: (1) development of a desirable personal identity, (2) experiences of power and control, (3) adherence to cultural traditions, (4) experiences of social justice and (5) experiences of a sense of cohesion with others. In addition, Ungar et al. (2007) noted how accessibility to material resources and supportive relationships are critical to resilience at an individual level.

It's about finding a way out. Bullough, Renko and Myatt (2014) studied entrepreneurial intentions among individuals in Afghanistan, a war-torn context in which life expectancy was 44 years and infant mortality was at 16%. The authors found that resilience has a positive direct effect on entrepreneurial intentions and also positively interacts with perceived danger in encouraging entrepreneurial intentions. In other words, even during a terrible environment of war and strife, an individual's resilience has a key role to play in their exploration of new commercial opportunities.

It's about individuals' embedment in bigger groups.[1] Toland and Carrigan (2011) argued that resilience should be defined within a wider ecological context; a natural and dynamic progression of resilience with many cross-level factors embedded in individuals, families and communities. This is in line with an interactive model in educational psychology that describes collaborative work towards shared goals. These authors see resilience as a unifying construct, bringing together five core functions of the interactive model: consultation, assessment, intervention, training and research.

Contexts of studies about resilience at an individual level

Importance of culture and social context. A large body of resilience literature at the individual level has been developed in the Western context or mainstream populations (Ungar, 2008). However, in his cross-cultural study, Ungar (2008) found that resilience is a culturally and contextually sensitive construct. Projects that work well in one context do not necessarily work well in another. To avoid bias in how resilience is understood, Ungar (2008)

1 We will come back to this point in chapter 6

suggested employing a participatory approach to capturing the nuances of culture and context. Scholars also acknowledge that risk conditions affecting individual level resilience can be derived from a broader circulation of social contexts (i.e. social structures, discourses and resource distributions). Despite such recognition, Bottrell (2009) argued that resilience research principally focused on individuals' positive adaptation in the face of adverse conditions, rather than exploring mechanisms existing in social contexts. Challenging the traditional assumption, resistance-based resilience suggests that interventions for resilience building need to consider the embeddedness of resilience in social identities and collective experiences. By studying social inequalities in a group of young people, Bottrell (2009) found that cultural practices, social processes and the nature of individual–social relations are all aspects of the context for resilience.

Natural disasters. The impact of natural disasters such as flooding, earthquakes and hurricanes on an individual's existence and condition has been the focus of a number of resilience studies. Any traumatic event during one's lifetime can be significantly associated with depression and post-traumatic stress. An example is the study by Lowe, Sampson, Gruebner and Galea (2015) of 418 household residents in the aftermath of Hurricane Sandy. This showed that resources at the individual and community level are interrelated and shape post-disaster coping and survival. The findings showed that demographic characteristics and disaster-related stressors are associated with higher post-traumatic stress. Living in an area with higher social capital is associated with higher post-traumatic stress. Higher community economic development helps in reducing risk of depression, this only being found in participants who do not experience any disaster-related stressors.

Frontline workers and health care. Individuals in a job such as policing that involves being first on the scene of traumatic events (e.g. mass shooting incident, fire or traffic accidents) are often referred to as first responders. First responders are likely to suffer negative physical and mental effects as a consequence of their role. In a study of resilience within first responders, Pietrantoni and Prati (2008) found self-efficacy, collective efficacy and a sense of community to enhance resilience. Self-efficacy is the degree to which an individual feels capable to deal with the challenge they face. Collective efficacy is an indicator of whether the wider organization is able to deal with the challenges arising in daily operations. Sense of community involves the individual having an emotional connection with a community, feeling a sense of belonging and believing one's needs are being met through community membership. Pietrantoni and Prati (2008) found females and older people within the first responder community more likely to suffer from burnout. Studies examine the issue of burnout in frontline healthcare, for instance in palliative care (PC) clinicians. Scholars in this field demonstrate that burnout is related not only to emotional exhaustion, depersonalization and low personal accomplishment but also to how systems and organizational structures work for those individuals (Maslach, Schaufeli and Leiter, 2001). Back et al. (2016) studied PC clinician well-being from the perspective of preventing burnout. These clinicians work day in day out on the most seriously ill patients. Over time, this can put the mental well-being of the clinician in danger.

Military deployments. Being deployed in battle can come with significant psychological costs for members of armed forces. The topic of coping with the stresses of warfare and the issues of post-traumatic stress arising as a consequence of an individual's engagement in warzones has received considerable attention, especially in the fields of psychology and psychiatry. Cornum, Matthews and Seligman (2011) used an approach drawn from the principles of positive psychology – Comprehensive Soldier Fitness (CSF) – to analyze resilience for members in a large army organization (1.1 million members). Meredith et al. (2011) studied psychological resilience against the backdrop of US Department of Defense (DoD) efforts to promote psychological resilience in the armed forces. In Bonanno et al.'s (2012) study of service personnel engaged in single and multiple deployments over time, resilience was seen in terms of a trajectory, namely, of low post-traumatic stress between pre- and post-deployment. Bonanno et al. (2012) identified preparedness and training within the US military as a factor for high levels of resilience among the sample. A higher level of resilience is reported for multiple deployers compared to single deployers, possibly indicating an ability to participate in multiple conflicts because of healthier physical and mental condition.

Innovation projects. Scholars have examined resilience in innovation projects in view of their high termination and failure rates (Todt, Weiss and Hoegl, 2018). There are a number of challenging factors in the context of innovation projects that necessitate resilience, including their complexity and the fact that they can be highly chaotic, that they are knowledge intensive, and that there are often multiple stakeholders involved, all with a view on how the project should unfold (Richtnér and Södergren, 2008). Moenkemeyer, Hoegl and Weiss (2012) studied individual resilience in the context of innovation project failures; such failures are seen as setbacks that can adversely impact an individual's wellbeing. The authors used data from a case of termination of a real-world innovation project to develop a construct of innovator resilience potential (IRP), this being made up of self-efficacy, outcome expectancy, optimism, hope, self-esteem and risk propensity (see also: Todt, Weiss and Hoegl, 2018). Todt, Weiss and Hoegl's (2018) study showed IRP to be strongly linked to psychological safety and leadership support. In itself, IRP is a transmitting mechanism, transmitting the 'protective effects' of these factors towards future project commitment. In a similar line, Richtnér and Södergren (2008) identified four sets of resources as preconditions for resilience: (1) structural (clear structures and mandates), (2) cognitive (skills, experience and competences), (3) relational (networks of people providing support) and (4) emotional (friendship, support and collegiality). Their study suggests project leaders should draw on different resources at different times in order to make progress.

Children and youth. Work on resilience in children and youth (defined as 18 or younger) is found in fields such as psychology, social studies and sociology. It centres on the inherent vulnerability of children and youth in society to trauma and disaster. Such vulnerability can be physical or psychological, and it can have long-term effects on their education and development (Peek, 2008). As Peek (2008) noted, children are naturally different to adults in terms of their needs and their lack of power. However, they do have capabilities and capacities to help contribute to preparing for disaster, for instance by educating them in schools and allowing them to share knowledge through their family and friend networks. They may also have creative and practical ideas to help deal with disasters (Peek, 2012). In a study of African American youth, Hare (1988) found that the causes of being 'at risk' emerge not only from individuals themselves but also from the racism, classism and sexism that black families faced. Hammond and Yung (1991) examined the issue of interpersonal violence among African American youth. This group was seen as a vulnerable population more likely to be affected by injury or death through violence than the wider population. The authors noted prior work identifying links between poverty and violence and how a child's continual exposure to violence will increase the likelihood of adult violence. The research suggests preventative interventions should be based around training in social skills such as giving positive and negative feedback, accepting negative feedback, resisting peer pressure, solving problems, and negotiating. Noteworthy is that school suspensions due to violence dropped for those who received the training.

Understanding resilience at an individual level

There are numerous examples of studies that identify factors that enhance resilience in individuals. We group the main insights into attributes of the individual, links to broader social environments, and the processes for developing resilience.

Attributes of the individual. Meredith et al.'s (2011) study was a systematic literature review to identify factors promoting psychological resilience. At the individual level, salient factors include positive coping, positive affect (including positive emotions and optimism), positive thinking, realism (i.e. realistic outcome expectations, self-esteem and self-efficacy), behavioural control (i.e. self-regulation, self-management and self-enhancement), physical fitness and altruism (i.e. selfless concern for the others and motivation to help without reward). Moenkemeyer, Hoegl and Weiss (2012) studied the negative impact of innovation project failures on individuals and how project members manage such setbacks and adjust themselves for subsequent innovation projects. They found six resilience components that are important for individuals to deal with failures and maintain project members' innovative capabilities. These are self-efficacy, expectancy, optimism, hope, self-esteem and risk propensity. Todt, Weiss and Hoegl (2018) developed these first-order codes into a second-order scale in a construct validity exercise.

In the context of clinicians, Back et al. (2016) argued that well-being is influenced by personal resources and work demands. The authors developed a prevention paradigm for addressing burnout and approaching clinician resilience. The paradigm, including a conceptual model and curriculum for improving clinician resilience, emphasized the early stage of intervention through developing individual resilience skills and assessing workplace engagement factors that enable clinicians to proactively respond to common challenges. The resilience skills include: (1) leveraging personal strengths; (2) tracking activation during the day; (3) setting healthy external boundaries; (4) self-regulating emotions, recognizing cognitive distortions; (5) developing realistic expectations for one's own performance; (6) finding meaning in daily work; and (7) committing to long-term development. The workplace factors consist of: (1) enabling control; (2) structuring rewards; (3) building community; (4) promoting fairness; (5) recognizing values; and (6) calibrating workload. Similarly, Pietrantoni and Prati (2008) demonstrated a high level of compassion satisfaction and a low level of burnout and compassion fatigue with the use of three resilience mechanisms: self-efficacy, collective efficacy and sense of community.

Embedment in social systems. Sippel et al. (2015) stated that individual resilience depends on many demographic, psychosocial and biological factors within and around the individual. Developing effective interventions to enhance resilience requires not only consideration of a wide range of factors such as family units, organizations, communities, neighbourhoods and social networks but also matching individual needs with these resources in time. Relatedly, Southwick et al. (2016) highlighted how individual resilience relies on factors in multiple individual-level systems, which are embedded in larger social systems. The role of social support in individual resilience, especially the support from one's community, is critical. The authors argued that individuals' coping strategies are strongly affected by the capacity of the broader organization and community. Individuals who are connected to organizations and communities that are well prepared for dealing with adversity tend to fare better than those who are not. Similarly, Liu, Reed and Girard (2017) used a multi-systems model of resilience to examine an interactive process of resilience between individuals and their larger socio-ecological contexts. They concluded that resilience is a dynamic and interactive process through three structures: (1) core resilience, (2) internal resilience and (3) external resilience. Core resilience refers to trait-like characteristics of an individual that are relatively static over time. Internal resilience focuses on individual factors that are often attributed to psychological resilience within an individual, as well as skills and resources emanating from interpersonal experiences and exposure to adversity. External resilience emphasizes the larger socio-ecological contexts from which resilience is developed and facilitated over time.

Meredith et al. (2011) identified family support, positive command climate (i.e. building pride/support for the mission, positive role modelling) and belongingness (i.e. integration and friendship) as evidence at the levels, respectively, of family, unit and community.

In their study of emotional carrying capacity (ECC) in relationships, Stephens et al. (2013) found emotional expression in relationships to be a source of resilience in individuals and teams, leading eventually to long-term virtuousness in organizations. They suggested that encouraging more constructively emotional expression across an organization allows individuals and teams to be more open to each other's emotions, both negatively and positively, and thus better able to anticipate the needs that are necessary for individuals and teams to recover from adversity. Additionally, leaders in organizations play an influential role in shaping the work environment where individuals and teams can safely share their emotions in both good and difficult times.

Cornum, Matthews and Seligman (2011) pointed out that building individual resilience requires proactivity rather than just waiting to see who has a negative outcome following stress. Implementing similar interventions may help to improve individual resilience in other large organizations. There are four elements in CSF, including (1) assessment of emotional, social, family and spiritual fitness; (2) progressive training on techniques to improve resilience in self and subordinates; (3) individualized training in different aspects of resilience; and (4) trained master resilience trainers (MRTs) who become the teachers of their subordinates to instil better thinking skills and resilience.

Processes for individual resilience. In addition to the identification of these types of effects on individual resilience, scholars have framed antecedents of resilience explicitly in terms of processes. Shih (2004), for instance, investigated processes involved when individuals successfully overcome harmful consequences of stigmatization in an essay on stigmatized individuals. She found that successful individuals adopt an empowerment model, rather than a coping (or depleting) model when dealing with stigma. Three processes (compensation, strategic interpretations of the social environment and foci of building multiple identities) help stigmatized individuals handle prejudice and discrimination. Rutter (1987) identified four protective processes that make individuals resilient: (1) altering the risk or avoiding exposure to it in order to reduce risk impact; (2) reducing the negative chain reactions that happen when an individual is exposed to risk; (3) establishing and maintaining self-esteem and self-efficacy (a "well established feeling of one's own worth . . . together with a confidence . . . that one can cope successfully with life's challenges" (p. 327)); and (4) exploring new opportunities that may provide experiences that help with protection against risk later on. In a study of executives in a public health agency, Grant, Curtayne and Burton (2009) found coaching to be a valuable way of helping people deal with stress during organizational changes. Participants reported an increasing level of self-confidence and personal insight, as well as skills in managing organizational change following coaching. Similar findings – that solution-based coaching fosters and enhances personal resilience – were reported by Green, Grant and Rynsaardt (2007). These studies suggest that executive coaching focusing on professionals may be an effective method of building individual resilience, enhancing workplace well-being and reducing depression and stress. This can be achieved through a self-regulation cycle involving acting, monitoring, evaluating and modifying towards ultimate goals.

CASE #1: G-Unique Designs: individual resilience on a small remote island

In March 2019, Giselle Richards, 34, mother of one child and owner and sole proprietor of G-Unique Designs, a small jewellery micro-business on St Helena,[2] one of the world's remotest inhabited islands, was reflecting on her business venture over a cup of strong St Helena coffee on the waterfront in the capital, Jamestown. With the waves of the South Atlantic breaking on the rocks, she pondered how to deal with the latest set of disruptions she had been facing.

With a population of 4,500 and a new government-led economic development strategy for the island based on growth in tourism and air access through a newly built airport, the island offered an opportunity for entrepreneurs like Richards to follow their entrepreneurial dreams and aspirations. Richards had started the business as a part-time hobby. She grew the business to one that consumed all her time and employed five islanders in 2018. However, storm clouds were gathering on the horizon in 2019. Sales of jewellery products were under pressure because the economic boost given to the island during the airport construction phase was over and the anticipated number of tourists arriving by air was not forthcoming.

In March 2019, with profits under pressure, Richards saw a reduction in staff to four people. She was still personally involved in all aspects of the business, design, manufacturing and selling, something she had started to limit between 2016 and 2018 because she wanted a less hands-on role within the business. She had not paid herself a proper salary in 2017 and 2018 in order to maintain staff salaries, preferring instead to pay herself a minimal salary to cover basic living expenses. She had to decide on an effective response and considered: (1) finding ways to grow exports, (2) moving with her family to the Falkland Islands where the economy was stronger, and (3) selling the business outright.

How should she proceed?

2 St Helena was one of 14 British Overseas Territories (BOTs)

Business inception and the early years

Giselle Richards was always interested in jewellery. She had been a consumer and buyer of jewellery, and, on returning to St Helena in 2008 after studying for a degree on the United Kingdom (UK) mainland, she spotted an opportunity. There were only two people making jewellery on St Helena, and Richards found their designs old-fashioned and too formal. In 2009 she started experimenting with a bead kit to create jewellery for herself. Being raised and schooled on the island of St Helena inspired her to make her designs reflect some of the island's natural wonders. By January 2010, Richards found herself creating unique jewellery in a small workshop at home and selling the products informally to friends and family. By April of that year she had set up her own business and started selling in small volumes through a retail outlet called The Hive, situated in the island's main town, Jamestown. The name of the business – G-Unique Designs – reflected Richards' first name initial as well as her philosophy of creating jewellery items that were truly distinct, just like St Helena. A mix of locals and a small number of tourists arriving by boat would buy her creations at The Hive.

Establishing the business was helped in part by a small grant from the St Helena Development Agency (SHDA). SHDA worked with entrepreneurs on the island to develop their ideas and brands. They offered Richards an initial loan to help develop branding and a business plan. They also offered a 'youth loan' that was used to buy raw materials. This latter loan had to be paid back. All raw materials were imported, mainly from the UK. Shipments of raw materials typically took three months to arrive. All imports to the island required a levy of 20% to be paid. Issues with defects and other problems with imported goods were a major problem for entrepreneurs on St Helena because of the time and cost it took to return them and re-order them. In most cases, the value added tax (VAT) paid could not be claimed back as the materials were sent to a freight-forwarding address based in the UK which was not recognized by many suppliers as a VAT-exempt address. If return time exceeded three months VAT could not be claimed back. This deadline meant many items could not be returned, incurring an unwanted cost to Richards. Of the materials used by G-Unique Designs, 95% were imported. The remaining 5% included items such as local seeds and sea glass.

Between 2010 and 2013, the business grew gradually. In 2010 Richards personally did all the manufacturing in a spare bedroom at her home. She moved out of this room and rented a small workshop on Ladder Hill (a settlement at the top of a hill outside Jamestown) in 2011. Selling expanded out of The Hive and into other retailers between 2010 and 2013. These retailers would take 20% from all sales they made of Richards' products. Revenues doubled between 2011 and 2013. Richards added one part-time employee in 2011, another in 2012, and a third in 2013. Her approach was to upskill workers straight from school, coaching and mentoring them in all aspects of the design–manufacture–sell process. Exhibit 2.1 shows the G-Unique Designs product range in 2013. Exhibit 2.2 shows examples of products in 2019.

Early success for Giselle

By 2013 the effects of the airport construction project on St Helena were starting to be felt in the economy. The main contractor was a South African company called Basil Reed. Hundreds of construction workers from South Africa and other countries were relocated to St Helena for months on end, and locals working on the airport project received salaries that were double a typical local income. A significant part of their earnings was spent on the island, including in grocery stores and the island's restaurants and bars. While some purchased local craft items such as Richards' jewellery, the boost to the overall economy meant locals'

Exhibit 2.1 Giselle Richards' product range in 2013

Product type	Product
Designed and manufactured for all customers	Beaded earrings Beaded necklaces Beaded bracelets Rings Wire-wrapped jewellery Fused glass jewellery Metal clay jewellery
Targeted at tourist market	Jewellery with charms of local images Beach glass jewellery Expanded range of jewellery with local horse beads Fused glass and fine silver jewellery Metal clay jewellery

Sea theme bracelet

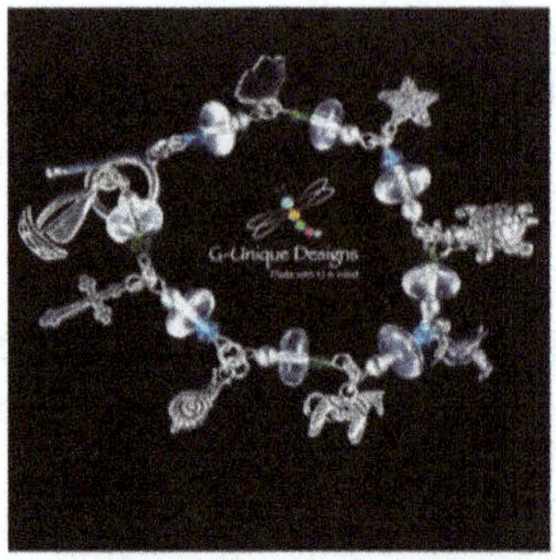

General St. Helena theme bracelets

Fine silver leaf earrings

Whale shark necklace

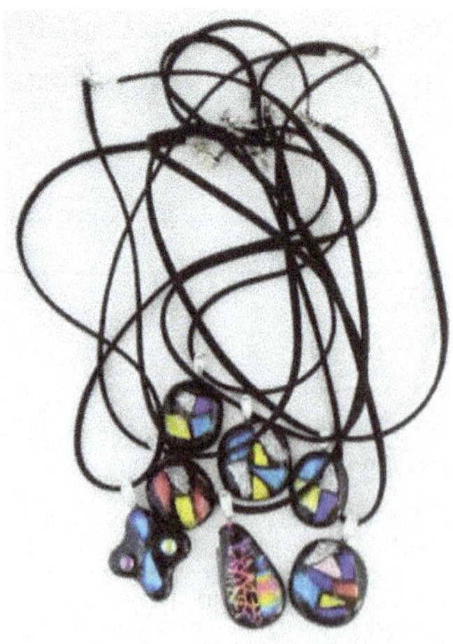

Fused glass necklace

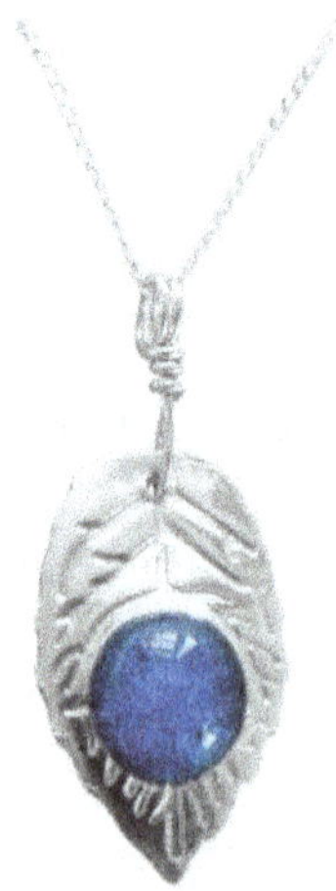

Fused glass and fine silver

Exhibit 2.2 Examples of Giselle Richards' products in 2019

demand for gifts and presents increased. G-Unique Designs experienced year-on-year sales growth every year between 2013 and 2017. Revenues doubled between 2013 and 2017.

In 2012 Richards moved to another workshop on Ladder Hill; one where she could also display and sell her products. She also continued to sell through various retailers in Jamestown. In late 2014 she became aware of a retail unit becoming available in the old market hall in Jamestown. This building dated back nearly 200 years and was in a state of disrepair. It was due a complete renovation, but this had not started yet. Richards wanted to have a sales presence in Jamestown, which was more accessible to both locals and tourists and generated greater foot traffic. With her name registered against one of the units in the market hall, Richards moved into an old café in Jamestown and waited for the renovation of the market hall to be carried out. She had three types of outlet at that point: the direct outlet at the workshop on Ladder Hill, the various retail stores in Jamestown, and the old café. However, in 2015 she decided to scale back on selling through other retailers. These had started to stock competitor products and Richards wanted to be seen to have a distinct market position, with sales made directly with herself or her staff.

In October 2015, while the Jamestown market hall was closed for renovation, Richards moved from the old café into The Consulate Hotel in Jamestown. The Consulate Hotel was one of the oldest and most famous buildings on St Helena, containing a restaurant and bar as well as accommodation. It was popular with locals and tourists alike. In June 2016, she finally moved into her unit in the renovated market hall.

Between 2014 and 2017, Richards took on two full-time employees and reduced one of the part-time headcounts. At the start of 2018 she had 5 staff in the business: three full time and two part time. In 2016, Richards gave birth. As a result of being medically evacuated to South Africa due to a pregnancy complication, she was away for two months in total. However, she was pleased with the performance of the business while she was away.

Exporting had also grown between 2014 and 2017. This was initially to St Helenians living abroad, mainly in the UK and on the other inhabited South Atlantic islands of Ascension and the Falkland Islands. Many St Helenians went from St Helena to Ascension and the Falkland Islands for work, and news of G-Unique Designs' products spread through the communities on those islands. Richards also used a Facebook webpage to promote her products.

In 2017 G-Unique Designs featured on American TV channel CBS News on a feature called 'Island Hopping'. Anchored by US TV host Connor Knighton, the feature described life on different remote islands around the world. Sales to the US received an immediate boost, and through 2018 and early 2019 the US was the largest export market for Richards. Her approach was to use a distributor in the UK that maintained a small inventory of G-Unique Designs' products. Selling these products through this distributor to consumers in the US and UK meant a much shorter delivery time. Before the St Helena Airport opening in 2017, there was a monthly boat service (on the 'Royal Mail Ship' or RMS) to the island from Cape Town in South Africa, in itself a five-day journey. The RMS was decommissioned in 2017. It could literally take months to ship a necklace from Jamestown to the US; holding stock at the UK distributor created a buffer and enabled orders to be fulfilled more quickly. It was this stock that was marketed to the US. By 2018 Richards was receiving one or two orders a month from the US, and she found that most of her customers there had little connection with St Helena; instead, they were fascinated by the island's British connection. Orders from the US were small in volume but relatively high in value.

In 2017 the airport runway on neighbouring Ascension Island was closed because it had fallen into disrepair. This had an immediate effect on Richards' aspirations for selling to the Falkland Islands because shipments to the islands came to a sudden end. Richards commented: "The close of the Ascension runway simply took out the Falklands market."

A new reality

The financial year ending March 2018 saw the first ever loss for G-Unique Designs, albeit a small loss. Sales had stagnated across all outlets and market segments. First, the economic boost that the island was given during the construction of the airport was over. The disruption of the airport construction project was initially a good thing. Hundreds of construction workers had provided an impetus to the local economy even before the first plane landed. This boost was now gone. Second, the forecasted number of air passenger tourists for the island was not realized because of an alteration in the air access strategy. There had been a change in the type of plane (smaller) and frequency of flights (fewer) compared to the original plan because of an unforeseen discovery of dangerous wind shear during the test flights. Entrepreneurs across the island felt the effects of this sudden disruption.

Nevertheless, Richards made key capital investments in machinery in 2018. She purchased a larger kiln, using a new development grant from the government agency Enterprise St Helena (ESH). Richards described this grant for the kiln as a "major help". One of the full-time employees left in late 2018 and Richards had no plan to replace that person due to the financial situation. Exhibit 2.3 shows the key events at G-Unique Designs.

Exhibit 2.3 Key events

Date	*Event*
2010	Started trading as sole proprietor of a cottage industry, crafting items at home, selling through local retailers. Richards still working full-time as a counsellor in Education Dept.
2011	Moved from spare bedroom to a workshop space – still selling through local retailers. Took on first part-time employee. Completed a course in Fused Glass and Metal Clay – bought first kiln.
2012	Moved to a larger workspace/ studio – starting selling direct as well as through local retailers. Richards working four days a week in Education Dept, one day full time in G-Unique Designs.
2013	Took on two full-time apprentices. Won 'Innovative Business of the Year Award' 2012/13.
2014	Moved into own retail space – G-Unique Boutique was formed. Temporary space before renovations in 2015. Richards working three days in Education Dept, two days in G-Unique.
2015	G-Unique Boutique moved temporarily. Took on two full-time employees after their apprenticeship. Medical evacuation of Richards off-island for two months. Business overseen by family members. Richards working two days in Education Dept, three days in G-Unique. Highest number of employees.
2016	Took on another apprentice. Richards on maternity leave Feb–June. From June: Richards working two days in G-Unique, one day at home (as parent). Started downsizing number of part-time employees.
2017	Launched website with e-commerce facilities. Awarded Queens Badge of Honour for 'Inspiring Young People in Business'. Changed tagline of business from 'Made with U in mind' to 'Your piece of St Helena'. Richards becomes full time in G-Unique.
2018	Bought larger kiln. Reduced number of full-time employees.

With the opening of air services, some raw materials could now be shipped in as air freight. In early 2019, Richards predicted imports of raw materials would be 50% by air and 50% by ship. This allowed returns to be made more quickly. However, shipments by air were more expensive than shipments with the RMS boat service.

By early 2019 G-Unique Designs' sales were still skewed towards the local market and tourism. In the first three months of the year, 60% of sales were to local islanders, 30% to tourists, and 10% to the export markets mostly in the UK and US.

Richards experienced another small loss for the financial year ending March 2019. While sales were constant, expenses – predominantly freight costs and utility bills, including telecoms bills – had increased.

Exploring new opportunities . . . abroad

Richards had learnt about alternative export markets such as China. Her maiden name was 'Yon', a name quite common on St Helena. It was said that it derived from the Chinese name 'Yong' and originated from when some 600 Chinese workers came to St Helena to work in various industrial roles during the 19th century. Many stayed on. There is even a small road in Jamestown called China Lane. In 2019, Richards made contact with an entrepreneurial incubator in Xiamen, China, to explore opportunities for sales in China. However, she soon realized there would be impediments to this strategy. First, she learnt that the demand would be for high volumes and selling on a wholesale basis to compete with large, international brands. She simply did not have the capacity to do this. Second, it was suggested that the manufacture of some of her designs would be done in China. Richards felt uncomfortable with this, commenting, "My jewellery is unique to the place it is based." She reflected on this initial learning from the Chinese market and felt it had sharpened her philosophy: "It taught me how my messaging needs to be specific as I approach the wholesale market . . . a lot of the work I do is really not scalable."

Richards was also planning to attend an annual sports event organized by the St Helena Association in Reading, UK, in late August 2019. This event had been running for over thirty years and was the biggest social gathering of St Helenians anywhere in the world. This would be her first time attending. She planned on taking selected jewellery stock in suitcases and setting up a stall at the event. Some components (such as chains) could be sourced in the UK and she would actually do some making at the event itself. She noted that the winter months on St Helena (June, July, August) were usually a quiet time for sales: "St Helenians don't spend much money during the winter." While there was a significant air fare cost for her and her family, she hoped a presence at the event would pay off.

Choices being considered by Giselle Richards

Richards was considering three main options.

Option 1 – Find new ways of growing export markets

Richards wanted to expand export markets as a way of overcoming the sales issues her business faced on home territory. Sales to the US had started, but they were small in volume. Sales to the Falkland Islands and Ascension Island had been disrupted. Potential sales to China were fraught with risk. Growing sales on the UK mainland involved considerable personal effort and cost. However, Richards was aware of growing interest in bespoke and crafted products and was keen to tap into such markets where possible. She had changed her original slogan of 'Made with U in Mind' in 2017 to 'Your piece of St Helena' and was keen to preserve the essence of making jewellery about St Helena in her export strategy.

Option 2 – Relocate to the Falkland Islands

Richards had seen how fellow St Helenians had left St Helena for greater economic prospects elsewhere, commonly to the UK mainland but also to other islands in the South Atlantic, including Ascension and the Falkland Islands. She was particularly interested in the Falkland Islands, which were experiencing an economic boom due to an emerging oil extraction industry. She felt she could set up a smaller version of G-Unique Designs on the Falklands, although she was aware of other craftspeople on the islands and did not want to 'step on their toes'. The Falklands had an established and sustainable agricultural sector, a small military presence and also a growing tourist industry.

Option 3 – Sell the business outright

Richards considered exiting and selling the business outright. She had not paid herself a proper salary in two years and the anticipated number of tourists to the island was not materializing. Perhaps now was the time to exit the business and start a new venture. Richards had become interested in upcycling glass products (glass bottles from wine, beer, jars) and had conducted some small-scale experiments. Using natural capital was also high on the St Helenian government's agenda. She was thinking about the possibility of starting a new venture, a small eco-business with one other partner.

Case reflection

The options identified by Giselle Richards all have profound implications: stay and take on new risks for the business, possibly seeing its slow demise, leave the island for a new life, or completely exit a business which she loves. Each of these options may bring new disruptions in the future. However, like many entrepreneurs in challenging circumstances, Richards has shown an ability to respond to multiple crises over time. This opening case, therefore, allows an examination of different resilience actions as well as different types of disruptions. It also illuminates the issue of experience and knowledge gained over time. Such experience in dealing with disruptions may stand her in good stead for the future.

Table 2.1 lists examples of actions taken by Richards in the case, grouped by proactive and reactive forms. In a proactive form, the entity under threat identifies, predicts and defends against the change in resisting the spread of disturbances before adverse consequences occur (Hollnagel, Woods and Leveson, 2006). In a reactive form, there is a response to a disruption, normally by finding immediate ways of recovering and implementing effective reaction plans (Ponomarov and Holcomb, 2009). What is interesting is that she actually showed a higher amount of proactive resilience than reactive resilience. Many of the key decisions she made were for the long-term, and decisions that would buffer against future shocks. Perhaps this is a consequence of growing up and living in such a remote place. Society generally in such locations has learnt how to survive by being proactive, forward thinking and resourceful.

While these different aspects of resilience are discernible in the case, a deeper question is whether these were the right choices. After all, the

Table 2.1 Examples of resilience exhibited by Giselle Richards in the G-Unique Designs case

Proactive resilience	*Reactive resilience*
Securing a loan from the St Helena Development Agency (SHDA) in anticipation of a growth in tourist numbers	Scaling back on selling through retailers (who took a share of the sale) when Richards learnt they were stocking competitor products
Planning and executing the various location moves in Jamestown (and Ladder Hill) around the opening of the Market Hall – this required Richards to be well connected with the agencies involved in the renovation of the building	Not paying herself a proper salary for two years in order to keep the business afloat and to cover the costs of staff, importing raw materials and shipping
Planning to attend the annual St Helena Association in the UK as a way to boost export sales at a time in the year when, in the Southern Hemisphere where St Helena was located, tourist numbers were traditionally low	Getting personally involved again in design and manufacturing at a time when she would have preferred taking a more hands-off approach
Making new capital investments (e.g. the kiln) in order to expand the product range	
Upskilling and training school-leavers – these being people who could contribute to the business's vision and operation for many years	
Holding stock at a UK distributor in order to reduce shipment times and costs for UK and US customers	

business had not performed well in the last two years, despite an encouraging start. Richards' response at the end of the airport construction phase was to make a capital investment, a long-term investment that could expand the range of products made. Was this a wise choice? If there were fewer tourists, who would buy these new products?

The specific disruptions that Richards faced are also interesting:

- Issues and defects with imported raw materials and parts: Richards has to absorb the cost (no real choice here because of the time it takes to send items back)

- Retail outlets starting to stock competitor products: scaled back on selling through retailers
- Jamestown Market Hall closed for renovation: moved from old café into The Consulate Hotel in Jamestown
- Needing to be medically evacuated to South Africa: one other full-time employee and one part-time employee continued operations
- Time taken to ship products on the RMS St Helena ship: set up distributor in the UK
- Economic boost of construction project over (an anticipated disruption): key capital investment in a kiln.

Newly occurring disruptions which require a response are mentioned in the case, and these can be classified as follows:

- Closure of Ascension Island runway (this was a very sudden disruption, not anticipated; it was also moderately severe because it effectively closed the Falklands market)
- Growth of tourist numbers not as high as anticipated in the government's original Sustainable Economic Development Plan (SEDP) from 2012 (it can be argued that this was a mounting pressure that developed over time – once the wind shear situation was discovered it was a number of months before it became clear which aircraft would be used and at what frequency[3]; it was also severe because Richards' business plan depended on adequate tourist numbers)
- Increase in freight and utilities/telecoms costs (this was quite sudden, although it could be argued it was not entirely unexpected; and it was high in terms of severity).

We can also reflect on how Richards appears to view disruptions as she goes about addressing them. For instance, Richards has not been addressing them all individually each time. But it does appear she has been addressing them collectively. This she has done by continually reassessing her strategy

3 Joshua, Kirsty and Williams, Christopher. "St Helena: Landing a future for a South Atlantic island", Ivey Publishing (2018) (product ID: 9B18M034)

for increasing sales abroad. This includes exploring opportunities to sell into China using a partner, although, as noted in the case, she then decides against this. It also includes preparing for the St Helena Association event in the UK. The former was an explorative mode. The latter was an exploitative move, utilizing existing capabilities and markets. Such decisions help buffer against the overall effect of multiple disruptions rather than address any specific disruption in isolation.

Option 1 – Finding new ways of growing export markets

Benefits of this option may include:

- Boosting sales with new products to existing customers
- Boosting sales through new customers
- Diversifying revenue streams to avoid over-dependency on any one market
- Finding new distributors to reduce the dependence on the single UK distributor
- Learning about trends and needs in new markets – this learning can be used efficiently to guide new product designs
- Identifying new market niches and potentially undiscovered customer segments that have an affinity to St Helena
- Utilizing advice, guidance and networks through the development and tourism promotion agencies on St Helena
- If successful, increased export sales helping to alleviate the problem of dwindling sales among islanders
- Being able to use the internet (e.g. her Facebook page) to promote and sell products.

Increasing the export orientation may have the following drawbacks:

- It will likely take considerable time for Richards to research new geographic markets
- There will be significant financial costs if she decides to visit new markets – or even existing markets such as the UK – personally; she will need to fly from St Helena via Johannesburg to destinations in the Northern Hemisphere

- It may be difficult to coordinate and manage disruptions as they occur in new export locations
- There is immense competition in the jewellery sector around the world
- The historical or cultural connection with 'St Helena, the place' will not be strong in many countries
- New distributors or partners could act opportunistically and it may be difficult for Richards to establish and enforce contracts, putting an onus on her to invest time and money in building new trustworthy relationships.

Option 2 – Relocating the business (as well as her family) to the Falkland Islands

This move would have a number of potential benefits:

- The Falklands appears to have a stronger and more diversified economy than St Helena, one that may enable her to grow sales
- There would not be the problem of losing the Falklands market when the Ascension runway closed for repairs
- There is an established cultural and social connection between St Helena and the Falklands by virtue of their British status
- There is a base market of St Helenians already living and working in the Falklands
- It would engender a sense of adventure for Richards and her family
- She would still be able to export to the UK and the US, as well as potentially other markets
- She could still keep some part of her business on St Helena – manufacturing and sales in particular – because she has already upskilled and trained a number of islanders who could keep the business going
- She could seek out government loans and incentives to establish a new business enterprise in the Falklands.

While disadvantages and uncertainties also exist:

- It would involve uprooting herself and her family, with a significant distance between the Falklands and St Helena and no direct flights; indeed, flights to return to visit family and friends would be extremely expensive and time-consuming

- There is no guarantee that buoyancy in the Falklands economy will last; assumptions about population and economic behaviour could change, as it did on St Helena after the airport construction project
- It may be more difficult, in terms of time and cost, to import raw materials
- If she intended to employee people, Richards would need to learn about the employment market on the island – she might be competing for skilled labour with other enterprises and organizations who may pay more
- There will be sudden and unforeseen disruptions that she is not aware of
- She may lose a sense of identity for the business as her inspirations would now come from the wider South Atlantic and not just from St Helena itself.

Option 3 – Selling the business outright

Pros of exiting the business in 2019 could include the following:

- She could cut her losses; the last two years of losses could signal an enduring and sustaining downward trend, perhaps indicative of an uncomfortable truth – namely, that the business was only viable during the phase of the airport construction and its positive effect on the St Helenian economy
- She could focus on new ventures, such as the interest she had in natural capital and, specifically, in upcycling glass products; such a new venture could be related to what she has done in jewellery and she would be able to transfer a lot of her skills and capabilities
- It would free up time to spend on other interests, including not-for-profit work, work in the community and the like.

While downsides of exiting in 2019 would include:

- She may need to find a new business model for selling any new products and services should she exit G-Unique Designs to start a new business – there is no guarantee that a new business model would work

- It may be premature to exit at this point; the two years of losses were relatively small, and there had been talk of an extra flight each week that might bring in more tourists; there could be an upswing in the market that she would miss out on
- If she did not start a new venture, she might have to find a job on St Helena as an employee again – this could be a difficult adjustment following nine years of entrepreneurship.

Insight from Keith McCoy, mental health specialist and author

Inspiring voices

Keith McCoy kindly provided the following anecdotes relating to how decisions influence our preparedness for resilience and well-being at an individual level. Keith has over 25 years' experience in healthcare, much of it in the area of mental health. He has seen at first hand the hardship and suffering caused by mental illness. His book *Hello Larry Barry* (published in 2020 and available on Amazon) is a dark comedy set in Ireland and dealing with issues related to stigma and the unrelenting challenges of sufferers' overcoming obstacles in everyday life. Keith's inspiration comes from his interests in sport and theatre. He tells the following:

> Hugo MacNeill played rugby for Ireland in the 1980s. He became the managing director of Goldman Sachs Ireland. When he was back at an alumni event at Trinity University Dublin, he was asked by students what he thought was the best degree a person could do. He advised that if you want to be a doctor that you have to do medicine, and if you want to be an engineer, you have to do that degree, but other than these types of scenarios you do have a genuine decision to make, you can be pragmatic and do a course you think will lead to a well-paid job even if you dislike the subject, or you can do something that you really love and really develop your mind, and then when finished, turn your brilliant mind to business.
>
> Brian O' Driscoll is arguably Ireland's greatest player ever. In 2008, he wasn't playing as well as he once did, and by his own admission wasn't enjoying rugby. He met the sports psychologist Enda McNulty who had helped the successful Armagh Gaelic football team. He was asked to recall a time that he really loved the game and Brian mentioned when

he first broke onto the international stage as part of the British and Irish lions, citing how he attacked space, beat players and had pace. McNulty realised that Brian had spent years trying to lessen his weaknesses and that this had created a dissonance of some kind. The advice he was given was to stop working on his weaknesses and instead focus on improving his strengths, as it was these strengths that had differentiated him from others and had given him his raison d'être. He did and won a grand slam with Ireland the following year and was nominated for world player of the year.

The lessons here are about the positivity and enjoyment that comes from playing to your strengths and choosing to do things that interest you. You don't have to, but you can appreciate the logic here in terms of how this can assist you with remaining positive and being content, thus leading to better resilience and stronger mental well-being.

Personally, something that assisted me is a play. In 2015 I saw an RSC production of Arthur Miller's *Death of a Salesman*. I got more understanding of life and mankind from that than any book, film or advice ever. It helped me to chill a bit and accept aspects of myself and led to a refocus. I say I chilled which is true, but this did coincide with what became a busy and successful period of time for me, I made a big decision to leave London, then completed an MBA with Durham University, became a Director for Culture and Wellbeing, and then wrote a novel, a mental health dark comedy, *Hello Larry Barry*.

Where you find your inspiration can be subjective.

Implications

Our brief review of academic literature on resilience at an individual level, along with the case of Giselle Richards and G-Unique Designs on St Helena and the insights from author and mental health practitioner Keith McCoy raise a number of points worthy of reflection. There is a wide range of contexts in which individuals find themselves in a position of vulnerability. Sometimes people are born into such situations and sometimes they choose to follow career paths or other life choices that increase the likelihood they will be confronted with disruption. The following five points are highly relevant for our understanding of the broader question of organizing for resilience.

First, the ways in which individuals are confronted with adversity are both numerous and complex. In some cases, adversity affects an individual for no other reason than fortune (or misfortune). Humans have no influence on the social and economic predicament – indeed the location – that they are born into. But this can have a big impact on the likelihood of adversity as a child or youth (Ungar, 2008; Winfield, 1991). On the other hand, regardless of birthplace and the location of childhood, individuals may find themselves facing adversity and trauma in the workplace later on in life (see the fourth, related, point below). In some cases they are highly trained professionals and even expect to confront (what for many would be) terrible situations on a regular basis. But they may still suffer psychological reactions and possible long-term mental ill health – including stress and burnout – as a consequence. There is a sense in the literature, captured nicely by Van der Vegt et al. (2015), that it is not possible to foresee all possible sources of risk and forms of disruption that can affect an individual throughout their lifetime. There are differences in terms of impact, some being relatively short term and easy to overcome (e.g. through training or proactive investments in preparedness), others being significant issues that endure over long periods of time (e.g. long drawn-out wars and social unrest; the effects of poverty and crime that go unresolved; problems attributable to isolation and remoteness).

Second, the extent to which an event is experienced as traumatic or disruptive may vary from individual to individual; the view of the experience can be highly personalized. If it were possible to take an overview of the disruption, one could say it exerts a degree of favouritism in terms of who it affects. From the individual's point of view, the disruption appears to pick out an individual (or missed an individual altogether). A natural disaster like Hurricane Sandy will disrupt everybody in a particular region in some shape or form. One of the effects of a disaster such as this is power outages; sub-stations explode and even some nuclear power stations are temporarily shut down. But not everyone is directly affected by a power outage. Indeed, local municipal authorities produce maps of where the outages occur. Some homes may actually retain power while the wider community is severely affected. Similarly, in times of flooding, some homes and businesses in a particular locale are badly damaged, others miraculously survive relatively unscathed. With the 2019/20 outbreak of coronavirus, many suffered the deadly consequences of the COVID-19 disease, others became infected by the virus but were asymptomatic. The question of whether an individual will be affected by a wider trauma disrupting a whole society raises again the question of blind luck. In a slightly different sense, the issue of defective materials arriving on the remote island of St Helena for Giselle Richards to use in her business is clearly a challenge. When the materials are unusable, a lot of time and money has been wasted. If the same business was based in a mainland economy in Western Europe or North America, the owner would not think twice about returning the materials and demanding a replacement or refund. For small businesses on St Helena this is generally not possible due to the time taken for shipments (often measured in months). Entrepreneurs on St Helena have come to accept this and, while they acknowledge it as a disruption, it is seen as something they just have to live with. An entrepreneur based in a major economy would likely take a different view of the disruption and seek redress from the supplier as soon as possible. What we see here is that, for entirely different reasons, different individuals may view the nature of disruption and trauma quite differently.

Third, coping strategies that individuals use also vary. On the one hand coping is seen as a capacity of the individual; their life experience, psychological and biological condition, and their assets and capabilities can all play a role in how individuals bounce back from trauma and disruption. On the other hand, the ability to cope is dependent on the social systems and structures in which the individual is embedded (Todt, Weiss and Hoegl, 2018), including the training and preparedness that is invested in them before they are exposed to trauma (Bonanno et al., 2012). These are not mutually exclusive alternatives, but the role of individual-level attributes and the role of the social systems surrounding the individual will co-exist and coalesce in a cross-level manner (Toland and Carrigan, 2011). Following Meredith et al.'s (2011) identification of factors that promote psychological resilience, positive coping, positive affect and positive thinking will all vary from individual to individual. Similarly, individuals will vary in their degree of realism, behavioural control, physical fitness and altruism. While there may be more commonality in family-level, unit-level and community-level factors, the juxtaposition of individual characteristics and environmental characteristics is highly distinctive and unique. Individuals will vary in terms of the extent to which they rely on their own characteristics and capacities to deal with trauma, versus whether and how they rely on their social environment. Likewise, the extent to which they explore new opportunities as a consequence of disruption (Rutter, 1987), express emotions (Stephens et al., 2013), have personal resources they can draw on (Back et al., 2016) or respond to coaching (Grant, Curtayne and Burton, 2009) can all vary from individual to individual. Keith McCoy used the process of writing a book about the theme of mental illness partly to share knowledge and awareness and partly as a consequence of being many years on the front line. He explored a new opportunity and expressed emotions at the same time. He was also a source of inspiration for others. Similarly, Giselle Richards shared her story to use in this book, and she has also received awards and recognition for being an inspiration to younger generations on St Helena.

Fourth, individuals can determine their own fate; they can put themselves in situations in which they are more (or less) exposed to trauma and disruption at a personal level. In many instances, there is path dependency; prior decisions made by the individual affect future likelihood of exposure to traumatic experience. On this point, Keith McCoy emphasizes playing to one's strengths. Giselle Richards takes a careful approach vis-à-vis extending her business to China while also considering uprooting and moving to the Falkland Islands. Individuals with the knowledge of an impending natural disaster (like Hurricane Sandy) and who have the means to escape are able to put themselves and their loved ones out of harm's way. Brave military personnel sign up for service, and receive training before entering the theatre of war. Individual managers and engineers may decide to enter and engage in innovation projects that are inherently chaotic and risky and which can produce negative side effects if they fail (Richtnér and Södergren, 2008). However, despite these prior decisions that an individual makes to determine and manage risk, unforeseen effects of disruption can still occur. With it comes psychological cost and loss of mental well-being (Meredith et al., 2011), exhaustion, burnout and depersonalization (Back et al., 2016; Maslach, Schaufeli and Leiter, 2001) as well as financial cost such as with the victims of a natural disaster (Lowe et al., 2015). If an individual has sufficient self-awareness to identify if they are beginning to – or likely to – suffer as a consequence of a prior decision to pursue a particular path in life, then they might be able to draw on the help and support of others in order to mitigate the risks and dampen the effects of adversity. As Back et al. (2016) noted, early (upstream) intervention is a useful and practical way of developing skills and coping. Our point here is that the individual has an important role to play in calling out for intervention, in the same way as they had a pivotal role to play in choosing a path that led to greater exposure to trauma.

Fifth, and linked to the previous point, individuals often have to evaluate multiple options when dealing with adversity. This evaluation capability is an essential aspect of the coping mechanism and the resilience of an individual. It goes beyond the self-awareness point in the previous paragraph, which is more about detecting the conditions for – and then calling for – intervention as early as possible. Instead, this is more about standing squarely in the face of disruption and being as clear as possible about the alternative pathways that could be taken. We see this clearly in the Giselle Richards case, where she was very clear about the three choices facing her (growing export markets, relocating to the Falkland Islands or selling the business outright). At a basic level, even individuals with few assets or little scope to create options for themselves may have decisions to make in terms of whether and how they accept help and assistance from family, their work units or the wider community. So the question becomes how to identify the available options and how to evaluate them in order to select the most optimal one. In the central case in this chapter, Giselle at least has some time to stand back and weigh up the options. She has time to draw on both her own experiences and resources and insight from the community level in order to come up with the right way forward. In other situations, when adversity strikes in a sudden way (such as with natural disasters – Lowe et al., 2015), individuals do not have the benefit of time. They may have to make critical decisions concerning the availability of options and their evaluation very quickly. This information-processing capability will be critical for enabling an individual in such pressing circumstances to pull through (and not make things worse!).

Finally, we started this chapter with the observation that individuals are the basic element of organizational systems. While the individual-level resilience literature highlights numerous ways in which the individual draws on the environment for support, it also highlights how individual-level capabilities can contribute to the overall resilience of broader organizational systems. In other words, it is a question not just of an individual 'taking' from higher levels or from the environment to help them with their own resilience but also of 'giving back' to the system and others in the system. Giselle Richards gave back to the community on St Helena in many ways, including promoting the brand of the island in her products as well as recruiting and training school leavers on the island. We also see this in various places in the literature. As Pietrantoni and Prati (2008: S15) stated: "first responders' occupation is aimed at protecting the local area, at alleviating suffering (and saving lives) of individuals and groups, which may belong to their own community". Stephens et al. (2013) highlighted the importance of being open to each other's emotions. For each person sharing their emotions (and exposing themselves to vulnerability), there will be others on the listening end, devoting their time and empathy to receiving those emotions. Ungar's (2008) definition of resilience in his study of youth across different cultures highlights the importance of the cultural context to provide "health resources and experiences in culturally meaningful ways" (Ungar, 2008: 225). Again, it will be important for each 'receiver' of help from a local culturally unique environment to have access to other individuals who are part of that cultural context. This role of the individual as a community member relates to the critical role of providing support to others, and ultimately, this happens between individual human beings.

Table 2.2 provides a summary of these themes.

Table 2.2 Key themes from the literature and cases on individual level resilience

Theme	*Sub-themes*	*Selected references and examples*
Complex sources: wide-ranging nature of disruptions facing individuals	Adversity due to the situation at birth and in childhood; adversity in the workplace; short-term vs. long-term effects on the individual	Ungar (2008); Winfield (1991); Van der Vegt et al. (2015) Giselle Richards case
Personalized reality: different individual views and experience of the same adversity	Blind luck, one-sidedness and chance; subjectivity; pre-existing condition and position of the individual	Hurricane Sandy COVID-19 pandemic
Individualized coping: coping strategies varying from person to person	Life experience; psychological and biological condition; individual-level training received; exploring new opportunities and seeking inspiration; expressing emotions; dependence on social systems and structures that vary from person to person	Meredith et al. (2011); Grant, Curtayne and Burton (2009); Rutter (1987); Stephens et al. (2013); Todt, Weiss and Hoegl (2018) Keith McCoy

Theme	Sub-themes	Selected references and examples
Self-awareness: understanding one's own choices and path dependencies	Career choices leading to exhaustion, burnout, depersonalization; undermining of psychological well-being as a result of career choices; self-detection and early upstream intervention to develop coping skills	Back et al. (2016); Maslach, Schaufeli and Leiter (2001); Back et al. (2016) Keith McCoy
Evaluative capacity: working out choices	Multiple and alternative options; continual evaluation; choosing whether to accept help from others; decision-making under time pressure	Lowe et al. (2015) Giselle Richards case
Reciprocity: individuals as receivers and givers of support	Giving back to the system; volunteering amidst a crisis; openness to others' emotions; cultural embeddedness of givers and receivers	Pietrantoni and Prati (2008); Stephens et al. (2013); Ungar (2008) Giselle Richards case COVID-19 pandemic

Learning points

This chapter provides the following learning points:

- Resilience is a topic that has received a great deal of attention at an individual level
- Studies highlight cultural and contextual embeddedness of individual resilience
- Work has been conducted in a wide range of contexts, including: natural disasters, frontline workers and healthcare, military deployments, innovation projects, children and youth
- Resilience at an individual level can be influenced by characteristics, traits and capabilities of the individual, by embedment in wider social systems including family, work and community, and by the processes individuals use to cope
- Themes that we will take forward in our broader understanding of organizing for resilience relate to: complex sources of adversity, personalized reality, individualized coping, self-awareness, evaluative capacity, and reciprocity

Suggested activity and assignment questions

1. Identify a situation in which you needed to be resilient in the past.
2. What was the nature of the disruption or adversity that you were facing?
3. Reflect on how you coped with the situation and what the outcomes were:

    a. Identify the main variables that helped and/or hindered your actions and responses.
    b. How are these variables interconnected (with each other and with the outcome you experienced)?

4. What features of the literature and examples covered in this chapter resonate with your own experience?
5. Conduct additional literature review to gain further insight into the variables you identify in your case and reflect on how well the academic research explains the outcome.

3

SMALL FIRMS, BIG SHOCKS

When shock is overwhelming

For small firms, disruptions can be crushing. Their size and relative lack of resources compared to larger firms puts small firms at a natural disadvantage. And it is not just about financial reserves; small firms may not have the scanning capabilities that larger firms have to detect imminent threats before they occur. It might be argued that small firms need to devote their limited resources to the specialized and narrow focus for which they were formed. This narrow attention can make them vulnerable. An example is micro-businesses and sole proprietors in the construction industry being exposed to the effects of extreme weather events (Wedawatta et al., 2010). Small firms are less likely to have the deep pockets and financial buffer needed to cover the costs of a response once a crisis has occurred. Small firms are more likely to go bust following a prolonged drop in cash flow. Consequently, we might be led to believe that it is only in the realm of large firms that we can truly understand resilience. As noted by Sullivan-Taylor and Branicki (2011), large firms have traditionally been the focus of empirical and theoretical work on resilience.

However, scholars in the field of small business research have noted that small firms do have an ability to be flexible and adaptive and be able to respond quickly (Smallbone et al., 2012). They tend to have fewer levels of managerial hierarchy and clear communications channels between the strategic apex – often the founder entrepreneur – and all parts of the organization. Small firms can have capabilities in being sensitive to disruption. Parker and Ameen (2018) referred to this as disruption orientation, a capability that allows them space to develop proactive risk management capabilities should disruption occur (Parker and Ameen, 2018). According to Blatt (2009), entrepreneurial teams have certain traits such as communal schemas and contracting practices that underpin trust and creativity. Both trust and creativity within smaller cohesive units positively influence resilience (Blatt, 2009). Branicki et al. (2018) noted how entrepreneurs are used to working in uncertain environments (a point underlined by Sullivan-Taylor and Branicki, 2011), and they are often highly resilient because of their direct experience of adversity.

These sorts of features, then, set small firms apart from large and bureaucratic organizations and suggest we need to pay particular attention to the question of how 'smallness' is crucial for our understanding of resilience in the context of the complex world we inhabit.

Literature on resilience in small firms

Definitional considerations

What is resilience in small firms?

It's about survival and avoiding decline of a weak economic actor. Liao, Welsch and Moutray (2008) examined factors leading to entrepreneurial discontinuance in small firms, focusing on various forms of capital: human capital, social capital and financial capital. In their study of 830 nascent entrepreneurs they found education and having relevant management experience to be important for survival in tech-based start-ups. Otherwise, human capital is not important and social capital also has no role to play. Financial capital in the form of personal funding does increase the likelihood of avoiding failure. Darnhofer et al. (2016) argued for the importance of relational resilience to understand resilience in family farms in Europe, these businesses having been in decline for many years in Europe. Smallbone, North and Kalantaridis (1999) examined the different types of strategy employed by manufacturing SMEs (small and medium-sized enterprises) to successfully adapt themselves to the local environment in peripheral rural regions. The findings showed that survived firms are those that proactively respond to local market opportunities by developing new products and seeking opportunities in non-local markets.

It's about a shared cognition. Blatt (2009) investigated the antecedents and mechanisms for resilience in entrepreneurial teams. Communal schemas and contracting practices facilitate resilience in entrepreneurial teams through trust and creativity, as well as clarity and accountability. Communal schemas in a small organizational unit mean that team members care about each other and value relationships. Contracting practices, such as activity transparency and explicit expectations in the team, are critical to team resilience in highly uncertain situations.

It's about the meaning of crisis under constraint. Herbane (2010) used case studies from four SMEs to explore the meaning of crisis for SME owners. He identified three dimensions for interpreting crisis in SMEs: (1) a lack of control; (2) a lack of cash; and (3) compressed time to respond. The results showed that owners of SMEs narrowly focus on cash flow and succession and tend to concentrate on the effects of the crisis rather than the cause. Additionally, owner managers who frame crisis based on their personal experience and knowledge use a chronological approach in three key areas: crisis threat, crisis response and crisis impact.

It's about sustainability. Moore and Manring (2009) pointed out that adopting sustainability strategies helps SMEs gain competitive advantages by: (1) becoming valuable sustainable investment targets for larger firms; (2) utilizing the effects of creative destruction and information technology to create highly competitive networks with other SMEs where large enterprises are less successful; (3) playing a role in creating and maintaining sustainable practices in local/global supply chains. They indicated the importance of SME networks, a theme echoed by Colovic and Henneron (2018) in their work on the links between internationalization of SMEs and corporate social responsibility (CSR). Colovic and Henneron (2018) noted how SMEs face challenges related to CSR in foreign markets as they internationalize, these being compounded by their resource deficits at home compared to larger firms. SMEs need to understand different cultures and different interpretations of what CSR is in different countries. Nevertheless, SMEs can internationalize successfully based on their interpretation and adoption of CSR strategies, these being influenced by host country actors and stakeholders.

Contexts of studies about small firm resilience

Academic studies on resilience in small firms have been conducted in a wide range of contexts and settings. Some of these are outlined below.

Economic crisis. Smallbone et al. (2012) studied how SMEs responded to the international economic and financial crisis in 2008/9, based on surviving SMEs in the UK and New Zealand. The empirical evidence showed a similarity with respect to methods of financing among the surviving firms, namely self-financing rather than tightening any bank credits. Despite these similarities, the NZ SMEs were more reliant on self-financing while with the UK SMEs there was a higher propensity to experience currency fluctuation. Although SMEs in both countries employed a combination of revenue-generating and cost-cutting measures, the results showed that resilient SMEs are less likely to adapt to recession conditions by cutting costs through, for example, reducing prices or employees. Instead, they adapt by attempting to generate revenue. Lai et al. (2016) studied the extent to which an economic downturn impacts firms' operational activity, and explore whether or not the existing human resources practices influence firms' response to recession and employees' job experience. Based on large-scale survey data, they found that SMEs were more vulnerable during the financial crisis when compared to larger firms.

Industrial context. Garmestani et al. (2006) examined how functional richness influences the survival of industries being challenged by economic change. Each of the industrial sectors differs with respect to the amount of clustering, firm diversity and richness of diversity across size classes. The findings showed that manufacturing industries with greater functional richness are more resilient to employment volatility. Garmestani et al. (2006) also realized that diversity may not contribute to resilience at smaller scale.

Resource supply and climatic context. Parker and Ameen (2018) examined SME resilience in the context of power supply disruption to small firms in South Africa. Wedawatta, Ingirige and Amaratunga (2010) highlighted a number of effects that adverse climatic conditions can have on SMEs in the construction industry. In the UK, where the study was set, a large proportion of construction firms are SMEs, the majority being sole proprietors. As a consequence of climate change, extreme weather events have become more common. Given the complex nature of the supply chains for construction services, extreme weather events such as flooding interrupt SME activity in construction in a number of ways. These include disruptions to site works as well as supply chains. Extreme weather events contribute to the failure of construction SMEs as viable businesses.

Family firms. Chrisman, Chua and Steier (2011) studied resilience in family firms. The results showed variation; some family-run firms are more resilient than others. These variations include: (1) arranged marriages as a management succession strategy; (2) long-term orientation and multi-temporal perspectives; (3) knowledge and opportunity identification; and (4) internal social capital and social exchange. Acquaah, Amoako-Gyampah and Jayaram (2011) examined differences in ways to build resilience between family firms and non-family firms in Ghana. The results showed markedly different approaches to cost-leadership and differentiation in a developing country; flexibility being important for family firms pursing differentiation and for non-family firms pursuing cost leadership. The central reason for these differences is argued to have its roots in differences in core resources, capabilities and absorptive capacity between family and non-family firms. The authors noted how family firms see it as important to meet delivery promises and provide faster deliveries under hostile conditions; this leading to lower long-term costs and good relationships with customers. In the Ghanaian environment, a differentiated strategy requires a complex logistical approach and the viability of delivery promises; faster deliveries within a differentiation strategy are brought into question. Non-family firms on the other hand can manage long-term costs through changes to capacity. These studies highlighted the importance of treating resilience in family-run firms as a special case, particularly in developing countries.

Formal vs informal firms. In an empirical study of enterprise resilience in the reef tourism industry (a setting which is highly vulnerable to natural disasters as well as economic and political shocks), Biggs, Hall and Stoeckl (2012) found that informal enterprises (e.g. small-scale self-employed entrepreneurs) reported better conditions during the crises (e.g. 2004 tsunami and 2008 political crisis) in three components of resilience than formal enterprises (e.g. licensed and registered for taxation): (1) financial capital; (2) social capital; and (3) the level of reported lifestyle benefits. Despite both informal and formal enterprises enjoying high lifestyle benefits, a higher proportion of formal enterprises with foreign business partners felt life in the reef tourism industry had become harder than informal enterprises, which tended not to be part of foreign ownership and management. Some formal enterprises expressed a greater inclination to look for other opportunities outside. The authors concluded that informal enterprises are more resilient than formal enterprises in the face of crises, highlighting the nuances of lifestyle benefits and enterprise flexibility.

Understanding resilience in small firms

In reviewing characteristics of entrepreneurial resilience, Hedner, Abouzeedan and Klofsten (2011) pointed out that entrepreneurial resilience, just like entrepreneurship, is a dynamic interaction of attitudes, activities and aspirations that vary across stages of economic development and societies. The authors argued that the characteristics of entrepreneurial resilience are associated with both internal and external factors. According to the American Psychological Association (2010), internal factors associated with resilience are the capacity to (1) have self-confidence and a positive self-image; (2) make realistic plans and exhibit communication skills; and (3) manage strong feelings and impulses. Regardless of internal or external factors, the primary factor is "to have relationships that provide care and support, create trust, and offer encouragement, both within and outside the family" (Hedner, Abouzeedan and Klofsten, 2011: 1).

In a comparative study, Sullivan-Taylor and Branicki (2011) found that SMEs have a distinctive perspective and approach to resilience that differs from that of larger firms. They employed Weick and Sutcliffe's (2001) four-category framework to examine how SMEs understand their own capabilities for managing threats and actuality of extreme events. The findings showed that *resourcefulness* (the capacity of managers to identify problems, establish priorities and mobilize resources to avoid damage) is a key driver of SME resilience. The second aspect in the framework is an *organizational* aspect, focusing on the preparedness of managers to make decisions and to take action to reduce disaster vulnerability and impact. SME managers tended to talk about 'muddling through' when extreme events occur.

The third category, *technical* systems, focuses on the ability of managers to ensure organizational system functioning. It was found that SME managers tend to prioritize day-to-day ongoing supply and infrastructure processes over preparing for extreme events. There was a recognition that dependence upon external organizations such as supply chain, infrastructure provision and customers are critical. The last category – *rapidity* – refers to the capabilities of managers to make decisions on threats without delay. SMEs demonstrate timeliness, agility and rapidity in practice. Relatedly, Parker and Ameen (2018) found that proactive risk management, resource reconfiguration, disruption orientation and investment in risk-averting infrastructure generally enhance resilience. The better able the small firm is to reconfigure resources, the more resilient it will be. The findings also show that proactive risk management mediates the influence of disruption orientation on firm resilience as well as risk-averting infrastructure on resilience.

Also comparing by size, Lai et al. (2016) noted that HR practices in terms of responding to crisis demonstrate a positive influence on resilience in SMEs. However, actions taken by HR in SMEs are significantly different to those in larger firms. For example, larger firms are more likely to reduce headcount – for example, through compulsory or voluntary redundancies or freezing recruitment – while SMEs are more likely to freeze or cut employees' wages. The finding also showed differences in workers' job experience during recession to be moderated by the level of management formality.

Branicki, Sullivan-Taylor and Livschitz (2018) employed an inductive approach and examined how entrepreneurial behaviours support SME resilience. The findings showed that entrepreneurs' experiences operating in uncertain environments and their ability to cope with uncertainty and crisis differ significantly from best practices as understood in larger firms. Specifically, one-way communication that emphasizes the need for crisis planning is unlikely to foster SMEs resilience. However, the characteristics of resilience discovered among participants are associated with individual resilience, such as self-efficacy, social connections and well-being. The model showed that both entrepreneurial and individual resilience characteristics provide a basis for SMEs to become more resilient.

Some scholars have developed frameworks that take a holistic view of resilience in small organizational units, including small firms and small teams. Gunasekaran, Rai and Griffin (2011) conducted a literature review and small-scale empirical study to identify factors that affect resilience in SMEs. SMEs have to grapple with challenges in the areas of succession planning, knowledge retention, personal relationships, cost, quality, delivery, flexibility, people management and IT integration, as well as governance of sustainable production within the global supply chain. By categorizing these factors into internal, external and enabling factors, the authors developed a framework to understand resilience and competitiveness of SMEs. The findings from the exploratory empirical work showed that, in order for SMEs to be resilient, they should firstly be proactive in terms of offering competitive products/services through various channels (e.g., strategic alliances, networking) and using technology to effectively communicate with various stakeholders (e.g., through IT and internet-enabled supply chains). The resilience of SMEs is inextricably linked to the concerns of top management in the firm. Suitable communication channels need to be established so that top management can be informed of changes in both internal and external environments.

Similarly, Furniss et al. (2011) developed a 'resilience markers framework' for understanding resilience in small teams. Many micro-sized firms (fewer than ten employees) and smaller SMEs can be seen through the lens of small teams. Furniss et al.'s (2011) framework put an emphasis on resilient performance from a system perspective, promoting "things that the system does well so that it is better able to cope" (p. 2). The framework consists of two parts. The first part is a three-level hierarchy made up of: (1) marker (a higher-order construct to describe generic types of organizational behaviour, e.g. managing workload), (2) strategy (see below) and (3) observation (a lowest level example of what actually happens in practice, e.g. a supervisor asking an employee to take care of an alarm). The second part expands the strategy level to reveal specific mechanisms of resilience (see Furniss et al., 2011: 6–7):

- *Resilient repertoire*: the range of competences that allows a system to respond to threats and vulnerabilities. These can be either created anew (an innovative response) or re-used from previous deployment (an adaptive response).
- *Mode of operation*: the way the system is organized and structured such that resources can be brought to bear to deal with the problem. The

mode of operation is dependent on the perceived threat and different interpretations may lead to different outcomes.

- *Resources and enabling conditions*: these are the conditions that allow the strategy to be carried out and include availability of staff and physical space.
- *Vulnerabilities and opportunities*: prior literature and cases have exposed a wide range of possible vulnerabilities; these making the system 'unsafe'. Opportunities, on the other hand, relate to other areas in which performance may be improved.

Case #2 – Expatica Communications: leading through tragedy

IVEY | Publishing

9B17C001

EXPATICA COMMUNICATIONS: LEADING THROUGH TRAGEDY

On a camping trip to Italy in July 2014, Mark Welling, managing partner and co-founder of Netherlands-based Expatica Communications B.V. (Expatica), received a message on his cell phone from his office in Haarlem, the Netherlands. The somber message said: "We think Antoine and his family were in the plane that crashed." Antoine van Veldhuizen was the other managing partner and joint owner of Expatica. He had been on Malaysia Airlines flight MH17, which had been shot down over Ukraine with a loss of all 298 people on board.

Within hours, the news was confirmed. Van Veldhuizen had been killed along with his wife, two children, and mother-in-law. Welling and van Veldhuizen had been involved in the business for over 15 years, and worked closely together over that period. Welling considered van Veldhuizen a close friend and brother. Following a long drive back to the Netherlands, and after visiting shocked family members, Welling found himself alone in the Haarlem office. It was Sunday and employees were due to return to the office the next morning. Welling felt like pulling out of the business. How should he prepare for the next morning? How should he approach the meeting with his employees? What actions should he take regarding the business in the short and medium term?

COMPANY BACKGROUND

Expatica was a "born global"[1] firm established in the Netherlands with the aim of providing information and services to expatriates (expats) living abroad. The company was founded in 2000 with the help of funds provided by a government incubator (called Twinning). It had a business model based on online advertising revenues. The website users were expats, and the original offering was high-quality local and international news delivered in English, for free.

In 2006, van Veldhuizen and Welling, two Dutch entrepreneurs involved in the original venture that became Expatica, were presented with an opportunity to acquire the majority of the company's shares and take control. They saw great potential in Expatica and aspired to set a new course for the company based on their understanding of the opportunities created by emerging technologies and the changing needs of expats living abroad.

By 2011, the main Expatica website was live in 11 countries. There were eight online offering areas: jobs, housing, listings, community, ask the expert, classifieds, forum, and dating. The online dating product was launched in 130 countries simultaneously in 2010. The income generated by online advertising contributed 90 per cent of Expatica's total income. In addition to its online products, the company offered events, of which the "i am not a tourist" Expat Fair was by far the most popular and expensive. Other events included education fairs, human resources seminars, and social events. Expatica also offered a "survival guide" for expats, which

1 A company establishing international operations at or near its founding.

was published in countries in which the "i am not a tourist" Expat Fair was held. The company had seen how the fair led to an increase in survival guide sales.

In July 2014, Expatica had eight full-time, permanent employees, including van Veldhuizen and Welling. Van Veldhuizen and Welling spent 100 per cent of their working time at Expatica, and were not actively involved in any other ventures. There were also six freelance staff members, employed on a renewable contract basis.

The six full-time, permanent staff members were located at the office in Haarlem. They consisted of one Dutch national and five expats living close by. Two were devoted to sales and had been working closely with van Veldhuizen. One worked on events, most recently concentrating on the upcoming "i am not a tourist" Expat Fair. One was responsible for social media, while another was responsible for website traffic management—vital to the business given the dependency on advertising revenue. Finally, there was one office manager, responsible for running the office.

The six freelance staff members were located outside the Netherlands. Three were situated in Bulgaria and were responsible for information technology system development and infrastructure. Three others were employed as editors, responsible for content across Europe.

Apart from van Veldhuizen and Welling, who had been associated with the company for 15 years, the shortest tenure among employees was 18 months, while the longest was six years. All permanent and freelance staff members had reported directly to van Veldhuizen.

There was also one intern who had started an internship at the company after Welling departed on his vacation in July 2014. The first time that Welling met this intern was on his return to Haarlem after curtailing his vacation. Along with the other employees, the intern was distressed and in tears.

RECEIVING THE SHOCKING NEWS AND INITIAL RESPONSE

Welling was enjoying his vacation and had not followed any news for a while. On this particular day, Thursday, July 14, 2014, he had gone swimming and had not taken his phone with him. When he returned from his swim, he checked his phone. He found a somber message from his office in Haarlem. It read: "We think that Antoine and his family were in the plane that crashed." What plane? Had there been a crash? Welling had no idea, and initially could not recall when van Veldhuizen was travelling. After calling the office, he found out that when the news of a plane crash reached the office, they suspected it was the plane in which van Veldhuizen was travelling. They tried calling van Veldhuizen and his wife but were not able to reach them. They had to conclude that this was actually the plane that he was on with his family—the MH17.

The family had been heading to Indonesia for a holiday and flying from Amsterdam to Kuala Lumpur for a stopover. The plane crashed in Eastern Ukraine. It was a mystery why the plane crashed, but soon the suspicion arose that it had been shot down. The location suggested a connection to the East Ukrainian–Russian border dispute. But why was a passenger airplane targeted?

The Netherlands was in shock—it later emerged that 196 Dutch nationals lost their lives in the crash. In Malaysia, the news was met with perhaps even more disbelief: this was the second disaster in a row for Malaysia Airlines. Malaysia Airlines flight MH370, a Boeing 777-200ER carrying 227 passengers and 12 crew members, had gone missing between Kuala Lumpur and Beijing on March 8, 2014.

Late at night on July 17, the sad news was confirmed. Welling did not sleep that night. The next morning, he and his family started on the long drive back home to the Netherlands. Under normal circumstances, they would have driven without stopping, leaving at around 5:00 a.m. and expecting a drive time of about 14 hours. This time, Welling decided to leave later, at around 10:00 a.m., and to stay overnight along the way. Welling felt the need to be careful and did not want the journey back to be too exhausting. He wanted to be as fresh as possible on his arrival on the Saturday. Processing the terrible news and answering the many phone calls related to it was already straining. He did not want to risk any fatigue and loss of attention needed for driving the car.

During the drive, he was constantly making and receiving calls. It was a hectic and confusing journey. He spoke with current and former employees, and with journalists. He even had a long conversation with an old colleague who was in Australia, later recalling how he had referred to this person using the wrong name for the entire conversation.

On Saturday evening, he arrived home. He did not stop calling people, informing them about the news. On Sunday, he visited van Veldhuizen's family, who had come together to mourn. Whereas the family was grieving and showed their sadness, he had not given himself time for that at all, having been consumed by organizing the trip home and informing others. This frame of mind appeared to stay with him: being alert and not giving in to emotions.

On Sunday afternoon, he went to the office alone. Entering the historic building in which the office was located and going over the many memories he had of van Veldhuizen, he wrote an "In Memoriam" tribute to van Veldhuizen, which was published on the company's website:[2]

> After a two-day trip back from Italy and a day spent with Antoine's family, I am now at the Expatica office. It is Sunday afternoon; no one is here besides me and a server exhaling loudly trying to counteract the heat.
>
> Alone at the office, I see everything in a new light. I see so many things connected to Antoine, things I hadn't really noticed before. His desk, his chair, his papers, the photos of his children. Even Antoine and Simone's mirror in the meeting room, the paper cow he decorated during a team activity.
>
> Slowly, the knowledge that everything will be different from now on sinks in. I put on "If It Be Your Will" by Leonard Cohen and sit at his desk. An extremely uncomfortable and lonely feeling creeps up on me. Antoine will never return. Expatica will never be the same.
>
> At 17:53 on 17 July, while on holiday in Tuscany, I received a text message from the office saying: "We think Antoine was in the plane that crashed." In total confusion, I read the message again and again. Which plane went down? Antoine wasn't flying out till next week, right? What kind of text message is this, then? What's this all about? Yet, soon the realisation that no one at the office would send this message, for no good reason, hits me.
>
> What follows is a bizarre evening with a slow but steady stream of news, facts, half facts, and non facts. An evening on which hope all too quickly makes place for the unthinkable. Simone, her mother Christiene, Quint, Pijke, and Antoine have died in a disaster that never should have taken place, leaving a vast emptiness behind.

2 Mark Welling, "Antoine van Veldhuizen—In Memoriam," Expatica, July 21, 2014, accessed September 8, 2016, www.expatica.com/nl/news/Antoine-van-Veldhuizen-In-Memoriam_428856.html.

Antoine has meant a great deal for Expatica. He is the personification of the Expatica Family. He co-developed Expatica almost from the very start. He started the "i am not a tourist" Expat Fair, which is now in its 11th edition. It is impossible to mention everything he has done for Expatica over the last 12 years. His boundless and infectious energy has led to many initiatives and successes. At times chaotic, at times ad hoc, but always with the best intentions and ideas.

Expatica was his dream, his baby, his passion. Even when times were rough or situations difficult, he stood for Expatica, the Expatica Team, its quality and its readers. The sheer amount of heart-warming reactions from readers and former colleagues spread out across the globe prove this to be true.

I have had the pleasure of working with Antoine over the last 15 years, during which we have been through a lot together, both good and bad. We have never had a disagreement; Antoine always acted in harmony and with respect for everyone involved. To me, Antoine was not only a partner at Expatica, he was my good friend. A friend whom I was not ready to part with; we still had so many great plans for the future. He and his family had such a wonderful life ahead of them.

Antoine will never return, but he will always be part of the Expatica family, forever known as its most important, energetic, loyal, likeable, committed, sympathetic, best member with the loudest laugh. He will never be forgotten.

Antoine will never return, but will always be one of my very best friends. I am grateful to him for our cooperation and friendship. I will never forget him.

I wish Antoine and Simone's family, their friends, and everyone who was close to Simone, her mother Christiene, Quint, Pijke, and Antoine the strength it will clearly take to get through this.

Mark Welling
Founder & Managing Partner Expatica
Communications B.V.

EVALUATING SCENARIOS

After writing the piece, Welling's immediate thought was, "I am pulling out." He could not go on without his business partner who had been so influential.

Van Veldhuizen was a passionate entrepreneur who loved his work–life balance. He sometimes did what he felt like doing most, such as sports at hours that others might spend at the office. He was excellent in establishing relationships and maintaining contact with stakeholders and friends alike. As a result, the company had excellent client and business relations.

Welling foresaw many situations that he felt he could not handle without van Veldhuizen. Van Veldhuizen was the operational and commercial partner, whereas Welling focused on new business and technical details, especially the dating site. Welling felt he could not take on all the roles that van Veldhuizen had fulfilled, particularly in the way van Veldhuizen accomplished them over the years. Together, they had taken on the leadership roles harmoniously, with little disruption or tension, each fulfilling aspects of leadership that were most natural to them.

Clients and partners were highly appreciative of what van Veldhuizen did in the company. How would they react to his death? Could anyone else do the work in the same spirit? This spirit had led Welling and van Veldhuizen to think constantly about next steps for the business. They had recently thought about moving to a smaller office and becoming a more compact business that would involve new projects they would enjoy, even projects that were unrelated to Expatica's core mission.

Welling also felt increased pressure because Expatica was approaching its busiest time of the year—the "i am not a tourist" Expat Fair for 2014 had to be organized and managed. The fair was to take place in October in central Amsterdam. It was an annual highlight for the company, attracting around 4,000 guests. How was Welling going to handle all the activities for the fair while at the same time making the all-important decision about the future of the company? That afternoon in the office, Welling contemplated many options, of which four stood out.

Option 1: Pull out of the business and sell everything to an interested party

The company was in good shape, and others would be able to transform the business and build on it. This option would make it possible for Welling to move on and start something new.

Option 2: Sell the part of the business that van Veldhuizen had focused on

This option would allow Welling to focus on the dating site, a part of the business that was growing. Welling had concentrated his efforts over the previous years on this side of the business, and had been set to continue on this road in the future.

Option 3: Step in and take on van Veldhuizen's role himself

This would ensure stability and the possibility of building van Veldhuizen's legacy, keeping alive what they had set out to do together. However, it was not an easy option. Would others accept Welling's decision to take on a broader role in the company? How would he be able to stay in contact with all clients, partners, and employees while continuing to do the work he normally did? What about the excellent relations that van Veldhuizen had established? Could he live up to what van Veldhuizen had managed to do? Welling would not look forward to fulfilling van Veldhuizen's role, particularly in the area of sales.

Welling had never focused on sales at Expatica, having found out in a previous job that it did not particularly suit him. The world of sales was not the most interesting part of the business to him, and he felt he was not a typical salesperson. He had always felt more comfortable in the technical and supportive roles that required problem solving and creative thinking. The complementarity of the two partners had actually been an important asset for the company. Would he be able to combine the two roles into one?

Option 4: bring in a new person from outside the company to focus on sales

If sales remained stable or grew, this would help Expatica stay afloat and give Welling time to think about important decisions concerning the company. Sales involved a considerable risk if not handled well. Welling contemplated recruiting a salesperson and training this person to take on van Veldhuizen's role in the long run. At least a stable income would be ensured, reducing the company's commercial risk. However, this option involved other risks. Welling was concerned that it would take some time to identify, train, and socialize this new person. The impact on actual sales would not be known for some months—at which point it might be too late: if sales were slow, there would be no time to recover, and the company might not survive. A new recruit might not have known van Veldhuizen personally, whereas everyone around the recruit would, both internally and externally. Would clients remain loyal?

DECISION POINT

Welling sat alone and tried to organize his thoughts. Following the journey back to the Netherlands, and witnessing the emotions of grieving family members, he needed to find a way to cope. He recognized that the employees had been dealing with the situation on their own since the previous Thursday. He thought about what they might be going through, probably feeling insecure about the company and their jobs. He was worried about giving the impression that he did not believe in the company anymore, and believed he had to set the right example. If he could not convey his belief in the company, then Expatica's employees would not be able to deal with any of the tasks ahead, whatever the decisions about the future might be. Welling recognized the need to be clear in his words and actions. However, he was unsure about how to move forward. How should he approach the employees the next morning—what should he say to them? What actions should he take regarding Expatica's future?

Case reflection

The challenge facing Mark Welling as he reflected on the sudden shock of Antoine van Veldhuizen's death cannot easily be put into words. The shock would have been exacerbated by the fact that family members, including children, had also been killed, as well as a large number of fellow countrymen and individuals from different countries. All were victims. All were innocent. None had any interest in the conflict in Ukraine at that time. There would have been the national and international press coverage and national and international outpourings of grief constantly in the news. There would have been nowhere for Welling to hide. Van Veldhuizen was very active in the local community in Haarlem and he was well known and well liked. Within the organization itself, employees would have also suffered from the news; there would have been a common sense of trauma affecting all employees and freelancers. The impact on stakeholders would not be clear, and all who knew van Veldhuizen or who had business dealings with him would have felt a sense of loss; emotions would be running very high. Beyond this psychological impact would have been the more practical challenge of how to keep the business going. There was the obvious question of van Veldhuizen's capabilities, his networks, his knowledge, his acumen, his talent, his motivation and drive, his ability to communicate and inspire. How could these be replaced? What impact would this loss have on business operations and future strategy? Understandably, these strategic and operational aspects would have been clouded by the high level of emotion and shock that stakeholders were feeling. And at the individual level, Welling was also fatigued. He had driven back to Haarlem from Italy. He had not slept. He was facing numerous and constant calls and messages. He was also in a state of high emotion and shock. He considered exit as an option.

The case has some useful features to aid our analysis of organizing for resilience. For small firms such as Expatica that face existential threats and sudden shocks that bring into question their survival, the impact is intensely felt at a number of levels. Because the firm was small, the impact on the individual (Mark Welling and colleagues) is also very strong. There are no additional layers or barriers to buffer the shock from the individuals leading and working in the firm. These individuals have a strong psychological contract with the firm; what impacts the firm, impacts them.

In Blatt's (2009) terms, there would have been a shared cognition in the entrepreneurial team, and this could be a source of strength and coping. Also, because the firm has an operating model that puts it at the heart of a network of other actors, as well as one that puts it at the heart of a specific community (a geographic community in Haarlem, as well as broader expat community), the shock is also felt at a wider stakeholder and community level. The care and support mentioned by Hedner, Abouzeedan and Klofsten (2011) applied across the wider communities in which Expatica was a part, would prove to be a source for coping.

Avoiding dealing with the shock simply was not an option for Welling. He had ownership rights to the organization as well as a deep commitment to its vision and strategy. While he might have felt like exiting the business – or at least considering this as one of a number of options – the hard reality was that he simply had to deal with the aftermath of the shock; there was no choice. While researchers emphasize prior experience of dealing with uncertainty as a basis for coping with disruption (Branicki, Sullivan-Taylor and Livschitz, 2018), Welling would not have experienced anything like this before. He would have to confront the situation and his employees would be expecting to see and hear from him on the Monday morning following his trip back from Italy.

The strategic and financial implications of the crisis would not have been all that apparent. It would not have immediately been known what the shock would mean in financial terms. Smallbone et al.'s (2012) comments about cost-cutting or additional revenue generating actions in order to cope with a significant crisis threatening the survival of the firm may prove to be useful, but not at the moment in time in which Welling was struggling to come to terms with the loss of his business partner. Similarly, Gunasekaran, Rai and Griffin's (2011) work on resilience in SMEs included aspects such as quality, delivery, cost and IT integration that simply would not have been at the forefront of Welling's mind at the moment in time the case is cut. However, other aspects such as succession planning, knowledge retention, personal relationships and people management were clearly issues that Welling had to grapple with in the short term.

Lai et al.'s (2016) note on the importance of HR practices in SMEs at times of crisis are especially useful. Although Lai et al.'s (2016) work examined SME vs larger firm responses in terms of HR practices in the face of a financial crisis and recession, the findings do highlight the importance of greater informality and caring for employees. For instance, small firms in the sample were less likely to pursue voluntary redundancies, freeze recruitment, reduce paid overtime or reduce use of temporary or agency workers. Similarly, from the workers' point of view, in smaller firms workers were less likely to move to another job, have their work reorganized or have their overtime restricted. However, they were more likely to have their contracted hours reduced (Lai et al., 2016). This research suggests strongly that at least some changes in HR eventually will be necessary but that Welling would be caring for his employees at that moment in time.

Overall, the leadership qualities that Welling needed to show are put under the spotlight. He would have had little time to prepare. And as noted above, this was a situation he could not hide from. Bass and Bass (2009) discussed different leadership styles. These include: (1) laissez-faire leadership, i.e. allowing subordinates to make their own decisions with a minimum of supervision; (2) autocratic leadership, i.e. retaining tight control over subordinates and not really involving them in decision-making or listening to their opinions; (3) participative leadership, i.e. including employees and all stakeholders in defining and setting goals and involving them in decision-making; (4) transactional leadership, i.e. defining goals and rewarding employees according to the extent to which they attain those goals; (5) transformational leadership, i.e. inspiring people and motivating people with a clear vision; and (6) authentic leadership, i.e. leading with one's heart and being self-aware and genuine. Welling recognized later that what he actually did was a combination of these, including being authentic and participative in the first few days after the onset of the crisis, but then adopting a more transformational model in the months and years ahead.

Insight from Claire Agutter, Director, ITSM Zone

Adapting as a small firm

"Fail to plan, plan to fail." We all know this quote, attributed to Benjamin Franklin. But what happens when events outside of your control take a wrecking ball to your plans? How do you adapt as a small organization? I'm writing this from my perspective in 2020 – the director of a small e-learning company in the IT sector, against the backdrop of a global pandemic.

I believe there are two essential characteristics that a small organization needs in order to be resilient: (1) firm foundations and (2) an agile mindset.

By firm foundations I mean that you have to get the basics right. Understanding your value streams and processes, automating activities as far as possible and having clear, regular communication inside your team and with your customers all give you solid foundations to build on. If the basics take care of themselves and don't require extra attention, you and your team have more mental space to dedicate to your new situation.

Then, an agile mind-set allows you and your organization to react quickly and adapt to whatever your market is throwing at you. Create a culture of experimentation, based on small ideas that can be tested and either discarded or scaled up, depending on how successful they are. Encourage input from everyone to build a learning organization. Be alert to people saying things like "but we've always done it like that" or "we tried that before, it didn't work". You need to encourage a culture that is open to change, not resistant.

In 2020, coronavirus completely froze our business for two weeks. All orders stopped and our pipeline started to dry up. We were helped here by our firm foundations, including automated credit control to help with cash flow and immediate communication within the team to plan for what we did next. Our agile mind-set quickly created a new content strategy based around guidance for virtual workers and remote learners who didn't have our experience in this field, and a free course offer increased traffic when other sites were losing it. Our face-to-face marketing calendar switched to virtual, and we explored new partnerships in our sector of mutual benefit. We tried to see the opportunities in the situation to allow our company to grow.

Implications

While the previous chapter examined resilience in individuals, this chapter is the first of four chapters examining resilience in higher-order organization forms and systems – i.e. where groups of individuals are organized in pursuit of a specific purpose. The focus on small firms raises the fundamental question about size and whether a lack of it makes the organization more vulnerable and less able to cope with adversity. The case of leadership during a time of immense tragedy at Expatica Communications demonstrates the human cost of the most brutal form of trauma and the impact this can have on families, co-workers and communities. Being small meant the pain was shared acutely; everyone knew Antoine van Veldhuizen personally. He was not just a senior figure in an elusive C-Suite that the lower-level workers had never met. Similarly, at ITSM Zone we see the effect of the coronavirus pandemic acutely felt by all in the team.

This leads to a first point of reflection, namely, that size does matter. It matters because disruptions that might be easier to cope with in much larger organizations can be devastating in small firms (Lai et al., 2016). As in the Expatica case, members even question whether they want to carry on. Some of the factors mentioned in the literature on small firm resilience are arguably ones that are highly pertinent to organizations of small size. These include the lack of control over events as emphasized by Herbane (2010), external dependence on a supply chain and lower bargaining power as emphasized by Sullivan-Taylor and Branicki (2011) and Smallbone et al. (2012), less diversified product lines with which to spread risk (Smallbone et al., 2012) and an inclination of entrepreneurs in small firms to seek experiences in uncertain and risky environments (Branicki, Sullivan-Taylor and Livschitz, 2018). Size determines how serious the threat is or can become, and how keenly its impact is felt among all employees. This does not mean to say that larger firms have total control over events, are not dependent on supply chains or are successful at avoiding risks. What our analysis at the small firm level does suggest is that small firms are vulnerable to disruptions that larger firms will be able to resist without any major difficulty.

Second, the literature on small firm resilience provides useful insights into how the question of size is relevant as we consider responses to disruption. For firms that are very small (as Expatica was at the time of Antoine van Veldhuizen's death) and that can be considered micro-businesses (<10 employees) the idea that employees in the organization share the same team spirit and entrepreneurial mindset is useful. Blatt's (2009) description of communal schemas and shared cognition is relevant here. It is likely to be easier to develop a communal schema among a handful of people in a small firm than it is among a few hundred thousand employees in a large, diversified multinational enterprise. Individuals will care for each other's needs under a communal schema; there will be greater trust and commitment when it comes to the stresses of executing 'rapidity' (Sullivan-Taylor and Branicki, 2011) in response to an extreme event. Another feature of small firms is that they are often highly networked to the extent that collectively they can act as a larger firm (Moore and Manring, 2009). The resources, skills and capital that small firms need in order to deal with disruption can be made available through the network; utilizing personal contacts between the entrepreneur/founder of the firm and senior contacts in other organizations. In this sense the shared schema can be thought of as being externalized among network partners as well as internalized among employees. Taken together, small firms may have an edge when it comes to aligning trust and reciprocity with rapid responses to disruptive events. Smallbone et al.'s (2012) study on small firm resilience in the UK and New Zealand during the financial crisis is demonstration of this ability to respond quickly with a combination of people and marketing tactics. Multivariate analysis of responses associated with resilient outcomes included motivating staff (for the UK sample), wage freezes (New Zealand sample) and reducing numbers employed (both samples). These variables are in line with an argument that shared cognitive schemas are an important facet of small firms that allow them to make tough decisions with their workforce in order to survive. In the UK sample, it was found that selling more to existing customers was associated with resilience during a financial crisis. This is in line with the logic that externalized trusting relationships with customers (perhaps long-standing personal relationships between the owner/entrepreneur and customers) will matter.

Third, linked to the previous point, we see an interesting concept of 'muddling through' and 'prioritizing day-to-day tasks over preparedness' in small firms (Sullivan-Taylor and Branicki, 2011). Arguably, this is an intrinsic characteristic; their size, narrow focus and limited resources means they are more likely to muddle through compared to larger organizations with established, tried-and-tested structures and processes. Muddling through can have a negative connotation in the English language. But in this context it is quite the opposite – after all, human resource management (HRM) is less likely to be formalized in small firms. And small firms are used to competing amid uncertainty. Lai et al.'s (2016) research showed aspects like training more likely reduced during crisis in a small firm compared to a large firm. Changing employee roles or moving employees to another job were found to be less likely in small firms compared to larger firms (Lai et al., 2016). This profile is entirely consistent with the notion of 'muddling through', defined by Merriam Webster dictionary as "achieving a degree of success without much planning of effort".[3] Cutting or freezing wages could be seen as a way of muddling through during an extreme event (Lai et al., 2016; Smallbone et al., 2012). The Expatica case also provides some light here. At the time of the shock, there could not have been a tried-and-tested way of dealing with the situation, one that could be readily utilized. Welling had to respond quickly, and he had to monitor the situation with his employees, customers and partners, as well as those directly affected by the tragedy in the local community. This was a daily task, relying on his natural instinct and authentic leadership approach. In the long run, his approach was a success, and it was not due to a pre-determined or formalized succession planning or HR system being activated at the time of the tragedy.

Fourth, we see a line of thinking in the literature that small firms can develop the mindsets of 'disruption orientation' (Parker and Ameen, 2018). Quoting Bode et al. (2011: 837), Parker and Ameen described a disruption orientation as "a firm's general awareness and consciousness of, concerns about, seriousness toward and recognition of opportunity to learn from supply chain disruptions" (Parker and Ameen, 2018: 536). Studying small firm resilience in the context of power supply disruptions, Parker and Ameen (2018) operationalized disruption orientation in terms of being alert to disruptions at all times, disruptions showing the firm where it can improve, recognition that disruptions can occur at any time, the firm thinking about how it could have prepared better, and reviewing the firm's impact and response to disruptions in order to improve in the future. This operationalization clearly puts reflective ability and learning orientation at the heart of the capability to deal with disruption. Learning orientation is high when a firm views learning as an investment that is beneficial for sustainable competitive advantage and where managers are willing to question their views of the world (Braunscheidel and Suresh, 2009). Reflective ability – commonly used in areas as diverse as healthcare, teacher training, architecture and the arts, project management and even management

---

3 www.merriam-webster.com/dictionary/muddle%20through, accessed 18 April 2020

consultancy – is about stopping to take stock of events and outcomes, and to actively learn from them with a view to changing ways of working (Williams, 2019). Learning and reflecting do matter for small firms in their quest to becoming more resilient; they matter in a way that is explicitly focused on disruptions and the effects of responses to disruptions. In Parker and Ameen's (2018) study, disruption orientation was operationalized tightly within the context of power supply outages. This was a major source of disruption for small firms in South Africa, leading to some small firms failing completely. While learning orientation will undoubtedly benefit small firms, particularly in hostile and competitive environments, disruption orientation is a more explicit and precise form of learning that is tailored to the specific types of disruptions that the firm has had to deal with in the past.

Fifth, we see a thread in the literature linking organic structures in small firms as a means of bolstering resilience and survival chances. For instance, Biggs, Hall and Stoeckl (2012) found that informal enterprises (small firms operating in the 'informal economy') faired better in a study of small firm resilience during two highly threatening crises: the 2004 tsunami and the 2008 political upheaval. Informal firms were seen to have high levels of social capital with external actors in order to elicit support. Being part of the informal economy, they were more likely (and able) to shut down for short periods and then open up again. And their employees were more able to seek other forms of employment on a temporary basis. But they do not have the same access to finance that firms in the formal economy have. Organic structures tend to be more associated with innovation and entrepreneurial orientation than mechanistic structures, and more suitable in fast-changing competitive and hostile environments (Aiken and Hage, 1971; Burns and Stalker, 1961; Damanpour, 1991). We do see some examples of innovativeness being used by small firms to enhance resilience (Smallbone, North and Kalantaridis, 1999). Nevertheless, lateral and frequent communications, the ability to network beyond the firm's boundaries, and learning orientation (features associated with organic organization) are attributes that we see being linked with survival in studies of small firm resilience. The point above about shared cognitive schemas in an entrepreneurial team also supports this; managerial attitude towards change is associated with organicity and innovativeness (Damanpour, 1991). Nevertheless, it is interesting that some studies show resilience in SMEs not necessarily involving an innovative response; it may involve financial buffering from the owner and a reduction in expenditure on recruitment, overtime and training (Smallbone et al., 2012). This is suggestive of a move towards a centralized and controlled approach, at least during the period of the disruption. Note the Expatica case and how Mark Welling needed to take control. In these situations there is a hybrid of organicity and some elements of mechanistic approaches. As Damanpour (1991) noted: "in a population of organizations, some are continually innovative (organic), some are continually non-innovative (mechanistic), and others are intermittently

Table 3.1 Key themes from the literature on small firm resilience

Theme	*Sub-themes*	*Selected references and examples*
Size-related vulnerability: size does matter	Lack of control over external events; external dependence and low bargaining power; lower diversification; natural tendency to experience uncertainty	Herbane (2010); Sullivan-Taylor and Branicki (2011) and Smallbone et al. (2012); Branicki, Sullivan-Taylor and Livschitz (2018) Expatica case ITSM Zone case
Communal schemas: the small firm as an entrepreneurial team	Internally shared mindsets and cognition; team spirit; rapidity of response; external connectivity; good external relations with customers	Blatt (2009); Sullivan-Taylor and Branicki (2011); Moore and Manring (2009) Expatica case ITSM Zone case
Muddling through	Prioritizing day-to-day tasks; lack of formalized HRM; lack of formal crisis response capability; cutting or freezing employee wages	Sullivan-Taylor and Branicki (2011); Lai et al. (2016)
Disruption orientation	Learning orientation; reflecting on performance and outcomes following a crisis; focus on specific forms of disruption	Parker and Ameen (2018); Braunscheidel and Suresh (2009)
Intermittent resilience	Informal firms temporarily ceasing to trade before re-opening; entrepreneurs having other jobs and sources of income; centralized decision-making during crisis; organic vs mechanistic vs hybrid structures in use over time	Biggs, Hall and Stoeckl (2012); Damanpour (1991); Smallbone et al. (2012)

innovative (intermediate)" (p. 579). Small firms have an ability to switch easily between mechanistic and organic modes, and back again, or to blend elements of both, in ways that work for the specific type of disruption.

Table 3.1 provides a summary of these themes

Learning points

This chapter provides the following learning points:

- Resilience has received explicit attention by researchers of small firms
- Small firms are an interesting type of organization to study resilience because of their relative weakness as an economic actor and their lack of control and influence over external events
- Relevant studies have been conducted in a number of contexts, including: financial crises, industrial contexts, utilities supply and climate change, family firms, formal vs. informal firms
- The types of factors that have been shown to influence resilience in small firms include internal factors such as having a shared cognition or orientation towards disruptions, proactive risk management, HR practices and caring for employees, and effective multi-way communication channels
- Externally oriented actions also matter, including drawing on social connections, communications with external parties, trusting relationships with other organizations
- Themes that we take forward in our broader understanding of organizing for resilience include size-related vulnerability, communal schemas, muddling through, disruption orientation, and intermittent resilience.

Suggested activity and assignment questions

1. Identify a small-sized firm, either through your own networks or through published reports, that has faced a major disruption in the past.
2. Identify the main characteristics of the small firm (size, age, industry, location) and the nature of the disruption it faced.

3. Attempt to gain an insight into what happened in the situation, either by talking to contacts in your network or by examining published reports, and then:

    a. Identify the main variables that helped and/or hindered the company's actions and responses
    b. Try and work out how these variables are interconnected (with each other and with the outcome).

4. Identify ways in which the literature and examples covered in this chapter resonate with the case you identify.
5. Conduct additional literature review and reflect on academic research into the variables you identify.

4

BIG FIRMS, ISOLATED SHOCKS

When shock can be quarantined

The previous chapter looked at potentially overwhelming shocks impinging on organizations of a small size. Let's move along the spectrum of resilience now and consider larger firms. Let's not worry too much about the exact size of the firm in terms of number of employees or revenue, but let's assume a firm that is large enough to have evolved into separate business units, separate subsidiaries. The firm has grown and diversified, product-market-wise, geographically, or both. The inevitable shocks that come along may not confront the different parts of the firm in the same way. In the case of international firms, we find that even in the same host country different subsidiaries can feel the effects of – and respond to – local turbulence in different ways (Williams, Colovic and Zhu, 2017). They cope differently depending on their unique circumstances, strategic postures and management decisions. What may be an issue for Unit A or Subsidiary A may not be an issue (or may be less of an issue) for Unit B or Subsidiary B.

A disruptive force that might threaten the survival of Unit A or Subsidiary A might have little effect on Unit B or Subsidiary B.

Scholars have looked at this in various ways, often without using the framing or language of resilience. However, unit or subsidiary survival can be seen as a resilient outcome and relevant work from the field of corporate strategy and international business is useful. Outcomes are a consequence of strategic decisions and managerial actions relating to growth and diversification. For instance, in the international business literature, a significant stream of work has examined the reasons for foreign subsidiaries of international companies to fail, framing this in terms of foreign subsidiary survival (Delios and Beamish, 2001; Garg and Delios, 2007; Gaur and Lu, 2007; Li, 1995). Work has also looked at why some subsidiaries in some locations succeed in their innovation projects with local partners, while others fail (Williams and Du, 2014). As the case of Tesco's Fresh & Easy in the US in this chapter shows, large firms do not quit easily, especially when the investment and commitment has been large. But sometimes they do say to themselves "enough is enough", and they cut their losses and exit from a field of play they only recently entered. Meanwhile, the firm remains active, productive and possibly quite profitable in other places. This phenomenon is a proxy for resilience in *parts of large firms*. Shock is at least partially quarantined in one operating domain of the organization's universe, and in the worst case scenario can be dealt with by fully exiting from that domain.

Literature review on resilience in parts of large firms

Definitional considerations

What is resilience in parts of large firms?

It's about differential strain. There is an increasing acknowledgement from scholars that disruptions can generate a variety of strains on different parts of organizations rather than the whole; this being referred to as "differential strain" (Kahn et al., 2018). As Kahn et al. (2018) noted, some parts remain unaffected, while others bear significant strain. We therefore take our definition of resilience (i.e. "the capacity for an enterprise to survive, adapt, and grow in the face of turbulent change" – Fiksel, 2006: 16) and apply it to parts of large organizations. So, the definition becomes: "the capacity for *part of an enterprise* to survive, adapt, and grow in the face of turbulent change" (emphasis added). Similarly, our definition of disruption (i.e. an event occurring externally or internally to the organization that has the potential to negatively impact the operating strategy and performance of the organization) is adjusted to refer to an event occurring externally or internally to a part of the organization that has the potential to negatively impact the operating strategy and performance of that part of the organization.

It's about geographic demarcation. Nohara and Verdier (2001) pointed out that sources of resilience for firms are embedded in the societies where they operate; local industrial policies matter as does the nature of academic-industrial research links and the quality of higher education. For firms spread out across large countries such as China or the US, the localized environment provides sources of external and internal disruption that can affect the part of the organization established in that location. Williams and Du (2014) showed that when subsidiaries of foreign MNEs (multinational enterprises) operating in China engage in innovation projects with local partners, the success of the projects is determined by the nature of the location in combination with the type of trust adopted in the relationship with the partner. Dai, Eden and Beamish (2013) examined the effect of geography on foreign subsidiary survival where the subsidiaries were located in countries afflicted by political conflict. They found that the geographic domain of the MNE is fundamental to its performance and its survival. Subsidiary survival depends largely on the characteristics both of the place (the conflict) and of the space (distance) between the subsidiary and its peers.

It's about diverse governance norms. In a study of the post-industrial governance forms of organizations in developed countries, McCann, Morris and Hassard (2008) noted how some organizations have been forced to modify forms of governance due to global economic liberalization and information and communication technology (ICT) developments. Williams and Vrabie (2018) identified how different R&D characteristics of host countries influence the governance mode (in terms of ownership stake) taken by investing foreign MNEs. Differences in the nature of the external environment across countries are pressures that are keenly felt by strategists. In their study of the US and Japan, McCann, Morris and Hassard (2008) described two types of governance forms for managing capital: 'shareholder capitalism' in the US and 'managerial capitalism' in Japan. Although external threats have forced changes in these approaches, it is noted that shareholder capitalism in the US had intensified with an even greater emphasis on 'shareholder value', whereas managerial capitalism in Japan had taken on features more akin to the shareholder variety, with many of the HRM features of the Japanese model remaining. Dedoussis (2001) argued that Japan's distinctive HRM practices at both the intra-firm level and the inter-firm level are resilient amid change. Despite changes in the *Keiretsu* system of industrial organization in the 1990s, the relationship between large-scale enterprises and permanent workforces continued to be a distinctive management practice.

It's about differentiation. In an analysis of a set of resilient companies over two decades, Reinmoeller and van Baardwijk (2005) found that companies simultaneously employ a dynamic balance of several innovation strategies in order to enhance their adaptation in diverse and turbulent environments. These include commitment to strategic diversity in innovation, knowledge exploitation and exploration in a disciplined manner, entrepreneurial behaviour to drive innovation, as well as a balance between internal exploration and cooperation strategies. Although innovation has increasingly become a priority on corporate strategy agendas, it was found that only those companies that allocate sufficient resources to innovation can successfully overcome setbacks and adapt accordingly. Investments in innovation should not be driven by short-term returns or cost, but rather should focus on maintaining a dynamic balance of innovation strategies for the changing context in order to become a resilient high-performer.

In a study of British and American MNE disinvestments, Sachdev (1976) identified voluntary and involuntary disinvestment as two main ways of exiting from foreign markets. Voluntary disinvestment refers to the decision made by a firm to eliminate a part of or all of its ownership in a foreign country on a voluntary basis. Reasons include unsatisfactory performance, a lack of management and liquid resources, and disagreements in general policies. In contrast, involuntary disinvestments are those companies that had little choice other than having parts of them being taken over by the host government through nationalization, expropriation, or confiscation. Through a discussion of findings of four significant factors (financial, organizational, technological and special factors) impacting disinvestment decisions, Sachdev (1976) concluded that most MNEs are ill prepared and ill equipped to deal with the problems of foreign disinvestment. There tend to be 'closed attitudes' amongst the management; disinvestment is seen as a failure. In addition, there are many other reasons, such as poor investment appraisal at the time of original investment and too little involvement of lower-level managers and of the host and parent governments when making decisions.

Contexts of studies about resilience in parts of large firms

Examples include the following.

Conflict zones. Driffield, Jones and Crotty (2013) were some of the first to examine the decision made by international firms investing in conflict zones in other countries as part of their internationalization. Internal conflict in countries is a feature that can threaten the survival of local organizations and entrepreneurs (Bullough, Renko and Myatt, 2014), let alone international investors. But conflict does not deter all international investors; many are willing to accept the risk. Such companies will end up with parts of their global operations in conflict zones and other parts outside such zones. The authors found that where institutions are weak and there is less concern for CSR in the home country, then the firm is more likely to invest in a host country characterized by conflict. The extent to which those investments endure was examined by Dai, Eden and Beamish (2013), who looked at the effects of place and space on Japanese MNE subsidiaries in 25 conflict zones around the world. The geographic concentration with home-country peers (neighbours) helps outside-zone subsidiaries to survive, and a more geographically dispersed MNE network (far-away siblings) helps inside-zone subsidiaries to survive. The geographic concentration generates self-reinforcing agglomeration economies that boosts chances of survival. The study showed how geographic dispersion of the MNE's network in the host country can have different effects on the survival of the subsidiary.

Developing market firms. Thomas et al. (2007) studied how three forms of experience by emerging market firms – (1) alliance experience with developed market firms; (2) previous failure experience in developed markets; and (3) numbers of prior entries in developed markets – relate to market entry and survival in developed markets. The results showed that experience does influence emerging market firm success in developed markets but is subject to cognitive biases of managers. Alliance experience with developed market partners means there will be a greater probability of entering a host country although this decreases survival chances. It is argued that this is because knowledge gained from alliance experience with developed market firms in the emerging market firm's home market produces a false sense of confidence that is difficult to be transferred to a developed market. However, prior experience of failure in developed markets is usefully transferable, increasing the resilience of the subsidiary. The authors suggested that failures in a developed market can be a valuable source of learning assuming the firm is able to process this knowledge effectively. Consistent with other scholars (e.g. Hitt et al., 2005), emerging market firms might better engage in exploitative learning in other emerging markets first and later enter more challenging developed markets.

Global supply chains. An example here is Botes, Niemann and Kotzé's (2017) investigation into the underlying mechanisms through which buyer-supplier collaboration enables supply chain resilience. The findings suggested that collaborative activities between a focal firm and its suppliers do not directly influence resilience in supply chains, but enable the antecedents of supply chain resilience (SCR): visibility, velocity, and flexibility. More specifically, joint knowledge creation enables not only supply chain visibility but also velocity through process insights and preparedness based on past experience of disruption mitigations. Furthermore, collective effort and information sharing between the focal firm and its suppliers enable all three SCR antecedents. Visibility is enabled by collective effort and information available to network members, whereas velocity in response to supply chain disruptions is enhanced by collaborative communication that allows buyer and supplier to identify opportunities for streamlining and optimizing processes. Information sharing enables flexibility through the early identification of risks. This allows sufficient time to organize supply chain elements to respond effectively to a disruption. However, the extent of information-sharing is limited by legislation that indicates the types of information that can be shared without breaching competition law.

The survival of foreign subsidiaries: an ideal proxy for understanding resilience in parts of large firms

In international business and global strategy there is a specific literature on survival of foreign subsidiaries of MNEs. This can serve in understanding the topic of resilience in parts of large firms. There are a number of ways it can do this.

First, it provides an understanding of how different tangible and intangible assets possessed by the firm influence profitability and survival of parts of the firm. Delios and Beamish (2001) examined how a firm's intangible assets and experience impact the survival and profitability of its foreign subsidiaries. The results showed survival and profitability are determined by different factors. A multinational firm's experience in a host country has a direct effect on survival by (1) developing new capabilities that offset the liability of foreignness and (2) enhancing adaptation by utilizing existing intangible assets to be competitive in a new market context. However, host country experience does not have an independent relationship with foreign subsidiary profitability. The findings suggest that a firm's ability to exploit its intangible assets in specific parts of its global network is contingent on its experience in specific localities where it has a presence.

Second, the subsidiary survival literature shows how a firm's membership or affiliation to a broader organizational form (such as a business group) can help the resilience of a part of the firm. This is particularly relevant in developing economies in East Asia where business groups are prevalent and business group affiliation has been shown to be a driver of innovation performance in firms (Choi, Lee and Williams, 2011). This highlights the phenomenon of the transfer of advantages from 'outside' the firm (but within its home country) to parts of the firm that are in need of help. Garg and Delios (2007) investigated the survival rates of foreign subsidiaries of MNEs from India to test if affiliation to a business group affects a subsidiary's survival chances. The results showed that business group affiliation does not influence survival rates, but it does have a contingent effect depending on the host country's stage of development. More specifically, the effect of business group affiliation emerges mostly as a contextually related influence in which subsidiary survival rates for business group affiliated firms tend to be most strongly augmented when a subsidiary of a business group affiliated firm is founded in a developing country. A developed country context characterized by a strong institutional environment promotes market-based transactions rather than personalized exchange through relationships. However, the likelihood of success was greater when founded in a developing country as opposed to in a developed country. The authors pointed out that foreign ventures of emerging economy MNEs are better able to compete in other developing countries where they can exploit their firm specific advantages better suited to the developing country environment. In this sense, the domestic advantages of business group membership are transferable internationally and these advantages do impact resilience in parts of the firm.

Third, the international business literature examines the effects of distance on subsidiary performance and survival. Distance comes in various forms; geographic, administrative, cultural, economic (Ghemawat, 2001). This has often required the blending of different underlying theories. Gaur and Lu (2007), for instance, integrated institutional theory and the organizational learning perspective to examine how ownership strategies affect subsidiary performance. They found that, in institutionally distant countries, the effect of ownership is contingent on institutional distance and host country experience. The negative effect of host country experience is weaker if foreign parents have more ownership in the subsidiaries. Subsidiaries will be more resilient if foreign parent companies have larger ownership positions. Relatedly, Sousa and Tan (2015) investigated the determinants of a firm's exit decision from foreign markets based on Chinese outward FDI (foreign direct investment). They found that strategic misfit between a foreign affiliate and headquarters negatively impacts an affiliate's survival. Cultural distance acts as a moderating effect on the relationship between internal strategic fit and the exit decision, amplifying the likelihood of exit. However, firms that enter markets at a large cultural distance are less willing to immediately withdraw from the market if the affiliate is poorly performing. The authors suggested that the headquarters are aware of difficulties facing the affiliate and are sensitive to giving more time to it when there is a large cultural distance.

Fourth, work has looked at the relationship between entry strategy and subsidiary survival. For instance, Li (1995) examined how (1) diversification, (2) entry strategies and (3) organizational experience impact subsidiary survival. These initial strategic choices made by the firm are associated with various hazards of eventual exit. There is a higher exit rate with diversification into an unrelated product, i.e., away from the firm's main product. Foreign entry strategies through acquisitions and joint ventures have a higher exit rate than greenfield investments. Finally, there is a benefit from experience in foreign locations in terms of increasing the potential for success in future investment abroad.

Fifth, the subsidiary survival literature has examined corporate communications and public relations surrounding what for many would be perceived as a negative storyline of an exit from a market. Posnikoff (1997) found that US firms experienced a positive significant increase in returns immediately when they made a public announcement of plans to withdraw from South Africa during the 1980s. Trading volume for the disinvesting portfolio also was significantly higher than historical trends would have predicted. The effect of the announcement of withdrawal from South Africa was a good 'public relation' with audiences concerned about continued involvement in the South African economy. These findings showed a critical role of government and private investment policies, either directly (e.g. the US government's imposition of sanctions in October 1986 that restricted any further investment in South Africa) or indirectly (e.g. California's public funds divestment announcement of September 1986), in encouraging firms to withdraw their operations from South Africa.

Finally, the subsidiary survival literature also shows the importance of time and path dependency in understanding resilience in parts of large firms. For instance, Park, Lee and Hong (2011) studied the effect of MNE international order of entry strategies on the exits of their subsidiaries based on a set of 61 parent firms and their 500 foreign subsidiaries spanning 51 markets during the period 1999–2004. They found that, in the context of Korean business groups, the order of entry and the core competencies of these MNEs are interrelated. If the first-movers have stronger competitive advantages than late-movers, the pioneers' subsidiaries have better survival rates than do those of latecomers. Otherwise, the latecomers in international markets have greater survival rates than pioneers.

Case #3 – Tesco's Fresh & Easy: Learning from the US exit

IVEY | Publishing

9B13M126

TESCO'S FRESH & EASY: LEARNING FROM THE U.S. EXIT[1]

R. Chandrasekhar wrote this case under the supervision of Professor Christopher Williams solely to provide material for class discussion. *The authors do not intend to illustrate either effective or ineffective handling of a managerial situation. The authors may have disguised certain names and other identifying information to protect confidentiality.*

Version: 2014-12-17

In mid-April 2013, Philip Clarke, chief executive officer (CEO) of Tesco PLC (Tesco), the world's third largest global retailer headquartered in London, United Kingdom, was scheduled to make a formal statement to the company's stakeholders about the future of Fresh & Easy Neighborhoods Market Inc. (Fresh & Easy), the company's fully owned subsidiary in the United States.

Tesco had already discontinued its operations in the United States and reported this in the annual financial results for the year ending February

1 This case has been written on the basis of published sources only. Consequently, the interpretation and perspectives presented in this case are not necessarily those of Tesco PLC or any of its employees.

2013. This followed a decision after a December 2012 Strategic Review that Fresh & Easy "would not deliver acceptable returns for shareholders in an appropriate timeframe."[2] The U.S. exit was to be made public on April 17, while Clarke would be announcing the preliminary results for the year 2012/13.

Overall, this decision had raised three fundamental questions. First, was exiting the U.S. market in 2012 the right decision? Second, how should the company manage the process of exit? Third, what were the takeaways from the U.S. operations that Tesco could apply elsewhere in its global strategy?

CLARKE'S GLOBAL PUZZLE

When he took over as CEO in March 2011, after holding several commercial and marketing roles at Tesco for over three decades, Clarke had placed the U.S. operations on his list of priorities. Although Fresh & Easy was generating only about 1 per cent of Tesco's consolidated revenues, its potential had strategic implications for the company. The rate of growth in the United Kingdom, the home market that was generating over 65 per cent of group sales and 75 per cent of group margins, had been stagnant. International revenues had therefore become crucial to the company's profitability. In addition, the United States was the second largest food retail market in the world, making it strategically risky, in the long term, for Tesco *not* to have a footprint there.

Tesco had opened its first wholly owned greenfield store in the United States in November 2007 at Hemet, a city in the state of California, amid expectations that a presence in the United States, once established, would be as successful as the long-standing presence in the United Kingdom where Tesco was the market leader. Over the next five years, Fresh & Easy had expanded into a chain of 200 stores across three states of the U.S. West Coast — California, Arizona and Nevada. It had absorbed capital investments of £1.2 billion ($1.6 billion).[3] Fresh & Easy was growing its annual

2 Earnings conference call, Tesco PLC, April 17, 2013.

3 *Reuters*, *"Tesco Launches Strategic Review of US Chain," www.cnbc.com/id/100278039, accessed April 19, 2013.*

revenues every year, but it was also incurring losses. On sales of £628 million for the year ending February 2012, it had incurred an operating loss of £153 million.

Tesco had also been present since September 2004 in China, the largest food retail market in the world (see Exhibit 1), through a joint venture (JV) with a local retail chain.[4] Clarke was contemplating a measured approach characterized by a "focus on stand-alone retail sites in the three regions of China where we have critical mass and good margins."[5] He had decided, in January 2012, to pull out of Japan, the third largest grocery market, because even after nine years of operations, Tesco had not turned the corner in that country; in fact, it had incurred losses of about £30 million. Tesco sold 50 per cent of its stake in the JV to Aeon Co, the second largest retail group in Japan, as part of an exit plan.[6]

Tesco had leading market positions in Thailand, South Korea, Hungary, Malaysia and Slovakia. However, it was struggling in Poland, Turkey and the Czech Republic.[7]

TESCO — COMPANY BACKGROUND

Tesco was founded in 1919 by Jack Cohen, a Polish immigrant who was operating a wholesale business from a market stall in London's East End. The first own-brand product sold by him was tea; it was called Tesco. The name was taken from the initials of T.E. Stockwell, who was a partner in the firm of tea suppliers, and the first two letters of the founder's surname. It was later adopted as the name of the company that went on to become the third largest retailer in the world (see Exhibit 2).

Tesco had group revenues of £64.83 billion for the year ending February 2013 and net profits of £0.12 billion (see Exhibit 3). It had 6,784 stores and employed 416,441 people full time worldwide. In addition to the United

---

4 *Tesco Annual Report 2004–05, p. 6.*

5 *Earnings conference call.*

6 *www.aeon.info/common/images/en/pressroom/imgsrc/121128R_1.pdf, accessed September 12, 2013.*

7 *Earnings conference call.*

Kingdom, Tesco was operating in 10 countries: China, Czech Republic, Hungary, Malaysia, Poland, Slovakia, South Korea, Thailand, Turkey and the United States.

Tesco offered both products (i.e., foods, general merchandise, electrical goods, clothing, petrol and mobile phones) and services (i.e., online sales, telecommunication services and financial services) at its stores. The financial services (including credit cards, loans, savings accounts, insurance and mortgages) were limited to the United Kingdom and operated by Tesco Bank, a subsidiary. The company sourced many of its food, clothing and general merchandise globally. It also bought many products directly from producers and manufacturers. The company's group sourcing operations were headquartered in Hong Kong.

Tesco was operating in a competitive domain of retailing in which losing customers to competitors was the single largest threat. Customer retention was thus one of the major challenges. The company was also witnessing opportunities in three areas: emerging markets (e.g., China, India and Thailand), which offered long-term prospects for growth; online channels, which were growing rapidly, particularly with the onset of smart phones; and private labels, which were becoming a source of differentiation.[8]

Strategy

Tesco's corporate strategy had seven elements:[9]

- To grow the U.K. core,
- To be an outstanding international retailer both in stores and online,
- To be as strong in everything as it was in food,
- To grow retail services in all markets,
- To be responsible to the communities it serves,
- To be a creator of highly valued brands, and
- To build a team so as to create more value.

---

8 Datamonitor Report, March 27, 2012, www.thomsonone.com/Workspace/Main.aspx?View=Action%3dOpen&BrandName=www.thomsonone.com&IsSsoLogin=True, accessed September 26, 2012.

9 Tesco Annual Report 2012, p. 4.

Growing the U.K. core was critical because the United Kingdom was the largest business in the group and a key driver of sales and profit. The major issues the company was addressing in the United Kingdom were that "the shopping trip just hasn't been improving fast enough," and that "our standards haven't been as consistent as our customers have come to expect."[10] Tesco was implementing a series of improvements under initiatives designated as follows:

- Service & Staff: providing training and equipment to employees to help them deliver better service.
- Stores & Formats: making retail stores better places in which to shop and work.
- Price & Value: delivering value for money to customers through the right blend of price, promotions and loyalty rewards.
- Range & Quality: improving the quality and variety of products and services.
- Brand & Marketing: ensuring the right communication with customers.
- Clicks & Bricks: offering a combination of online and offline presence.

Becoming an outstanding international retailer was critical in the light of markets in Europe having become mature and those in Asia (with the exception of Japan) holding the promise of growth. International sales were generating 32 per cent of group revenue and 29 per cent of group profits. The focus in Europe was on consolidating existing stores. The focus in Asia was on investing in new stores.

Becoming strong in non-food businesses (e.g., general merchandise, clothing and electricals) was important because they were discretionary purchases; customers could withhold buying them, unlike food items, particularly when incomes were falling. Both Europe and Asia were delivering stronger performances in non-food businesses than the U.S. market.

As far as the other strategic elements were concerned, growing retail services was vital in the light of the fact that consumers were increasingly spending a larger proportion of their incomes on services (such as eating out, telecoms or financial services.) Being responsible to the communities

10 Ibid.

it serves meant providing customers with safe, good quality, affordable, nutritious food and creating good jobs and careers for its employees. Being a creator of highly valued brands was essential because brands attracted customers, and brand management skills could be leveraged in different markets. Building a team to create more value was central to the objective of leadership development at Tesco.

Tesco was deploying a multi-format approach to its store network in order to meet customers' needs for different types of shopping trips. The formats fell into four types: Tesco Extra stores averaging more than 60,000 square feet and offering a full range of groceries and home goods; Tesco Superstores averaging 50,000 square feet and offering a range of food and non-food items; Tesco Metro stores averaging 15,000 square feet and offering ready-made meals and sandwiches; and Tesco Express stores averaging 3,000 square feet and offering fresh produce, wines, spirits and bakery products. The company's business model, for many years, was based on the premise "We buy, move and sell products and services to our customers and use customer insight to do this slightly better each time."[11]

International Expansion

It was in the early 1990s that Tesco took a decision to internationalize its operations. In 2003, it ranked eighth among the top 10 retailers in the world by sales[12] and was progressively moving up in rankings.

In order to identify target countries for entry, the management used some preliminary yardsticks: the population size must be showing signs of growth; personal incomes should be on the rise; the local retail markets, in particular the grocery markets, should be fragmented; and large global retailers should not already be present. Countries of Eastern Europe and Asia qualified in the first round for further diligence.

In 1995, Tesco made its first overseas acquisition of S-Market's stores in Hungary followed by acquisitions in three new countries in the next year — Poland (Savia stores), the Czech Republic (K-Mart stores) and Slovakia

11 *Ibid., p. 25.*

12 *www.retail-week.com/tesco-joins-worlds-top-10/1725722.article, accessed October 26, 2013.*

(also K-Mart stores). Subsequently, it entered Thailand (Lotus stores) in 1998, South Korea (Homeplus stores) in 1999, Malaysia (in a JV with Sime Darby) in 2002, Turkey (Kipa stores) and Japan (C2 Network stores) in 2003 and China (in collaboration with China Resources Enterprise) in 2004. Its foray into the United States in 2007 was Tesco's first wholly owned greenfield venture.[13]

The underlying premise of Tesco's international expansion was "We will win locally by applying our skills globally."[14] The company believed that retailers going overseas had to be flexible, "thinking through the correct entry for each market, being selective in their focus and picking markets carefully in order to safeguard capital, management time and know-how."[15] Examples of localization included prayer rooms in Tesco stores in Malaysia and selling fresh frogs in China. It did not sell poultry, popular in the United Kingdom, in its stores in South Korea. Pork was a draw in Tesco's stores in China but not in Malaysia.

By 2012, Tesco had over 3,200 stores in 12 countries outside the United Kingdom, nearly equivalent to the number of stores it had in its home country. It was leveraging "group skill and group scale"[16] to move into the next phase of international expansion.

Drawing on group skill meant applying expertise from individual countries to *all* markets of Tesco. An example was the Clubcard, the company's loyalty program. Having invested millions of pounds to develop the program in the United Kingdom in the late 1990s, Tesco could introduce a loyalty scheme relevant to each market at a fraction of the original cost. Drawing on group scale meant using the size of the company to lower prices, improve quality and source new and different products from the best suppliers around the world. An example was the sourcing of bananas from a single source for the global market.[17]

---

13 *www.tescoplc.com/index.asp?pageid=306. accessed October 27, 2013.*

14 Tesco Annual Report 2012, p. 16.

15 "Tesco Takes Its Time to Build Global Empire," The Telegraph, November 21, 2005, www.telegraph.co.uk/finance/2926469/Tesco-takes-its-time-to-build-global-empire.html, accessed October 22, 2013.

16 Tesco Annual Report 2012, p. 16.

17 Ibid.

Tesco drew on a common pool of resources and tools in its international expansion. It applied standardized property blueprints and the same specialist team of designers to build each store at a new international location. It was thus able to reduce costs, lower the carbon footprint, ensure effective space utilization and make the store operational in less time. Tesco was also rolling out identical processes and systems as part of an approach it called "One platform, many markets: the best everywhere." It was improving back-office efficiency through a shared service centre located in India, which was monitoring store operations such as self-service checkouts for all markets. The company also had centralized the distribution and logistics at its depots in Poland and China for products procured globally.

South Korea was the largest international country by sales in which Tesco had been most innovative with technology. It had set up virtual stores in subways and bus stops where time-pressed customers could shop on-the-go using their smart phones. The displays, which included a range of daily items (from milk and apples to pet food and stationery), appeared on the pillars and screen doors at subway stations for commuters to scan the QR code beneath the product on their smart phones. They could pick them up at a designated store of their convenience or even have them home delivered at a time of their choice.

Tesco had near leadership positions in all Asian markets. The European markets were relatively smaller in size. Economic downturn in the region had made consolidation a priority over expansion (see Exhibit 4).

U.S. FRESH FOODS INDUSTRY[18]

The fresh foods industry in the United States had nine categories (see Exhibit 5). Some had shown static growth in volume in 2007 over the previous year, largely due to the recession. The industry had long-term prospects for growth because of concerns over the country's health card. Obesity, for example, was a nationwide concern. In 2009–10, a majority of the U.S. population — 35.7 per cent of adults and 16.9 per cent of children

---

18 www.portal.euromonitor.com.proxy1.lib.uwo.ca/Portal/Pages/Statistics/Statistics.aspx, accessed October 25, 2013.

and adolescents — were obese.[19] The poor health record of the country had been widely publicized in the media since mid-2000. Consumers were being prompted by both grocery retailers and the government to act.

Retailers were influencing the buying habits of adults in the United States by promoting sales of healthy foods such as fresh produce through new marketing techniques and store redesigns. They had two incentives: fresh food generated higher margins than packaged food, and it had a faster turnaround. The federal government was influencing the eating habits of children in different ways. One example was the revision of meal patterns and nutritional standards, based on the latest dietary guidelines, in the National School Lunch Program. The revision was aimed at increasing the proportion of fruits, vegetables and whole grains in the school menu.

The industry had other drivers in terms of the rising cost of health care in the United States, which was spurring consumers to take personal responsibility for health, and demographic changes, which meant that seniors and young working adults were both at the forefront of the dietary transition towards a higher proportion of low-cost/high-protein options. A major trend was the launch of private labels in fresh foods as a response to consumer need for low-cost alternatives. Veganism was another trend leading to demand for meatless proteins such as lentils in the United States.

Supermarkets and hypermarkets were the dominant distribution channels for fresh foods, accounting for more than 60 per cent of volume sales. They were remodeling their stores to offer an expanded assortment of fresh foods but were facing challenges from two segments: Internet retailers and farmers' markets.

Internet retailers in the United States were growing at 6 per cent every year. Their advantages were home shopping and home delivery. The largest of them all, Amazon.com, was planning to offer a wide range of groceries and fresh food online by leveraging its skills in logistics. Farmers' markets were growing in number every year by 10 per cent. They appealed to the desire on the part of consumers to control the origin of their food.

---

19 Cynthia L Ogden, et al., "Prevalence of Obesity in the United States 2009–10," NCHS Data Brief, January 2012, www. cdc.gov/nchs/data/databriefs/db82.pdf, accessed November 05, 2013.

Historically, fresh food was highly commoditized. Of late, however, there were innovations in packaging and labeling. There were also value additions such as produce traceability leading to brand building.

FRESH & EASY

Tesco was drawn to the United States not only because of its own growth aspirations but because it saw that country as a market that, in spite of "having enough grocery stores," rewarded "innovative retailers" with returns that were "quite good by international standards."[20] Innovation became a plank of Tesco's growth platform in the United States from the beginning. The company had done homework lasting over a year. Several Tesco executives stayed at the homes of ordinary Americans, following them as they shopped, cooked and ate. They took a "good look at what they kept in their fridges and their cupboards"[21] and made notes.

One of the surprises for Tesco managers was that while the United States was known as the land of plenty, the quality of processed fresh foods in its supermarkets was not high; they contained preservatives, flavours and colors that consumers would rather not have. Tesco saw an opportunity for a retailer that recognized the issues that Americans cared about — not only freshness of food but also their larger concerns about health, obesity, community and global warming.

California was the choice for a launch territory for four reasons. It was similar to the size of the U.K. market; it was described as a "food desert"[22] dominated by cheap, fast-food establishments; it helped pass off the warehouse where the store prototype was being built as a movie set, preserving the element of surprise among competitors; and together with Arizona and

20 Cecilie Rohwedder, "Tesco Studies Hard for U.S. Debut," Wall Street Journal, June 28, 2007, global.factiva.com. proxy1.lib.uwo.ca/ha/default.aspx, accessed September 29, 2013.

21 Ibid.

22 Romesh Vaitilingam, "Tesco Goes West," www.southampton.ac.uk/assets/imported/transforms/peripheral-block/ UsefulDownloads_Download/BB0D1F202B5242C58A80ADCC69A25C03/Britain_In_2012_Tesco.pdf, accessed April 26, 2013.

Nevada, California played host to many new housing development projects where new stores could be opened.

The format was decided in favour of a convenience supermarket because the pre-entry analysis pointed to a gap in U.S. retail in terms of a small store (of about 10,000 square feet), a format in which Tesco also had operating skills in its home market. The new format was positioned to offer the freshness of Whole Foods, the value of Wal-Mart, the convenience of Walgreens and a product range similar to Trader Joe's. Greenfield became the growth route because acquisitions complying with the differentiation that Tesco wanted in the United States were not easy to come by on the West Coast.

The format influenced the store size; it would be about 10,000 square feet, much smaller than a standard supermarket of 50,000 square feet. It also influenced the assortment; each Fresh & Easy store would carry about 3,500 stock keeping units (SKUs) as compared to about 40,000 SKUs available in an average U.S. supermarket. A bulk of the merchandise consisted of private labels sourced locally.[23]

Tesco built a state-of-the-art campus in Riverside, California, housing a distribution centre, which had the infrastructure to cater to the needs of 1,000 stores targeted over the long term on the West Coast alone, and a kitchen, where a large assortment of ready-to-eat" foods was prepared. The strategic view at the company was that once it reached a critical mass of 400 stores, Fresh & Easy would achieve break-even.

Tesco's Unorthodox Retail Concepts

Tesco brought concepts into its stores that were not only novel for U.S. consumers but went against the grain of U.S. retailing.

For example, Americans were used to being helped by a clerk at the cash counter who would also bag the groceries for them; Fresh & Easy stores had only self-checkouts. Americans were used to buying in bulk once a month; Fresh & Easy encouraged more frequent trips to its stores. Americans preferred variety and size in their merchandise; the displays at

---

23 articles.latimes.com/2013/sep/10/business/la-fi-burkle-fresh-easy-20130911, accessed November 07, 2013.

Fresh & Easy were limited in terms of the number of SKUs. Americans, in general, had large appetites; the servings of ready-to-eat meals were small. Americans preferred long expiry dates; Fresh & Easy products had limited shelf life. Americans preferred a store that was organized; the store layout at Fresh & Easy was unorthodox. Americans spent more on flowers than Europeans did; Fresh & Easy did not offer floral products. Americans shopped for bakery products; Fresh & Easy did not offer them. Customers in California shopped in shorts and T-shirts; the focus on freshness meant open deep freeze refrigerated cabinets in Fresh & Easy stores. Americans drove for shopping, expecting parking lots; Fresh & Easy stores were usually in walking distance in a neighbourhood. Americans were picky shoppers, examining each item before placing it in their carts; Fresh & Easy offered farm produce wrapped in cellophane bundles that could not be examined. All successful U.S. retailers had tailored their product assortments to fit the specific demands of demographic groups shopping at each particular outlet; Fresh & Easy employed a uniform product mix at each location.

Although each innovation was meant to change the buying habits of Americans and veer them towards health and wellness, Fresh & Easy was also regularly re-examining its innovations. For example, over time, it introduced bakery products in 30 per cent of its stores, offered floral products and put doors on all the cabinets to minimize the impact of refrigeration. It had also downsized its range of health and beauty products because U.S. consumers preferred to buy them at drug stores. Tesco had also rolled out a loyalty card —the Clubcard that was already successful in the United Kingdom — in its U.S. stores.

Early Results

A few months after the launch in November 2007, Tesco said that the new concept had been well-received by U.S. consumers and that 93 per cent of customers were satisfied with the overall shopping experience. The company also said that it was confident that its sales per square foot would ultimately be double that of conventional supermarkets and reach close to two-thirds of Trader Joe's, a leading U.S. retailer.

In March 2008, the board of Tesco convened in the United States to "enhance their understanding of the progress of the Fresh & Easy operation."[24] It was a pointer to the growing strategic importance of the U.S. operations for the company's leadership. The sales per square foot of Fresh & Easy stores, exceeding $20 per square foot per week, were ahead of the U.S. supermarket industry average. Fresh categories were selling well, confirming that the core offerings of Fresh & Easy had gained acceptance with U.S. consumers.[25]

2008 was also the period when the first signs of the deteriorating property market in the United States became evident, particularly in Arizona and Nevada. By the end of February 2009, Tesco had opened only 119 of the 1,000 projected stores on the West Coast. It was not even opening some stores that were fully built.

As the U.S. economy slid into a severe recession, the states of California, Arizona and Nevada were particularly affected. The national unemployment rate, for instance, which topped at 9.6 per cent in 2010, reached 12.4 per cent, 10.4 per cent and 13.2 per cent in California, Arizona and Nevada, respectively, in the same year.[26] Consumers were stretching their budgets; they were trading down to low-priced private labels and turning to retail channels that offered the lowest prices (i.e., hypermarkets, warehouse clubs and variety stores). The growth in the supermarket channel since 2008 in states such as California and Arizona was trailing most other states (and the national average) by a significant margin.

Fresh & Easy by then employed 5,000 people in its stores. It had a highly centralized organization in the United States, handling 85 per cent of the logistics on its own. The costs of central functions amounted to 5 per cent of sales in the United States as opposed to 1.5 per cent in the United Kingdom. Fresh & Easy was incurring overheads on unopened outlets in addition to paying for the lease of a huge area of land — bigger than Disneyland — which it had earmarked as a distribution centre in northern California.

Some financial analysts had begun to question the merits of U.S. expansion. "The main thing is that they underestimated how Americans shop,"

24 Tesco Annual Report 2009, p. 47.

25 Tesco Annual Report 2008, p. 11.

26 blog.euromonitor.com/2013/04/in-the-wrong-place-at-the-wrong-time-how-the-location-of-tescos-us-experiment-contributed-to-its-fai.html, accessed September 26, 2013.

said one, adding, "They didn't have a very clear proposition. Are they a convenience store? Are they a discount store? Who are they?"[27]

The ongoing recession brought the identity crisis at Fresh & Easy into sharp focus. As a mid-priced supermarket, it was being frequented by neither high-income consumers who, unaffected by recession, were shopping at specialty, gourmet and high-end supermarkets such as Whole Foods nor middle- and lower-income consumers who, affected by recession, were turning to retailers offering the lowest prices such as Wal-Mart. Fresh & Easy seemed caught in what a blogger called a "format muddle."[28]

RECENT EVENTS IN INTERNATIONAL MARKETS

Tesco had recognized in early 2013 that discipline in capital allocation was the key to unlocking value in international expansion. It decided to focus its international growth on "high growth economies with relatively less developed retail sectors."[29] Accordingly, it segmented its foreign markets into three groups.[30] The first consisted of those characterized by not only robust economic growth but also strong market positions for Tesco. Among the existing markets, Thailand, South Korea and Malaysia were part of this group and so qualified for priority in resource allocation. The second consisted of markets characterized by weak economic growth but in which Tesco held market-leading positions. The Czech Republic, Hungary, Poland and Slovakia fell into this group in which resource allocation would be targeted to designated growth sectors. The third consisted of China, India and Turkey and was characterized by strong fundamentals such as rising personal incomes and growing food demand. They, however, required a cautious approach to capital allocation because Tesco had to navigate its way through road blocks such as regulations for foreign direct investments.

27 online.wsj.com/article/SB10001424127887324640104578160514192695162.html, accessed April 26, 2013.

28 www.theweek.co.uk/politics/23805/fresh-easy-tescos-great-american-disaster. accessed April 26, 2013.

29 Tesco Annual Report 2013, p. 2.

30 Ibid., p. 8.

ISSUES

Clarke was facing various signals as he prepared to make the statement about the U.S. operations.

First, investors had reacted positively to the announcement of the Strategic Review as was evident in the rise in Tesco share price by 2.56 per cent the day after the announcement even though the FTSE index rose by only 0.24 per cent that day.[31] Analysts, on the other hand, had been forecasting a turnaround of Fresh & Easy by 2015 leading to improvements in revenue and earnings (see Exhibit 6).

Second, within the company, there was a view that the U.S. initiative "could one day get to profit."[32] However, there was also a sense that Tesco should focus on international markets and that it should stick to markets that were "growing, more-profitable and better-returning."[33]

Third, there was a sense of anticipation in the market that Tesco would exit from the United States, and analysts were concerned that exit would make a bid for re-entry, at a later date, difficult.

Overall, the decision to exit the U.S. market had raised three fundamental questions.

First, the U.S. strategy did not fit with the company's mainstream strategy despite several growth metrics showing positive signs (see Exhibit 7). The mismatch had brought the basis of segmentation of international markets into question. Was exiting the U.S. market in 2012 the right decision?

Second, the company had already written down the assets of the U.S. business and booked provisions for future liabilities, which had together impacted profit after tax by £1.2 billion for the year.[34] How should the company manage the process of exit from the United States?

Third, the costs of exit could be offset by utilization of learning and intelligence across other international markets. What were the takeaways from the U.S. operations that Tesco could apply elsewhere in its global strategy?

---

31 www.tescoplc.com/index.asp?pageid=36, accessed November 05, 2013.

32 Earnings conference call.

33 online.wsj.com/article/SB10001424127887324640104578160514192695162.html, accessed April 26, 2013.

34 Earnings conference call.

EXHIBIT 1: TOP 15 GLOBAL GROCERY MARKETS

	2012 Ranking		2016 Ranking (Forecast)		
#	Country	Size ($bn)	#	Country	Size ($bn)
1	China	1,082	1	China	1,582
2	United States	940	2	United States	1,118
3	Japan	408	3	India	566
4	India	375	4	Brazil	468
5	Brazil	329	5	Russia	467
6	Russia	314	6	Japan	423
7	France	284	7	France	302
8	Germany	271	8	Germany	297
9	United Kingdom	243	9	United Kingdom	278
10	Indonesia	168	10	Indonesia	247
11	Italy	165	11	Italy	166
12	Mexico	123	12	Mexico	154
13	Spain	122	13	Canada	133
14	Canada	111	14	Spain	131
15	Australia	108	15	Turkey	128
	Total	5,046			6,460

Source: The Institute of Grocery Distribution, www.igd.com/Media/IGD-news-and-press-releases/Chinas-grocery-market-reaches-US1trillion/, accessed June 12, 2013.

EXHIBIT 2: TOP 10 RETAILERS WORLDWIDE 2011

#	Name of retailer	Country of origin	Retail revenue ($millions)	Retail revenue growth (%)	Net margin (%)	Return on assets (%)	No. of countries of operation	Foreign revenue (%)
1	Wal-Mart	United States	446,950	6.0	3.7	8.5	28	28.4
2	Carrefour	France	113,197	(9.8)	0.5	0.8	33	56.7
3	Tesco	United Kingdom	101,574	5.8	4.4	5.5	13	34.5
4	Metro	Germany	92,905	(0.8)	1.1	2.2	33	61.1
5	Kroger	United States	90,374	10.0	0.7	2.5	1	–
6	Costco	United States	88,915	14.1	1.7	5.8	9	27.0
7	Schwarz	Germany	87,841	5.8	–	–	26	55.8
8	Aldi	Germany	73,375	3.7	–	–	17	57.1
9	Walgreen	United States	72,184	7.1	3.8	9.9	2	1.5
10	Home Depot	United States	70,395	3.5	5.5	9.6	5	11.4
Top 10			1,237,710	4.4	2.9	6.2		32.9

Source: "Global Powers of Retailing 2013 Retail Beyond,"
www.deloitte.com/assets/. . ./Deloitte_Global_Powers_of_Retail_2013.pdf, accessed October 24, 2013.

EXHIBIT 3: TESCO — GROUP INCOME STATEMENT

Year ending February (in £ millions)	2013	2012	2011	2010	2009
Revenue	64,826	64,539	60,931	56,910	54,327
Cost of Sales	60,737	59,278	55,871	52,303	50,109
Operating Profit	2,188	3,985	3,811	3,457	3,206
Profit before Tax	1,960	3,835	3,535	3,176	2,954
Net Profit	120	2,814	2,671	2,336	2,166
Business Segments (Revenue)					
United Kingdom	42,386	42,248	40,117	38,558	38,191
Asia	11,462	10,793	9,159	8,439	7,068
Europe	9,957	8,826	10,241	8,704	8,862
United States	–	628	495	349	206
Tesco Bank	1,021	1,044	919	860	–
Total		64,539	60,931	56,910	54,327
Business Segments (Operating/TradingProfit)					
United Kingdom	1,007	2,704	2,360	2,458	2,540
Asia	661	737	570	474	343
Europe	329	529	527	440	479
United States	–	(153)	(186)	(165)	(156)
Tesco Bank	191	168	264	250	–
Total	2,188	3,985	3,535	3,457	3,206
Retail Indices					
Number of stores	6,784	6,234	5,380	4,811	4,332
Sales area ('000 sq. ft.)	116,236	112,433	103,616	93,985	88,451
Average employees	537,784	519,671	492,714	472,094	468,508
Average FTEs	416,441	406,088	384,389	372,338	364,015

Note: Each year's data is as per the annual report for that year. Recast of financials in successive years has not beem considered for the purpose of the exhibit.

FTE: full-time employee

Source: Tesco Annual Report 2013, pp. 72. 85. 136; Tesco Annual Report 2012, pp. 90, 102, 152; Tesco Annual Report 2011, pp. 93, 106, 146; Tesco Annual Report 2010, pp. 70, 82, 121; Tesco Annual Report 2009, pp. 68, 79, 125.

EXHIBIT 4: TESCO — INTERNATIONAL EXPANSION

#	Country	Year of Launch	No of stores	Revenue £ million	Market/Consumer characteristics	Main features of Tesco operations	Current strategic stance
1	Hungary	1995	216	1,606	• Net exporter of farm products • Preference for local produce • Value for money • Phone shopping	• Sourcing local products • Facilitating exports of local vendors	Becoming more profitable while retaining market leadership
2	Poland	1996	446	2,176	• Prefer products sourced locally • Value for money	• Online • Clubcard • Sourcing local products • Facilitating exports	Putting a hold on new store launches and expanding online presence
3	Czech Republic	1996	376	1,356	• Rapid technology adoption	• Online	Refocusing on a more profitable approach
4	Slovakia	1996	136	1,114	• Value for money • Buy local produce	• Local sourcing of non-foods for global sales	Retaining a strong position in a weak market
5	Thailand	1998	1,433	3,742	• Value, convenience, health and safety • Convenience format popular • Online	• Local sourcing • Listed on local stock exchange • Promoting "Taste of Thailand" campaigns	Sustaining leadership and enhancing the current 15% market share
6	South Korea	1999	520	5,311	• Value, freshness, health and quality • Online	• Virtual stores • "Taste of Korea" campaign • Korean food range	Making new capital investments
7	Malaysia	2002	47	937	• Value, freshness and quality • One stop shopping • Ready to eat meals	• Local sourcing of private labels	Maintaining growth in sales and margins
8	Turkey	2003	191	745	• Median age <29	• Digital Clubcard	Putting a hold on new store launches and expanding online presence
9	Japan	2003	121	Divested in January 2012			
10	China	2004	131	1,432	• Largest grocery market in the world • Growing preference for brands • Price and value	• Sourcing center for 60% of clothing and 40% of non-food purchases by the Tesco group	Refocusing on a more profitable approach
11	United States	2007	200	700	• Second largest grocery market in the world • Price and value	• Health and wellness • Value for money • Economic downturn	Under review

Source: www.theguardian.com/business/2013/apr/18/tesco-empire-uk-and-beyond, accessed October 28, 2013; www.tescoplc. com/index.asp?pageid=400, accessed October 28, 2013.

EXHIBIT 5: U.S. FRESH FOODS MARKET — VOLUME GROWTH

		Actual					Forecast				
#	Category (in '000 tonnes)	2008	2009	2010	2011	2012	2013	2014	2015	2016	2017
1	Meat	24,987	25,057	24,788	24,289	23,783	23,514	23,629	24,062	24,452	24,696
2	Vegetables	18,772	18,848	19,009	19,278	19,443	19,670	19,958	20,285	20,622	20,928
3	Fruits	16,906	16,686	17,479	17,599	17,769	18,030	18,252	18,473	18,733	18,969
4	Starchy Roots	5,585	5,461	5,262	5,101	5,062	5,055	5,039	5,016	4,978	4,964
5	Eggs	4,395	4,434	4,456	4,485	4,525	4,568	4,624	4,665	4,697	4,715
6	Sugar & Sweeteners	3,384	3,434	3,622	3,651	3,547	3,519	3,496	3,525	3,540	3,558
7	Fish & Seafood	1,619	1,601	1,557	1,539	1,569	1,600	1,628	1,654	1,675	1,707
8	Pulses	999	944	970	926	951	964	976	986	999	1,010
9	Nuts	361	365	371	377	387	394	401	408	414	418

ource: US Fresh Foods, Euromonitor Report, www.portal.euromonitor.com.proxy1.lib.uwo.ca/Portal/Pages/Statistics/Statistics.aspx, accessed October 25, 013.

EXHIBIT 6: TESCO — ANALYST FORECASTS 2010 TO 2017

	2010	**2011**	**2012**	**2013**	**2014**	**2015**	**2016**	**2017**
Sales by Geography								
United Kingdom	39,104	40,766	42,798	44,780	45,929	47,160	48,422	49,627
Rest of Europe	8,719	9,192	9,866	9,760	10,309	10,851	11,406	11,965
Asia	8,465	10,278	10,828	11,545	12,512	13,366	14,286	15,249
United States	**349**	**495**	**630**	**788**	**1,048**	**1,280**	**1,449**	**1,584**
Total	57,497	61,650	65,166	68,043	71,064	74,033	77,033	79.984
EBITA by Geography								
United Kingdom	2,413	2,504	2,480	2,194	2,068	2,081	2,116	2,112
Rest of Europe	474	527	529	541	587	625	670	700
Asia	440	570	737	749	811	858	906	945
United States	**(165)**	**(186)**	**(153)**	**(104)**	**(33)**	**33**	**54**	**65**
Total	3,412	3,679	3,761	3,605	3,700	3,880	4,043	4,121

Note: EBITDA: earnings before interest, taxes, depreciation and amortization.

Source: Morgan Stanley Research, Exhibit 33, p. 19, May 10, 2012, www.thomsonone.com/Workspace/Main.aspx?View=Action%3dOpen&BrandName=www.thomsonone.com&IsSsoLogin=True, accessed September 21, 2013

EXHIBIT 7: U.S. ECONOMY — GROWTH METRICS 2009 TO 2017

		Actual				Forecast				
Metric	Unit	2009	2010	2011	2012	2013	2014	2015	2016	2017
Unemployment rate	%	9.3	9.6	8.9	8.1	7.5	7.0	6.6	6.5	6.5
Labour cost per hour	$	34.2	34.8	35.5	36.1	36.8	37.7	38.6	39.5	40.6
Gross Domestic Product (GDP)	($ bn)	13,974	14,499	15,076	15,685	16,277	16,972	17,680	18,443	19,277
GDP per head	($)	45,516	46,872	48,383	49,959	51,453	53,231	55,019	56,943	59,046
Personal disposable income	($ bn)	10,722	11,127	11,549	11,931	12,243	12,770	13,294	13,894	14,544
Private consumption	($ bn)	9,846	10,216	10,729	11,120	11,551	12,044	12,535	13,085	13,644

Source: The Economic Intelligence Unit Country Forecast, May 2013, country.eiu.com.proxy1.lib.uwo.ca/US, accessed November 2, 2013.

Case reflection

There are a number of relevant themes in the Tesco's Fresh & Easy case that can help develop understanding of organizing for resilience. Some of these relate to the fact that the company's investment in the US was an entrepreneurial one; it was one that explicitly took on risk. Other themes are more generic, related to the issue of this chapter. Sometimes shocks and disruptions just hit parts of large organizations and they can be dealt with by making decisions at the level of the part of the organization that is affected.

Resilience of an international entrepreneurial venture. By developing and investing in a new international venture, Tesco was exposing itself to new disruptive forces. If it had not invested in Fresh & Easy, it would not have had any disruptions from the US market – it did not have a presence in this market previously. Headquarters-driven entrepreneurial ventures in international companies are never without risk, and by pursuing them, the firm will create new entrepreneurial knowledge (i.e. knowledge of the opportunity, knowledge of how to evaluate the opportunity, and learning from outcomes) (Williams, 2018). Also, the company did take steps to mitigate the risk of this new venture, including gaining knowledge of the US grocery market and shopping habits prior to entry, as well as making adjustments in its marketing mix once the initial performance results were available. This ongoing incremental adjustment was necessary and to be expected as a consequence of any new entrepreneurial venture by an international firm in a new market.

In addition, timing plays a key role in entrepreneurial venturing (Srivastava and Lee, 2005). The company entered the US market right at the start of the global financial crisis, and exited just as the economic situation was improving. It could be argued Tesco should have stayed a few more years in order to see profit in the US. Many entrepreneurial ventures fail, and others take many years to reach a break-even point. Research has shown that prior experience in the venture domain can bring forward the break-even point (Oe and Mitsuhashi, 2013). Tesco had little experience of the US market and, given the venture was a new grocery format, it had little experience in this format too. Expecting a break-even within the first five years – during a global financial crisis – might have been viewed as optimistic.

Resilience at the unit level. The case reinforces Sachdev's (1976) description of voluntary disinvestment by an international firm in a foreign market. Clearly, performance was unsatisfactory, but the company could have tried over a longer time period to rectify the situation. It was a voluntary decision to exit, and it applied just to the Fresh & Easy brand in the US, not to other international markets. Indeed, in a separate case of Tesco's entry strategy into India, the company had a completely different approach to India – at more or less the same period of time – India became a global hub of IT and service operations for Tesco, as well as ultimately a new market for groceries through a partnership with Star Bazaar, part of Trent Hypermarkets (Chandrasekhar and Williams, 2014).

The case seems to echo the sentiment of various studies in the foreign subsidiary survival literature, especially concerning knowledge and experience in a host country. This literature can be seen as an analytical proxy for studying resilience in parts of large organizations. For instance, Delios and Beamish (2001) found an important effect of host country experience on survival. This, as noted above, was something that was absent prior to Tesco's entry into the US (although it did have in-depth experience in India by the time the Star Bazaar partnership was launched in 2014 (Chandrasekhar and Williams, 2014)).

The case also runs counter to the subsidiary survival literature in some respects. For instance, Li (1995) noted foreign entry strategies through acquisitions and joint ventures to have a higher exit rate than greenfield investments. Of course there is no data on acquisitions and joint ventures by Tesco into the US; they did not exist in the case. However, the suggestion that (wholly owned) greenfields somehow bring with them some advantages – from the home country or other parts of the international firm – that help overcome risks of acquisitions and joint ventures, can be met with some counter evidence. This was an example of a greenfield that clearly failed.

The case provides a good basis for discussing Nohara and Verdier's (2001) assertion that organizing for resilience in international firms is inextricably linked to the nature of the local societies in which parts of the firm's operations are located. While these authors discussed this in terms of industrial policies, academic-industrial research links and higher education, elements that are not so prevalent in the Tesco case, having good-quality relationships with local stakeholders in the communities in which the subsidiary was located in is vital. The case does highlight the top-level mission to help alleviate obesity levels in the US. This is a tall order and one that raises questions in terms of the informal institutional environment of the host country and broader governmental and societal policy and lifestyle trends. If Tesco was not able to understand this aspect of the local society fully, its relationships with key community actors would be put under pressure, leading to performance issues.

Insight into resilience in the face of COVID-19 in parts (but not all) of a large university

The global coronavirus pandemic wrought devastation and destruction to countless lives and industries. One industry that was particularly affected was the higher-education university sector. And perhaps nowhere was the damage felt more acutely than in the UK, where many large institutions – from the famous prestigious ones to the less well known – had built a financial dependency on income from foreign students. Fees for foreign students were considerably higher than for local (home) students, and even though the total proportion of foreign students to total students was low in many cases, the contribution of their income to total fees was substantial. It was not unusual for this to be in the order of hundreds of millions of pounds per annum. As a consequence of the lockdown there was suddenly an enormous risk that foreign students would not be allowed to travel into the UK to study, or might not want to, until the pandemic was declared over. Quite naturally, universities started to consider ways in which programmes could be delivered on an online basis. Indeed, this had already started in the immediate aftermath of the lockdown – there had been no choice.

What is interesting for the current chapter is that, in at least one case, not all departments and courses across the whole university were affected in the same way by the forced switch to online delivery. At one end of the spectrum, programmes that had already been running in the university's business school on an online basis were much less affected by the shock. There had been some students enrolled on modules to attend in-house lectures and international visits. These were cancelled. But other offerings were available, and less than 10% of the total number of students on this 'already online' programme were adversely affected. At the other end of the spectrum, courses that required lab work were no longer able to offer these experiences while the lockdown was on. Similarly, with courses in sports science where a great deal of the learning and assessment is done in practice there was suddenly an absence of learning opportunity. While other aspects of these types of courses were made available online, hands-on lab and gym work was suddenly totally out of bounds for students.

This example shows how a large institution that had evolved over time into different parts (faculties, departments, courses) was not affected in a uniform and constant way. More by luck than judgement, resilience to the issues surrounding lockdown and restrictions on travel was lower in some departments and courses and higher in others. In this case, it could be argued that the quarantining of the disruption around certain parts was not a binary or dichotomous attribute; there was a scale ranging from parts that were less affected to parts that were more affected. Consequently, the parts that were more affected needed to draw on the resources, knowledge and capabilities from the parts that were less affected when considering how to build a buffering capacity over the longer term in an attempt to counter the risk of a drop in income should the lockdown persist.

Implications

Recent reviews of the field of organizational resilience do not place a great emphasis on resilience in *parts of large firms*, despite academic focus on this aspect (Kahn et al., 2018). But cases like Tesco's Fresh & Easy illustrate how real the phenomenon of differentiated resilience (and differential strain) is (Kahn et al., 2018). Linnenluecke (2017) talked in a general sense about organizational resilience, not about parts-of-organization resilience. However, she did raise some pertinent questions relating to how organizations need to balance demands for reliability and experimentation, as well as the impact of institutional characteristics (note the plural here). As a reflection of many years of prior work on resilience, this suggests organizational resilience scholars previously had a tendency to view the organization as a whole, rather than in parts. In the field of corporate strategy and international business, on the other hand, scholars have taken a much more differentiated view of strategizing and organizing for sustainable competitive advantage (and survival) in different units and under different institutional characteristics of countries. The Tesco's Fresh & Easy case reminds of the reality of diversification in large firms, and how difficult it can be to enter new markets with new types of offerings. Tesco's did not survive in the US, although they did survive as an international enterprise. As noted by Li (1995), there is a higher exit rate when large organizations enter new markets that are unrelated to the firm's main product line. The following themes are worth highlighting.

First, the literature on subsidiary performance, survival and exit, as well as the case of Tesco's Fresh & Easy highlight an important link between resilience of parts of organizations and resilience in the whole organization. While the shock may only initially affect a delineated part of the organization, without swift managerial attention and action, the knock-on effect and drain on resources (financial and non-financial) impacts the whole organization. We refer to this using the military analogy of collateral damage. In effect, the part of the organization that is under stress the most can become a wound that, if left untreated, will bleed the whole organization to death. The effect of the shock will cascade around the wider organization as managerial attention is diverted towards 'fighting a battle' in one part of the organization. This cascading effect is highly dangerous for the entire organization; there is an opportunity cost for the resources and attention spent on a particular unit that could be invested elsewhere. Sachdev's (1976) early work is a reminder that survival and exit may not even be choices that the organization makes; in certain unstable and volatile contexts, firms can have their assets expropriated by host country governments. If these local assets are part of a wider global value chain (GVC) for the firm, they contribute to its overall performance by being integrated in a global value creation process. Sudden expropriation and loss will have adverse ripple effects both upstream and downstream.

Second, the literature shows how the part of the organization that is put at risk as a consequence of the new investment can rely on various sources of help and assistance when dealing with adversity and disruption. The Tesco's Fresh & Easy case would have involved headquarters' managers from the UK assisting the subsidiary in its efforts to boost sales and reduce costs, including through the transfer of established corporate competences such as the company's Clubcard loyalty program. Kahn et al. (2018) noted how inter-group relations among different parts in organizations are critical, enabling the focal part to quickly access resources and capabilities possessed by other parts of organizations in coping with the pressing situation.

Delios and Beamish (2001) highlighted the importance of intangible assets and experience of the parent company. What is important in this theme is the ability of the company to transfer help and assistance in times of crisis. Many have argued this can happen more efficiently when the part of the organization under duress is under full or majority ownership of the parent. Indeed, Gaur and Lu (2007) showed how subsidiaries that are wholly owned tend to have a higher chance of survival than joint ventures. However, this point about being a part of a collective applies not just to ownership advantages emanating from the parent company. We also see evidence of parts of organizations that are affiliated to business groups helping survival. Garg and Delios' (2007) study of foreign subsidiaries of Indian firms showed how business group affiliation boosted the chances of survival in developing (as opposed to developed) host countries. Similarly, Thomas et al. (2007) pointed to the importance of various forms of experience and in particular to prior experience of failure. They looked at this in research on emerging market firms entering developing countries. Experience of failure in other times or locations is seen as a 'transferable' asset that will alleviate future risks and boost resilience.

Third, literature highlights the role of distance between the part of the organization affected by disruption and the part of the organization (normally a headquarters) containing managers responsible for overall strategy. As an organization grows in size and presence, we can expect it to branch out into different locations both within one country and internationally. Large private sector corporations typically earn the majority of their sales and profits from outside of their home countries. The issue of distance between headquarters (home country) and the location of the foreign investment (host country) is a prominent theme in the international business literature. It has been broken down into different dimensions, such as in Ghemawat's (2001) CAGE model. The topic has been an attractive one in international business research partly because of the relative ease with which researchers can capture distance empirically. Cultural and institutional distances (sometimes referred to as 'psychic distance' (Kogut and Singh, 1988)) can be measured. While the language of resilience is not typically found in the international business literature, it is interesting that Kogut and Singh (1988) used the term 'disruptive' when describing the problem of integrating target acquisitions in culturally distant countries into the acquiring firm. Psychic distance (problems due to culture and language differences) disrupt information flows between local market and parent firm. Dai, Eden and Beamish's (2013) work on survival of foreign subsidiaries in conflict zones showed geographic distance between a subsidiary and its peers to be an antecedent of its survival chances (and thereby its resilience). Proximity to those who are under the same hierarchical control (of the organization) but do not suffer the same adversity is useful for building resilience. The parent can orchestrate the transfer of help and assistance as needed, and units can themselves call on forms of support without incurring coordination costs and delays attributable to distance. Gaur and Lu (2007) showed how subsidiaries are more likely to survive in countries that are institutionally distant from the home country as long as they are wholly owned. This exemplifies the use of distance in a contingency framework with forms of ownership or governance in explaining resilient outcomes.

Fourth, this chapter highlights how the initial decisions made by strategic leaders when they set up new units impact resilient outcomes in these parts of organizations. Such initial decisions can later be seen as mistakes made during the establishment of the unit, especially when things turn out bad. Such establishment decisions set the scene for whether the firm can withstand disruptions. In the case of Tesco's Fresh & Easy, this can be seen in terms of: (1) a 'go' decision to enter the US as the target market in the first place; (2) a decision on the timing of entry (prior to the start of the financial crisis); (3) a decision to focus within the US on the West Coast; and (4) a decision to diversify in the product offering (a fresh and green store format not used elsewhere in the world by the company). The case highlights micro-level decisions within the location to overcome teething problems, and, of course, the decision to exit after five years of losses and at a time when the US was actually recovering from the effects of the financial crisis. But the establishment mistakes were seen to matter, especially as they combine into timing, location and marketing approach. In the field of international business, the initial entry strategy decisions are often seen in terms of location, ownership mode (joint venture vs. wholly owned) and ownership stake (in terms of level of equity control), establishment mode (greenfield vs acquisition) and the extent to which expatriate managers are deployed to get the operation up and running. The preponderance of work shows that these initial conditions matter to the final outcomes. Park, Lee and Hong (2011) showed that first-movers with competitive advantages are more likely to survive. Li (1995) highlighted the danger of foreign entry strategies that entail a diversification into new product arenas. Sousa and Tan (2015) noted the role that internal strategic fit (or lack of it) has on the chances of survival. Internal strategic fit is defined as the degree of alignment between a foreign affiliate's strategy and that of the headquarters. This can be seen as a result of strategic decisions made by the organization during the establishment of the unit. According to Sousa and Tan (2015), the greater the degree of fit, the higher the chances of avoiding exit.

Finally, the literature points to the issue of how a large organization can respond to adversity in one of its units by quarantining the effect of shock in that one part of the organization. The concern is that the effect of the disruption can flow over into other parts of the organization (and risk collateral damage). Can shock (and its effects) be quarantined? The literature suggests it can as long as the organization is prepared to understand the factors that may expose a part of the organization to shock and then adopt a solution for that one part of the organization in order to deal with it. At one level, the decision to exit a market is perhaps the most drastic way of quarantining an issue. A medical analogy would be the amputation of a limb due to the onset of gangrene.[1] But there may be other ways to quarantine the issue. The Tesco's Fresh & Easy case teaches how diversification in the product market (i.e. the new store format) was unique and distinct to the specific host country (the US). Therefore, an initial condition had been set that meant any disruptions to the Fresh & Easy brand would be restricted by and large to the US. It would have been a different story if Tesco's investment in their global IT hub and call centres in India – which serviced multiple countries – were affected by a sudden disruption (imagine a natural disaster that wiped them out). In such a horrific scenario it would be difficult to quarantine the issue without building redundancy into the company's infrastructure. Managing distance may also hold part of the key to quarantining the impact of adversity. Dai, Eden and Beamish (2013) showed how proximity to peer subsidiaries not in a conflict zone can be useful for resilience of subsidiaries in a conflict zone. This speaks

1 While limbs cannot grow back in humans, new ventures in a previously exited market are entirely possible in the business world.

to the need for managers to design the parts of the organization in ways in which their exposure to sources of adversity are managed by alleviating the problems of distance and encouraging collective assistance to those parts in need.

Table 4.1 provides a summary of these themes.

Table 4.1 Key themes from the literature on resilience in parts of large firms

Theme	Sub-themes	Selected references and examples
Collateral damage: risk of the adversity cascading	Disruption in part of a firm influences the firm's overall performance; risk of expropriation and loss of assets in extreme cases; pressures to exit	Sachdev (1976); Kahn et al. (2018) Tesco's Fresh & Easy case
Collective effort: benefits of being part of a wider organizational system	Ownership advantages (including intangible assets and experience) of the wider organization; business group affiliation helping resilience; prior experience of failure in other contexts	Delios and Beamish (2001); Gaur and Lu (2007); Garg and Delios (2007); Kahn et al. (2018); Thomas et al. (2007) A university's response to the COVID-19 pandemic
Managing distance: between the unit affected and the controlling unit (headquarters)	Different forms of distance including cultural, administrative, geographic, economic; cultural distance can moderate the impact of internal misalignment on the chances of exit; institutional distance as a boundary condition for effect of ownership; proximity to sources of help	Ghemawat (2001); Sousa and Tan (2015); Gaur and Lu (2007); Dai, Eden and Beamish (2013)
Establishment mistakes: initial conditions and path dependency determining resilient outcomes	Sequencing of market entry; entry strategy (in particular greenfields over acquisitions) determining survival chances; degree of fit between subsidiary and headquarters	Park, Lee and Hong (2011); Li (1995); Sousa and Tan (2015)
Quarantining: ring-fencing the shock once it has occurred	Differentiated fit as a solution; dynamic balancing; the option of exit	Nohria and Ghoshal (1994); Reinmoeller and van Baardwijk (2005) Tesco's Fresh & Easy case

Learning points

This chapter provides the following learning points:

- Resilience is a topic of utmost importance to parts of large organizations; it will differ across the organizational units of a diversified firm
- Disruptions can hit large organizations in isolated parts because of their diversification in both geographic and product-market scope
- Relevant studies have been conducted in a number of contexts including: conflict zones, developing market firms and globally interconnected supply chains
- Resilience in parts of large organizations is determined by various corporate strategic decisions as well as management decisions made during the disruptive phase
- The strategy literature on survival and exit tends not to be framed in terms of resilience but nevertheless provides rich theoretical and empirical insights for understanding resilience in parts of large organizations
- Themes that we can use in our broader understanding of organizing for resilience include: collateral damage, collective effort, managing distance between parts, establishment mistakes and quarantining.

Suggested activity and assignment questions

1. Identify an organization that has been confronted by a major disruption in a specific part of its organizational system.
2. Identify key characteristics of the part involved (e.g. location, function, size, age) and the nature of the disruption.
3. Why did the disruption only affect this part of the organization?
4. Find out what happened in the situation and analyze your findings in order to:

   a. Identify the main variables that helped and/or hindered the organization's actions and responses
   b. Show how these variables are interconnected (with each other and with the outcome).

5. Identify ways in which the literature and examples covered in this chapter resonate with the case you identify.
6. Conduct additional literature review and reflect on academic research into the variables you identify.

5

BIG FIRMS, ENTERPRISE-WIDE SHOCKS

When shock cannot be quarantined

The previous chapter discussed the phenomenon of parts of large firms needing to be resilient; the localized societal and industrial conditions providing shocks to a relatively isolated part of the organization. In a worst case scenario, that part of the organization may need to be truncated, as happens when MNEs exit from foreign markets following periods of under-performance. Attempts to deal with the crisis sometimes turn out to be all in vain.

We now move along the spectrum of resilience to the scenario of a shock confronting the whole of a large organization. This proposition is undoubtedly more severe; the existence of the entire organization is under threat, not just a part of it. Despite the fact that the organization has previously grown in size and has had a winning formula in the past that has enabled it to expand and diversify into different units and territories, that winning formula's validity is under threat. Without some prompt action at a strategic level the organization will fail. Earlier in the book we mentioned the case of the collapse of Barings Bank, at that time the world's second oldest bank. The shock came from within: a rogue trader called Nick Leeson and the lack of internal checks that could have caught his fraudulent transactions. Other examples of large corporations failing as a result of fraudulent accounting activity are Enron and MCI (formerly WorldCom). Many other famous examples exist of large firms suffering as a result of external shock. Many instances were brought about by the global financial crisis and include Lehman Brothers in the US and Northern Rock in the UK. Airlines such as flybe and Virgin Australia went into administration as a consequence of the global COVID-19 pandemic.

The academic literature on this phenomenon is not new. As we shall see below, while some scholars have looked at the issue of corporate failure from the point of view of corporate strategy (Bowman and Singh, 1993; Hambrick and D'Aveni, 1988), others have looked at it through the lens of corporate governance and the way the organization is controlled (Clark and Demirbag, 2002; Craig and Amernic, 2004; Hambrick and D'Aveni, 1992; Parker, Peters and Turetsky, 2002). While both strategy and governance can be seen as culprits in the demise of an entire organization, without the presence of a disruptive force to nudge the company into oblivion (Jensen, 1993; Markman and Venzin, 2014), many large companies are able to continue as poorly conceived and badly run organizations.

Literature review on resilience in large firms

Definitional considerations

What is resilience in large firms? Are not all large firms resilient by default?

It's about 'liability of bigness'. The literature shows emphatically that large firms are not all resilient by default. Many collapse despite their size and historically impressive financial assets. Markman and Venzin (2014) referred to this as *liability of bigness*. They studied resilience in financial services, noting how 465 US banks failed in 2008–2012. In their study, Markman and Venzin (2014) defined resilience in the context of large financial services corporations as "no less than 10 years of persistent superior performance" (Markman and Venzin, 2014: 1097).

It's about avoiding complete financial collapse. In one area of the literature, scholars examine the financial survival of large corporations. Such studies imply that firms are resilient if they avoid financial distress and collapse, although authors may not use the term 'resilience' explicitly. In the financial distress literature, we see analysis of firms that are teetering on the edge of collapse (Parker, Peters and Turetsky, 2002) or struggling to recover during a financial crisis (Sajko, Boone and Buyl, 2020). And in studies of corporate collapse, scholars conduct historical analyses, identifying the reasons for the build-up and final execution of once well-respected firms. Examples include the collapses of Enron (Clark and Demirag, 2002) and Kodak (Cuthbertson, Furseth and Ezell, 2015).

It's about strategic self-renewal. Other corporate-level studies are subtler. For instance, Reinmoeller and van Baardwijk (2005), who studied Dutch companies listed on the Amsterdam Stock Exchange between 1983 and 2002, saw organizational resilience in terms of a capability to self-renew over time. The literature on corporate restructuring falls into this camp. Bowman and Singh (1993) showed that a wide range of methods and theories have been used in the field of corporate restructuring. The self-renewal perspective also puts a spotlight on innovation and the development of technological knowledge. In the context of China, Choi and Williams (2014) examined the effects of different aspects of innovation strategy on sales growth of firms, emphasizing different ways in which technological knowledge is developed and how this knowledge influences sales growth. Firms tend to survive when their sales grow. The authors found R&D intensity in firms and spill-overs to have a positive impact, while depth and diversity of knowledge to have U-shape and inverted U-shape effects respectively.

It's about changing the way we control our assets. Williams and Martinez (2012) were one of the first to examine the impact of the global financial crisis of 2008 on the entry strategies of international firms as they expanded abroad. Data from both before and after the onset of the crisis based on Dutch MNEs showed a change in the ownership strategies adopted after the crisis took hold. Pre-crisis, the widely accepted positive relationship between government effectiveness in the host country and ownership mode was supported – more effective governments allaying concerns about risk and exposure in host countries. However, in the context of the global financial crisis, this relationship changed to a negative one: increases in host country government effectiveness in the presence of the crisis were now more likely to lead to lower propensity for full control.

Contexts of studies about resilience in large firms

In parallel with the literature discussed in earlier chapters, scholarly work on resilience in large firms has been conducted in a variety of interesting contexts. These include the following.

Historic accounts and comparisons. Jensen's (1993) work reviewed the industrial revolutions of the 18th century (the first industrial revolution originating in Britain involving new energy sources in production) and 19th century (the second industrial revolution involving new transportation and communication systems, along with new methods of mass production) and drew on these experiences to enlighten our understanding of economic trends in the late 20th century. He argued that there are important similarities to the challenges facing corporations in modern times to the context of the 1800s. Jensen (1993) noted that while the 19th-century industrial revolution brought about great benefits, it also generated "substantial hardship, misunderstanding, and bitterness" (Jensen, 1993: 832). A key point stressed by Jensen is how increased productivity and over-capacity underlines the need for firms to exit industries, this having implications for human welfare. Jensen's specific focus was on how internal control systems bear some of the responsibility for failing to allow firms to exit and downsize efficiently.

Financial services and economic context. Markman and Venzin (2014) linked corporate resilience to countries with robust economies: Switzerland (e.g. Credit Suisse, UBS) and Germany (Deutsche Bank). Their study compared resilient firms to non-resilient ones in the global financial services industry. The authors developed a measure of resilience based on financial performance and volatility (called VOLARE). This is a specialized measure that relates specifically to the financial services industry, showing if a firm was able to withstand the global financial crisis of 2007/8. Markman and Venzin (2014) showed that size per se did not help a large bank survive the crisis. It was ownership advantages and international strategy that helped, rather than size. Many smaller firms were seen as more resilient than larger ones. There was also a home country effect: US banks, located as they were in the financial shock epicentre, experienced the greatest decline of all. Less developed countries actually supported their banks through more prudent lending principles and accountability. Finally, Markman and Venzin (2014) showed how product diversity was associated with greater overall resilience in this sector.

Collapsed companies. While some researchers (such as Markman and Venzin, 2014) utilized larger samples and high numbers of collapsed companies, others delve more deeply into specific cases. Clark and Demirag (2002) discussed issues relating to corporate governance in the case of the Enron collapse. Specifically, they highlighted how corporate culture and the company's influencing of policy to deregulate the energy sector contributed to the company's collapse. They also underlined the now well-known influence between Enron and its accounting firm, Arthur Andersen, in what the authors refer to as 'dubious' financial transactions. Arthur Andersen later also collapsed, voluntarily surrendering its licence to practice. Craig and Amernic (2004) went further by conducting a micro-level analysis of Enron's letter to shareholders in 2000 alongside the Andersen CEO's testimony in 2001. As stated by Craig and Amernic (2004: 813): "several of the corporate leaders implicated in the collapse of Enron were deceitful, deceptive, egocentric, arrogant, hubristic and harboured delusional complexes".

Understanding resilience in large firms

Corporate strategy. Markman and Venzin (2014) compared the most resilient banks with the least resilient banks on various characteristics: size, home-market solidity, and product diversity and service scope prior, during, and after the financial crisis. They found that large banks were actually less resilient than smaller banks and country effects such as GDP were important but not in the traditional way. Although conducting business in a stable and growing home market is important, when the epicentre of a significant economic crisis originates from the same location, proximity and exposure matter more. Finally, and contrary to expectations, they found no significant link between higher levels of regional scope or product-region diversity and resilience. Taken together, they concluded that internal operations, cost structure, business-model fit, and strategy are more likely to influence a bank's resilience than its size or international expansion.

Dundas and Richardson (1980) discussed the relationship between market failure and diversification and the impact on performance. The term 'market failure' in the paper refers to a transaction being performed more efficiently by a firm than through the market; the transaction is internalized. The authors used a taxonomy of four classes of corporate strategy – single product (100% of activities around one product market), dominant product (>70% of revenues from a dominant product-market), related product (<70% of revenues from any one product market but >70% of revenues coming from a group of related businesses) and unrelated product (<70% of revenues from any group of related businesses). These classes of strategy are seen as responses to different sources of market failure. Single and dominant product strategies are used under conditions of complexity, related product under uncertainty, and unrelated product under failure of capital markets. In other words, the existence of different sources of market failure results in different strategic responses. Drawing on the work of others (notably Rumelt, 1974), the authors showed that the highest performing firms are either dominant or related-product firms which constrain the scope of their diversification in comparison to those that diversify more widely.

Hambrick and D'Aveni (1988) identified four major characteristics of large business bankruptcies during the 1972–1982 period (domain initiatives, environmental carrying capacity, slack and profitability). They found that bankrupt firms show signs of relative weakness as early as ten years before they ultimately fail. This downward spiral had particular features including early weakness in slack and performance, extreme and vacillating strategic actions, and abrupt environmental decline. They also identified four phases in the failure process: (1) the seeds of weakness period, (2) the early impairment period, (3) the marginal existence period (a weak, break-even state) and (4) the closing period. When firms enter into the marginal existence stage with deficient potential slack and performance, these problems create stress, which in turn induces perceptual and process errors. The most apparent manifestations are strategic extremism (inaction or hyperaction), intensified in the final stage of death. Hambrick and D'Aveni (1988) concluded that these bankruptcies are culminations of long timeline declines, underscoring the problems of inertia, perceptual error under stress, or long strings of bad luck. Conversely, the relatively long process of decline suggests that turnaround managers may generally have more time to conduct their task than is often thought.

Several papers in the Bowman and Singh (1993) special issue on corporate restructuring in *Strategic Management Journal* show how restructuring can be seen as a successful adaptation of the firm to its environment. In Gibbs (1993) work, free cash flow in the firm was found to be a determinant of financial restructuring. Also, when there are more outsiders on the board, firms are less likely to restructure. Bethel and Liebeskind (1993) found block-holder ownership to correlate with corporate restructuring, especially the downsizing of the firm. Zajac and Kraatz (1993) showed how higher education institutions are more likely to outperform when they adapt to the changing needs of students. Similarly, Robins (1993) discussed radical organizational changes in major film studios as they outsourced film production in order to expand their market coverage.

A balance in corporate innovation. Reinmoeller and van Baardwijk (2005) showed that the most resilient companies are those that continually strike a dynamic balance between four innovation strategies: (1) knowledge management, (2) cooperation, (3) exploration and (4) entrepreneurship. More specifically, resilient companies' commitment to strategic diversity was constant but the balance and emphasis amongst the innovation strategies changed over time. For example, knowledge management and exploration strategies were implemented across all periods, but later periods showed a decreased emphasis on exploration and an increase in knowledge management. This is partially because all large companies that have accumulated considerable knowledge assets and skills focus on the efficient reuse and recombination of them, especially those that are tacit and unexplored. The attention paid to such knowledge management increased over a 20-year period. However, during the 2002 recession, more attention was paid to exploration through specialized units such as R&D centres and corporate think tanks. This is evident by an increasing number of employees in R&D laboratories and a widening of corporate R&D networks and is consistent with studies showing how technological knowledge development impacts sales growth of firms (Choi and Williams, 2014). In Reinmoeller and van Baardwijk's (2005) study, cooperation strategy remained remarkably constant but the resilient companies tended to be selective, targeted and purposeful in collaborative projects. In addition to internal exploration and external cooperation, resilient companies continually encourage entrepreneurial behaviour to drive innovation. Reinmoeller and van Baardwijk (2005) concluded that focusing on one innovation strategy to the exclusion of others may produce innovation, but it will not lead to resilience. The authors noted how a "resilient company employs a dynamic balance of all four strategies, continually revising its portfolio of innovation strategies to adapt to changing environmental conditions" (Reinmoeller and van Baardwijk, 2005: 65). A dynamic balance of all four strategies in time according to the changing context is crucial for a company to maximize its chances of remaining resilient.

Corporate governance and internal control. Lakshan and Wijekoon (2012), studying in the context of Sri Lanka, found CEO duality to be associated with corporate failure. This supports the notion that combining the chairman and CEO role in one person is counterproductive from a resilience point of view; there is a lack of independence between decision control and decision management. These authors considered a wide range of corporate governance factors, including board size, outside directors and presence of an audit committee. Governance factors found to be associated with surviving (i.e. more resilient) firms included having outside directors on the board, having a company audit committee, and remuneration of board members to profit and loss.

Kleinknecht (2015) studied how works councils and employee board-level representation influenced performance in European firms during the global financial crisis. The findings showed that firms with works councils and employee board-level representation have lower company value in good times but build a buffer against a loss of value in bad times. More specifically, firms that take less risk become more resilient when an exogenous shock occurs. Giving employees a voice in decision-making at board level seems to prevent excessive risk-taking in good times and increases a firm's resilience in bad times.

Hambrick and D'Aveni (1992) examined corporate failure from the perspective of characteristics of the firms' top management teams (TMTs). Based on 57 large bankruptcies matched with the same number of survivors, the study showed how deterioration of the TMT is central to the downward spiral of large corporations heading towards failure. More specifically, failing firms showed significant annual or cross-sectional divergences compared to survivors on several indicators of TMT composition, including imbalanced or inadequate expertise, inferior talent or disadvantageous social structure within the failing teams. Moreover, those divergences become more pronounced due to the fact that organizational decline is a lengthy process. During the downward spiral, a combination of factors, such as voluntary departures, the exhaustion of resources or limited resources for attracting executive talent and scapegoating, contribute to team deterioration, which brings about further corporate decline, through either strategic errors or stakeholders' dissatisfaction.

In Clark and Demirag's (2002) analysis of the collapse of Enron, corporate governance and control were identified as antecedents of failure. There was a corporate culture encouraging staff to influence public policy-makers to deregulate the US (and world) energy industry. Enron also led its accounting firm into endorsing financial transactions that were deemed 'dubious'. These culminated in the collapse of Enron and also contributed to the demise of Andersen. However, the Enron saga forced US financial markets into chaos and brought about reforms that most certainly would not have occurred had the company continued. Craig and Amernic (2004) examined (1) the letter to shareholders in Enron's Year 2000 Annual Report prior to its collapse and (2) the testimony provided by the CEO of Andersen, Joseph Berardino, to the US Congress in December 2001, to explore the micro-level discourse that serves as an ideology-sustaining rhetoric. The analysis of micro-discourse showed its capacity to inform the grand- or mega-discourse. There were examples of inconsistencies, irrationalities and rhetorical tactics at play in the micro-discourse of the shareholders' letter and Berardino's congressional testimony. CEOs can engage in a hubristic discourse, laden with arrogance, self-aggrandizement, hyperbole, deceit, puffery, egocentricity and single-mindedness.

Hybrid explanations. Some lines of analysis blend both strategy and governance aspects in examining large corporate survival. Parker, Peters and Turetsky (2002) studied financially distressed firms following the onset of an adverse financial event. They examined how attributes of corporate governance as well as financial characteristics influence the chances of the distressed firms surviving. They found corporate governance to be associated with resilience to adversity. Of note is that when a firm replaced its CEO with an outsider the likelihood of bankruptcy doubled. Relatedly, Jensen (1993) discussed factors preventing efficient exit of firms from industries. Specifically, he described the role of the market for corporate control in affecting efficient exit. Reflecting mainly on the period from 1973 to 1993, he noted that internal control systems failed to encourage timely exit and downsizing. The external product market or legal/political/regulatory system were the main ways to deal with excess capacity. Although overcapacity will ultimately be eliminated by product market forces, this solution generates large, unnecessary costs. Internal control mechanisms were seen to be largely ineffective. Consistent with the analysis made by Craig and Amernic (2004) more than a decade later, board culture is an important component of board failure. However, Jensen (1993) talked less about hubris and more of the dangers of too much consent and a lack of conflict. For instance, he emphasized "politeness and courtesy at the expense of truth and frankness" in boardrooms as a major problem (Jensen, 1993: 863). Information problems can also limit board effectiveness. There are limitations and constraints on the information available to boards – including a true awareness of the company's cost base relative to competitors. This severely hinders a board's ability to monitor and evaluate a CEO. And even then, as the author notes, if

> managers do acknowledge the requirement for exit, it is often difficult for them to accept and initiate the shutdown decision. For the managers who must implement these decisions, shutting plants or liquidating the firm causes personal pain, creates uncertainty, and interrupts or sidetracks careers.
>
> (Jensen, 1993: 848)

Furthermore, the author noted how legal liability often motivates boards, in particular class action suits initiated by shareholders, the plaintiff's bar, and others – lawsuits which can be triggered by unexpected declines in stock price. These legal incentives are more often consistent with minimizing downside risk than maximizing value. Boards want to avoid adverse publicity from the media, politicians and regulators. According to Jensen (1993: 864), "while these incentives often provide motivation for board members to cover their own interests, they do not necessarily provide proper incentives to take actions that create efficiency and value for the company".

Case #4 – Philips NV: dealing with a global financial crisis

Ivey | Publishing

9B13M011

PHILIPS NV: DEALING WITH A GLOBAL FINANCIAL CRISIS[1]

R. Chandrasekhar prepared this case under the supervision of Professor Christopher Williams solely to provide material for class discussion. The authors do not intend to illustrate either effective or ineffective handling of a managerial situation. The authors may have disguised certain names and other identifying information to protect confidentiality.

Version: 2013-02-07

In mid-October 2008, Gerard Kleisterlee, president of Koninklijke Philips Electronics NV (Philips), a multinational corporation headquartered in Amsterdam in the Netherlands, was weighing strategic options. Since taking over as president in 2001, the company veteran of 25 years had transformed Philips into a leaner but stronger enterprise with a progressively higher portfolio of consumer products and services. But a crisis

1 This case has been written on the basis of published sources only. Consequently, the interpretation and perspectives presented in this case are not necessarily those of Koninklijke Philips Electronics NV or any of its employees.

looming large in the global economy since mid-2007 had placed the company's core strategy of customer centricity under test.

Only a month earlier, Lehman Brothers, the U.S. investment bank, had declared itself insolvent. The 185-year-old institution had run out of cash and sought official protection from its creditors in what was billed as "the biggest bankruptcy in American history."[2] Governments in several countries, including the United States, had been bailing out their banks and financial institutions since the beginning of the year. Several governments themselves (e.g., Iceland) were seeking bailouts from governments of other countries (e.g., Russia).[3] Liquidity was shrinking in the banking system. Consumers had less money to spend; businesses had less money to invest. The rate of growth of gross domestic product (GDP) was falling worldwide (see Exhibit 1). A global credit crunch was taking hold.

The problem was that the credit crunch would reduce the revenues and margins of Philips, thereby rendering the company's declared goal of doubling earnings before interest, tax and amortization (EBITA) by end of 2010 difficult to accomplish. This goal was part of Vision 2010, a strategic initiative that had only just been unveiled in January 2008.[4]

How should Philips deal with the credit crunch in the short term? How should Philips come out of the global financial crisis as a more robust company in the long term?

PHILIPS — COMPANY BACKGROUND[5]

Founded as Philips & Co. in 1891 by Anton Philips and Gerard Philips at Eindhoven in the Netherlands, the company started manufacturing and

2 Andrew Clark, "How the Collapse of Lehman Brothers Pushed Capitalism to the Brink," The Guardian, September 4, 2009, http://www.guardian.co.uk/business/2009/sep/04/lehman-brothers-aftershocks-28-days, accessed on December 5, 2012.

3 Yuri Zarakhovich, "Why Russia is Bailing Out Iceland," TIME magazine, October 13, 2008, http://www.time.com/time/world/article/0,8599,1849705,00.html, accessed on December 4, 2012.

4 Philips Annual Report 2007, p. 16.

5 http://www.philips.ca/about/company/history/ourheritage/index.page, accessed October 15, 2012.

marketing carbon filament lamps. By the turn of the century, it had become one of the largest lamp producers in Europe. By 1910, it was also the largest employer in the Netherlands with 2,000 people on its payroll.

Philips set up its first research laboratory in 1914, marking its foray into basic research. The company introduced a medical x-ray tube in 1918, marking its entry into the business of medical devices. In 1925, Philips became involved in the first experiments in television and, in 1927, began producing radios. By 1932, Philips had sold one million radios to become the world's largest radio producer. A year later, it produced its 100-millionth radio valve and also started production of medical x-ray equipment in the United States, signaling the beginning of a new identity as a multinational corporation. By 1939, when it launched the first Philips electric shaver, the company employed 45,000 people worldwide.

Philips made major contributions to the development of the recording, transmission and reproduction of television pictures. In 1963, it introduced the compact audio cassette. In 1965, it produced its first integrated circuits.

The flow of new products and ideas continued throughout the 1970s. Philips made breakthroughs in the processing, storage and transmission of images, sound and data. These led to the inventions of the laser vision optical disc, the compact disc (CD) and optical telecommunication systems. The company started teaming up with competitors, such as Sony Corporation, which were working independently on consumer technologies till then. In 1972, the company co-founded PolyGram (in a 60 to 40 partnership with Siemens), which went on to become a successful music recording label.

In 1983, Philips achieved a technological landmark: the launch of the CD console developed in collaboration with Sony. Other milestones of the time included the production of the 100-millionth TV set in 1984. The company expanded its manufacturing base in the 1980s through the acquisitions of the television business of GTE Sylvania, a U.S. manufacturer, and the lamps business of Westinghouse Electric, another U.S. company, further consolidating its presence in the largest consumer market in the world.

Building on the success of its CD technology, Philips collaborated with Sony to introduce another innovation in 1997 that became the fastest growing home electronics product in history: the digital video disc (DVD). Personal computers had gained ground by then, and DVD brought a whole new world of entertainment, education and data to consumers.

By the end of the century, Philips had become a conglomerate with more than 120 businesses. To ensure that it did not become unwieldy, the company started working on a three-pronged strategy: focus on margins rather than revenue; close, fix or sell underperforming divisions; and invest spare cash in building up the strongest parts of the firm. The company believed, however, that basic research should continue to be the "soul" of the company. It came up with a novel way of financing research and development (R&D). Only 25 per cent of the R&D budget was sourced from the common expense pool while the rest came from ongoing "contracts" between R&D and the company's various business divisions.[6]

The renewed focus was also meant to carry forward the ongoing reduction in the size of the company. In 2004, for example, Philips had 140 production sites in 32 countries and employed 162,000 people. By 2007, it had 100 production sites in 29 countries with 123,800 employees. However, the company's revenues had fallen around €11 billion between 2000 and 2007 (see Exhibit 2).

The company continued to acquire businesses that had a strategic fit with its priorities and spin off businesses in which it was not doing well into joint ventures (JVs) with partners. In the five-year period beginning 2002, Philips had acquired 22 companies and floated eight JVs (see Exhibit 3).

There were two major developments at Philips during the decade beginning 2000. In 2004, the company unveiled its new campaign of "Sense and Simplicity." All subsequent advertising and promotions were built around the promise of ensuring that the company's products would make a difference in the lives of consumers because they were easy to use. In 2006, Philips sold 80.1 per cent of its semiconductors business to a consortium of private equity partners. The sale laid the groundwork for a new and independent semiconductors company, named NXP, which was founded on the heritage of over 50 years of innovation at Philips. The divestiture marked a milestone in the shift from cyclical products to those with day-to-day applications.

---

6 "The Shrinking Company," The Economist, May 6, 1999, http://www.economist.com/node/606895, accessed November 17, 2012.

The company had recorded revenues of €26.79 billion for the year ending December 2007. Its consumer electronics business generated the highest revenues (see Exhibit 4), while its medical systems business generated the highest gross profits (see Exhibit 5).

In January 2008, Philips communicated its Vision 2010 initiative, positioning itself as a market-driven and people-centric company. As part of Vision 2010, the organizational structure was simplified by consolidating all existing products into three lines of business: health care, lighting and consumer lifestyle (see Exhibit 6).

HEALTH CARE

The health care business was generating around 25 per cent of revenues for Philips. The company ranked fifth among the top 10 global medical devices companies by revenue in 2007 (see Exhibit 7). The health care business had been formed by combining the erstwhile medical systems division with the home health care and consumer health care solutions divisions. It was the fastest growing line of business for the company for the following three reasons[7]:

1. The integration of the divisions was consistent with the company's mission of improving access to health care with products and services at every stage in the care cycle covering hospital and home. The concept of care cycle was particularly evident in oncology, cardiology and women's health, which were widely considered to be the new growth areas for the medical devices industry.
2. The health care business was able to deliver, in its new form, better patient outcomes for its customers and drive down costs for them.
3. The integration reduced the peaks and valleys in annual demand. Targeting individual patients as consumers reduced seasonality of earnings wherein a large share of revenue was accruing, in tune with governmental budget spending, in the fourth quarter.[8]

---

7 Philips Annual Report 2007, pp. 18–25.

8 Ibid., p.14.

Hospitals and health care providers in the United States and Europe, in particular, were coping with pressures of falling reimbursements because budgetary constraints had reduced government spending on public health. They were also bringing capital expenditure under greater scrutiny because of tighter credit markets.

The Philips health care business had five market segments: imaging systems (x-ray, computed tomography, magnetic resonance and nuclear medicine equipment that was designed to create diagnostic images); home health care solutions; ultrasound and monitoring solutions (ultrasound imaging, patient monitoring and cardiac systems); health care informatics (picture archiving, clinical decision support information, cardiology IT and document services); and customer services (consultancy, clinical services, education, equipment financing, asset management and equipment maintenance).

Imaging systems had been witnessing slow growth in the U.S. market since the enactment in February 2006 of the Deficit Reduction Act, which had limited the payments, under Medicare, for imaging services performed in "non-hospital settings."[9] The other businesses were growing; health care informatics, for example, was growing at 15 per cent per annum.[10]

Philips was also focusing on categories in which it could aim for leadership positions. These included cardiac care, acute care and home health care. The company had made several acquisitions since 2005 to reinforce this shift.

Its most high profile acquisition, in December 2007, was Respironics, a U.S.-based provider of respiratory and sleep therapy solutions for use at homes. It was aimed at securing a global leadership position in a niche market: home health care solutions. Other acquisitions included Stentor, a U.S.-based health care information technology (IT) firm providing picture archiving and communication systems (PACS), which were used for storing, managing and distributing digital radiology images, in July 2005; Witt Biomedical Corporation, the largest independent supplier in the United States of monitoring and reporting systems used in cardiology laboratories,

9 Ibid., p. 69.
10 Ibid., p. 56.

in March 2006; Emergin Inc, a U.S.-based provider of software utilized to transmit medical alarm signals throughout hospitals, in August 2007; XIMIS Inc, a U.S.-based provider of radiology information systems on the Internet, in December 2007; and VISICU, a U.S.-based provider of patient monitoring systems in remote locations, in February 2008.

The health care business employed 27,000 people in 2007.[11] It procured 80 per cent of its materials from fewer than 100 preferred suppliers as part of optimizing supplies from low-cost countries.[12] The channels of distribution were mostly direct. Each market segment had a dedicated sales team. Key global accounts were managed by an international retail board. The top 20 accounts represented 12 per cent of total sales in 2005 and 18 per cent in 2006. The company had a strategic partnership program with 20 U.S. hospitals for an integrated package that had generated a $1 billion order portfolio every year. Philips was examining the rollout of this model in other international markets.

Health care was in talks since April 2008 with Medel SpA of Italy to acquire the latter's aerosol therapy business. There was demand for compact, lightweight, portable nebulizers for children and seniors with asthma. The global pulmonary drug delivery technologies market was expected to grow between 7 per cent and 9 per cent. Medel SpA had a manufacturing facility in Guandong, China for nebulizer compressor systems. The addition of the Guangdong facility would mean a significant expansion of Philips's footprint in China.[13]

Global Medical Devices Industry

The global medical devices industry was estimated at about $275 billion and expected to grow at a compound annual growth rate (CAGR) of 9.3 per cent over the period 2008 to 2013. The United States was the largest market

11 Ibid., p. 65.

12 Ibid., p. 97.

13 http://www.newscenter.philips.com/main/standard/about/news/press/20081215_aerosol_acquisition.wpd, accessed November 1, 2012.

at 43 per cent of global revenues, followed by the European Union (34 per cent) and Japan (10 per cent).[14]

The industry consisted of both pure plays (e.g., Boston Scientific) focused only on medical devices and diversified companies (e.g., Philips) for whom medical devices were a part, albeit significant, of their business. Seven of the top 10 were based in the United States, but 45 per cent of their revenues were derived from international markets. All the companies had a heavy manufacturing and R&D presence in Asian and Latin American countries not only for their low-cost base but also their proximity to local markets. The United States, in turn, was a magnet for companies from emerging markets because in addition to being the largest, it was also the most profitable market in the world for medical devices.

Demographics was an important factor driving industry growth. The world's population was ageing even while life spans were getting longer and birth rates were getting lower. The number of people aged 60 plus was forecast to grow from 688 million worldwide in 2006 to almost two billion by 2050, according to the *World Population Ageing: 1950–2050* report by the United Nations Population Division. The study also projected that this age group would represent 32 per cent of the total population in developed nations by 2050, up from 20 per cent in 2006.[15]

An ageing population spawned new trends in health care. Examples included the development of simpler medical kits for homes, less invasive treatments and an emphasis on preventive rather than curative medicine. New technologies were turning in-patient procedures towards out-patient settings, saving costs on hospital stays. The rising ratios of patients to medical staff had also created a demand for technologies (e.g., data monitors) with which patients could, on their own, access critical data while in hospitals. The convergence of mechanical and biological innovations, wherein

14 Robert Gold, "Industry Surveys: Healthcare Products and Supplies," September 18, 2008, http://www.netadvantage. Standard andpoors.com. proxy1.lib.uwo.ca/NASApp/NetAdvantage/showIndustry Survey PDF.do? task=show Industry Survey&code= hps&type=pdf&date=pdf/hps_0908. pdf, accessed October 29, 2012.

15 http://www.un.org/esa/population/publications/worldageing19502050/pdf/81chapteriii.pdf accessed October 16, 2012.

biologically active ingredients were incorporated into medical devices, was reducing treatment durations. In addition to new product development, the convergence was triggering changes in the strategies of several industries. For example, engineering-oriented companies were scrambling to gain expertise in medical devices.

Medical devices were broadly of two types: conventional and technological. Conventional devices (e.g., kits, trays, gloves, gowns, syringes, patches, dressings and disposables) had wide applications cutting across hospital departments; they were mass produced and low priced. Technological devices (which included not only products such as scanners but also a range of solutions built around patient care) were specific to therapeutic and diagnostic applications; they were priced at a premium and were often customized.

The manufacturers of medical devices did not have a direct interface with end users (e.g., physicians, nurses and medical attendants). They dealt only with non-medical professionals in hospitals, clinics, clinical laboratories, nursing homes and imaging centres as their frontline customers. But this situation was beginning to change because self-monitoring was on the rise and several technological devices were being targeted at individual patients as consumers. The long-standing business-to-business (B2B) orientation was beginning to acquire a business-to-customer (B2C) dimension.

LIGHTING

Lighting was generating close to 25 per cent of revenues at Philips. It was the company's oldest line of business with the mission of "simply enhancing life with light."[16]

Philips was gradually moving out of incandescent lighting and moving towards products based on light emitting diodes (LEDs), the state-of-art technology in lighting. It was gradually shutting down its incandescent factories worldwide. From 20 in 2001, the number of incandescent factories had come down to seven in 2007.

16 http://www.lighting.philips.com/main/connect/one-lighting-story-video.wpd, accessed January 8, 2013.

In order to drive growth in lighting, Philips had taken a three-pronged approach: making acquisitions (particularly in emerging technologies), focusing on applications (which would help in getting closer to customers) and segmenting the lighting business (both markets and customers).

Many of the recent acquisitions in the lighting business pertained to LED. They included Lumiled of the United States in 2005 (for high-powered LEDs and to gain entry into solid state lighting) and Bodine Company of the United States in 2006 (for a foothold in the niche market of emergency lighting). The year 2007 had witnessed five acquisitions so far: TIR Systems of Canada (for LED modules generating high quality white light); Color Kinetics of the United States (for LED lighting systems); Lighting Technologies International of the United States (to meet the needs of the growing entertainment industry); and Genlyte of the United States (for professional lighting applications).

The acquisition of Genlyte had moved Philips from the third largest to the second largest manufacturer of luminaires in North America. In addition to getting hold of an established brand portfolio, this acquisition had enabled Philips to gain entry into the *installment* business of innovative lighting solutions even as the *replacement* business was shrinking. It had also strengthened its proposition as a services-solution company by offering commercial energy audit together with a lighting upgrade program aimed at replacing the inefficient lighting systems found in 85 per cent of buildings in the United States.

Philips had sliced the market into six segments and its customers into seven segments in 2008. The more recent solid state lighting components segment and solid state lighting modules segment were technology intensive and had been growing largely by acquisition. The long-standing luminaires segment consisted of professional luminaires (involving city beautification, road lighting, sports lighting, office lighting, shop/hospitality lighting and industry lighting) and consumer luminaires (functional, decorative, lifestyle and scene-setting lighting). The lamps segment consisted of incandescent, halogen, compact fluorescent and high-intensity discharge products. The automotive lighting segment consisted of car headlights, car signaling and interiors. The special lighting applications segment covered projection, entertainment, purification and comfort heating. The customer segments consisted of homes, offices, outdoor, industry, retail, hospitality and automotive.

Lamps was the largest business, accounting for around 46 per cent of sales. The luminaires business accounted for 6 per cent. The remaining businesses generated between 10 and 20 per cent of sales.

Philips competed with GE and Siemens in the lamps segment globally, while in the luminaires segment, which was fragmented, it competed locally with many regional players in each country. A range of companies were getting into the business of components (involving transition to solid state lighting) and applications (involving finding customer solutions). Chinese companies were entering Western markets with energy-saving solutions, posing a threat to established players such as Philips.

Philips was trying to change the consumer mindset about an "expensive" LED bulb by positioning it as a durable good (such as an iPad, a TV or a car) rather than as a disposable good (such as Kleenex, pencils or toilet paper). It was recruiting marketers from durable goods firms (such as Honda) and consumer product firms (such as P&G). They were segmenting the market into categories including "young affluent," "pre-empty nest" and "green socialites" as part of offering specific value propositions. For example, the packaging of an LED bulb resembled how an iPod was packaged. Philips was also rating the bulbs on "lumens" (indicating brightness) rather than on "watts" (indicating energy utilization).[17]

Global Lighting Industry

Globally, lighting was a $65 billion industry segmented into luminaires, light sources and lighting electronics. Luminaires comprised 70 per cent of the market by value, light sources 24 per cent and lighting electronics 6 per cent.[18]

A luminaire was a lighting unit consisting of socket, housing and reflector. The luminaire market in the United States was concentrated among four players — including Philips — while it was fragmented outside the

17 Paul Glader, "Would You Pay $25 for This Light Bulb?" The Washington Post, October 16, 2011, http://www. thefiscaltimes.com/Articles/2011/10/16/WP-25-for-this-lightbulb.aspx#page1, accessed October 15, 2012.

18 Christian Rath, "LED Lighting," HSBS Global Research, http://www.research.hsbc.com December 13, 2011, accessed November 1, 2012.

United States with over 500 players in Europe alone. The market had reached maturity and was the slowest growing.

The light source was the bulb or lamp. Over 65 per cent of this market was shared among three companies worldwide — GE, Philips and Siemens. This segment was witness to technological shifts that were far reaching. The light electronics market had also become volatile, with many integrated electronics companies and semiconductor players, particularly from the Far East, moving downstream from chip production towards developing their own lighting systems and entering the market.

The lighting source segment was going through restructuring in a number of ways. First, since it accounted for 19 per cent of world energy consumption and 6 per cent of global carbon dioxide (CO_2) emissions, lighting had become one of the sheet anchors for improving energy efficiency and adoption of what was known as "green energy" practices. Rising energy prices were also contributing to this change. Second, traditional vacuum-based technologies were yielding to solid state lighting technologies. The incandescent bulb, which single-handedly had sustained the lighting industry since it was invented by Thomas Alva Edison over 130 years ago, was already being phased out in favour of compact fluorescent lamps (CFL). The more advanced LED technology, which was still evolving, carried higher upfront costs for the customer but was economical in the long run. LED also offered freedom of choice in terms of miniaturization, colour and architectural integration. Third, the point of value creation was shifting from products (such as bulbs and components) to applications and solutions (which were end-user driven). Customer-centric systems and solutions were becoming the new differentiator in the industry. Eighty per cent of the new value creation would be LED-based. Fourth, for decades, more than 90 per cent of the annual bulb and lamp volume was sold in the replacement market, but LED penetration was eroding the replacement market almost entirely.

The transition was being facilitated by law. The U.S. Energy Independence Act of 2007, for example, mandated that the 100-watt incandescent bulb would not be sold on retail shelves starting in 2012 and 40-watt bulbs would be phased out by 2014.[19] Similar legislation was already in place in parts of Europe; other countries were catching up.

19 http://www.thefiscaltimes.com/Articles/2011/10/16/WP-25-for-this-lightbulb.aspx#page1, accessed October 30, 2012.

CONSUMER LIFESTYLE

The consumer lifestyle business was generating about 50 per cent of company revenues. Formed by the combination of the consumer electronics and domestic appliances and personal care divisions, the consumer lifestyle business marked the evolution of Philips from a technology business to one that focused on individual well-being and also from a bulbs and television company to one that focused on fulfilling people's lifestyle needs. Consumer spending on lifestyle products was discretionary; therefore, the consumer lifestyle business was likely to be affected more sharply by a decline in consumer confidence and the consequent fall in consumer spending than the health care and lighting businesses. The business had six business segments in 2008 — television, shaving and beauty, audio and video multimedia, domestic appliances, health and wellness and peripherals and accessories. Television was the largest segment by revenue but was the least profitable.

Philips had developed a three-pronged strategy to gain market leadership in the consumer lifestyle business — focus, flexibility and differentiation.

As part of focus, Philips had taken a decision in April 2008 to license out the TV business in North America to the U.S. subsidiary of Funai Electric Company, a Japanese manufacturer of electronic goods. Funai was a major original equipment manufacturer (OEM) supplier for appliance, consumer electronic and computer peripheral companies on a global basis. Philips had been sourcing various products from Funai for nearly two decades.[20]

Under the five-year agreement, effective September 2008 and renewable thereafter, Funai would assume complete responsibility for Philips's TV business in the highly competitive markets of the United States and Canada and ensure uninterrupted supply of Philips TV brands in North America. The offloading of the TV business was viewed in trade circles as being decisive on the part of Philips in a year in which TV sales were expected to move up due to the 2008 Beijing Olympics.

As part of flexibility, Philips tweaked its business model in TVs: it would receive royalty payments in exchange for Funai's right to use the Philips

---

20 *Michael Steen, "Beleaguered Philips Take 'Lifestyle' Option," Financial Times, April 14, 2008, http://search.proquest. com.proxy2.lib.uwo.ca/docview/229060861, accessed November 6, 2012.*

brand name in North America.[21] The losses would be replaced by positive cash flow from royalties. A similar deal was being worked out not only for the rest of the geographies including Europe but also for other categories. For example, Philips was in talks for a brand licensing arrangement with TPV Technology Ltd. for the global distribution and marketing of personal computer monitors, digital signage and IT displays.[22]

As part of differentiation, Philips was offering a broad range of products — from high to low price/value quartiles — rather than limiting its offerings to particular income or demographic categories. This was expected to help deal with the imminent downturn.[23]

The lifestyle retailing landscape worldwide was undergoing change; markets of the developed world had become mature in many retail categories. Emerging markets of Brazil, Russia, India and China (collectively known as the BRIC nations) were the new destinations for global retailers. It was in this context that Philips had reorganized its local sales activities within three sales "clusters" — key emerging markets (China, India and Latin America), other emerging markets (in Central and Eastern Europe, Russia, Ukraine and Central Asia, the Middle East and Africa, Turkey and the ASEAN zone); and mature markets (Western Europe, North America, Japan, Korea, Australia and New Zealand). Key accounts management was also becoming a way of growing sales, particularly in emerging markets.[24]

Global Consumer Lifestyle Industry

The industry was diffused because lifestyle products covered a wide ground, incorporating products that were part of other established industries. For example, a shaving set was part of the personal care industry, and a washing machine was part of the domestic appliances industry, but both could be marketed as lifestyle products.

21 *Tarr Gerg, "Funai Licenses Philips' US TV Business," This Week in Consumer Electronics, April 21, 2008, http://search. proquest.com.proxy2.lib.uwo.ca/docview/232020363, accessed November 6, 2012.*

22 *Philips Annual Report 2009, p. 91.*

23 *Ibid., p. 91.*

24 *Ibid., pp. 42 and 71.*

The revenues generated by the top 250 companies manufacturing and marketing consumer products worldwide was in the order of $2.5 trillion in 2007.[25]

The industry was characterized by discretionary spending. The products revolved around making personal statements rather than around functional needs. Consumers could, therefore, defer buying to a later date.

Companies got around this limitation by segmenting their customers. They would develop distinctive profiles for each segment and tailor products that would fit them. The profiles were developed around attributes that, irrespective of current financial straits, were valuable to consumers. For example, spending time with the family was an important consideration for consumers caught up in busy schedules. A product or service that facilitated family time had a good chance of winning in the market place even if it was priced higher.

Another way of drawing in customers was to provide an element of experience at the point of sale. Customers were more inclined to buy a lifestyle product when the ambience in a retail store enabled them to engage with its features.

Several factors were driving the growth of the consumer lifestyle industry. The pursuit of health and well-being was a universal trend; the demand for technologically advanced but easy-to-use customer solutions was rising; consumers were conscious of product design; and they were also becoming aware of the ecological impact of their buying decisions.

ONSET OF GLOBAL ECONOMIC TURMOIL

The global economic crisis was sparked in early 2007 by the default of home mortgages on a large scale in the United States.[26] The trigger was a

25 Deloitte Touche Tohmatsu Ltd., 5th Annual Report, "Global Powers of Consumer Products 2012: Connecting the Dots," http://www.deloitte.com/assets/Dcom-Guam/Local%20Assets/Documents/Global%20Powers%20of%20CP%202012_Deloitte_Web.pdf , accessed January 8, 2013, p. 15.

26 Michael D Bordo, "An Historical Perspective on the Crisis of 2007–08," National Bureau of Economic Research Working Paper 14569, December 2008, http://www.nber.org/papers/w14569, accessed December 5, 2012.

financial instrument called mortgage-backed security, which had its beginnings in the early part of the decade.[27] A mortgage-backed security was a tool with which banks could gather loans provided to individual home buyers, bunch them together by the thousands and resell the bunch, in bits and pieces, to investors who were unconnected with the asset but had an appetite for the risks it carried.

The mortgage-backed security was a form of securitization[28] that had emerged as a financial engineering product. Hailed by Wall Street analysts as an innovation, securitization enabled a bank to create a new financial instrument by aggregating various assets. The bank could then market different tiers of the repackaged instrument to different investors, making it easy for them to purchase shares in an asset pool.

The concept was soon being extended beyond home mortgages to commercial, personal, credit card and auto loans. It led to new products (such as sub-prime loans) and new processes (such as credit default swaps [CDSs] and collateral debt obligations [CDOs]) and created a superstructure of

---

27 Mortgage-backed securities (MBS) were defined as "investments, somewhat similar to stocks, bonds or mutual funds. Their value is secured, or backed, by the value of an underlying bundle of mortgages. When you buy a MBS, you aren't buying the actual mortgage. Instead, you are buying a promise to be paid the return that the bundle will receive. An MBS is a derivative, because its value is derived from the underlying asset." http://useconomy.about.com/od/glossary/g/mortgage_securi.htm, accessed December 22, 2012.

28 One of the definitions of securitization was that it was "a transaction in which a special purpose entity, such as a trust, (a) issues certificates, promissory notes, or other securities to investors; (b) uses the cash received from the investors to purchase mortgage loans or other similar assets on which payments are expected to be made; and (c) ultimately uses those payments, if and when received, to repay the investors." Steven L Schwarcz, "What is Securitization? And For What Purpose?," http://scholarship.law.duke.edu/cgi/viewcontent.cgi?article=3127&context=faculty_scholarship&sei-redir=1&referer=http%3A%2F%, accessed December 21, 2012.

credit in the American economy. It was also finding its way into Europe and other developed markets.

By mid-2007, the defaults were gathering ground and causing damage in three ways: the value of securitized mortgage derivatives, into which the home mortgages had been aggregated, were showing up negative in the balance sheets of investment banks, hedge funds and other intermediaries who had bought into them; there was uncertainty about the exact value of the securities collateralized by home mortgages; and the element of trust, on which the banking industry was built, was fading not only within the banking community but even among customers. The latter came into sharp focus when, in August 2007, there was a run on Countrywide Financial, a U.S. bank with strong exposure to mortgages. In order to stem the crisis of confidence, the U.S. Federal Reserve froze the interbank lending market that month. To pre-empt a credit crunch, it also started injecting liquidity into the monetary system.

Things were taking a turn for the worse in the United States, the most important market for Philips. Bear Sterns, a premier U.S. investment bank, came to the verge of bankruptcy because its two subprime hedge funds had lost their value. In March 2008, the Federal Reserve financed the acquisition of Bear Sterns by JP Morgan; the move was a *volte-face* on the part of the Federal Reserve because only days earlier it had announced the grant of an interim loan to Bear Sterns in order to bail it out directly. In July 2008, the regulators seized the assets of U.S. mortgage lender IndyMac Bank. During the month, the government also nationalized two home loan agencies, Fannie and Freddie Mac, which had become insolvent. In September, the Federal Reserve let Lehman Brothers, another investment bank, go under while bailing out insurance major AIG the very next day. That month also witnessed the closure of operations of Washington Mutual, the largest savings and loan company in the United States, and also of Wachovia, the country's fourth largest bank. The U.S. government responded by announcing a $700 billion package called the Troubled Asset Relief Plan (TARP) to purchase mortgage-backed securities that had been discounted to rock bottom levels.

The impact of the crisis was felt beyond U.S. borders. In September 2007, the British bank Northern Rock sought an emergency loan from the Bank of England to address liquidity problems and pre-empt a run.

There was a cascading effect across Europe. Several countries showed signs of not just recession but depression. The most spectacular was Iceland, a country with less than half a million people, where the government used emergency powers to take over Kaupthing and Landsbanki, its two largest banks. Some countries of the developed world, such as Canada, were stable largely because their banking systems were characterized by regulatory oversight. Emerging economies, such as the BRIC nations, were also relatively unaffected largely on account of low consumer borrowing. For example, credit card penetration was less than 5 per cent of the population in India.

Property values started to fall in the United States, turning the liquidity crisis into a full-fledged credit crunch in the developed world. Many governments were tightening up provisions pertaining to governance and regulatory compliance in their banking system. They were also planning to stimulate public spending; the U.S. government had passed the Economic Stimulus Act in February 2008 providing tax rebates (of between $300 and $600) for individuals and tax breaks (such as bonus depreciation and higher tax deductions) for businesses.[29] The central banks were planning to reduce interest rates to spur spending by consumers and businesses alike.

ISSUES IN OCTOBER 2008

Philips derived nearly half of its revenues from four markets — the United States, Germany, the United Kingdom and France. In 2007, these markets had generated, together with the Netherlands, 48.3 per cent of the company's revenues. Worrying for Philips, the financial crisis was having a grave economic impact in these markets (see Exhibit 8).

Kleisterlee had to develop a short-term strategy to ensure that the company stayed on track with its strategic goals. In the long term, Philips had to emerge as a stronger and more robust multinational corporation.

---

29 http://stimulus.org/2008_stimulus, accessed December 22, 2012.

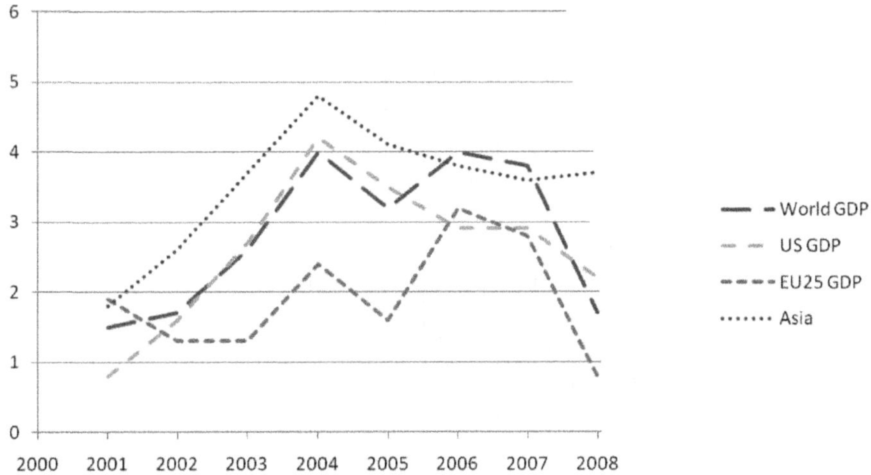

Exhibit 1 GDP growth (percentage)

Source: The Economist, Intelligence Unit Country Forecast reports, October 2008 http://www.eiu.com.proxy1.lib.uwo.ca/site_info.asp?info_name=corporate_landing_University_of_Western_Ontario, accessed November 10, 2012.

Exhibit 2
PHILIPS — REVENUES BY COUNTRY

(in € millions)								
Year	Netherlands	U.S.	Germany	France	U.K.	China	Others	Total Annual Revenues
1998	1,653	7,164	2,777	2,092	1,931	1,878	12,964	30,459
1999	1,619	7,535	2,727	1,962	2,281	2,023	13,312	31,459
2000	1,696	9,126	3,272	2,333	2,179	2,683	16,573	37,862
2001	1,555	8,901	2,648	1,990	1,560	2,205	13,480	32,339
2002	1,507	9,409	2,333	1,893	1,503	2,510	12,665	31,820
2003	1,181	7,532	2,184	1,952	1,258	2,699	12,231	29,037
2004	1,144	6,594	1,972	1,804	1,172	1,545	10,624	24,855
2005	1,036	7,133	1,916	1,680	1,126	1,816	11,068	25,775
2006	1,088	7,447	1,985	1,626	1,186	1,740	11,904	26,682
2007	1,159	6,725	2,014	1,784	1,250	1,707	12,154	26,793

Source: http://www.philips.com/about/investor/financialresults/annualreports/index.page; *Annual Report (AR) 2000 p 61; AR 2003 p 30; AR 2006 p 184; and AR 2007 p 139 accessed October* 22, 2012

Exhibit 3
PHILIPS — SPINOFFS AND ACQUISITIONS 2002 TO 2007

SPINOFFS

#	Year	*Joint Venture Partner*	*Country*	*Joint Venture Company*	*Strategic rationale for spin-off*
1	2004	Société Générale	France	Philips Medical Capital	Entering health care equipment financing business
2	2004	ST Microelectronics	Taiwan	Crolles2	Accessing skills of miniaturization of Systems on Chip (SoC)
3	2004	TSMC	Taiwan	SSMC	Accessing state-of-art wafer fabrication process technologies
4	2004	China Neusoft	China	Philips Neusoft	Securing foothold in Chinese market for medical systems
5	2005	Hewlett-Packard	U.S.	Lumiled	Extending footprint in light emitting diode (LED) technologies
7	2005	LG Electronics	Korea	LG Philips Display	Gaining access to manufacture of liquid crystal displays (lCDs)
8	2005	NEC Corporation	Japan	NEC Philips	Accessing enterprise communications technologies

ACQUISITIONS

#	Year	*Acquired Company*	*Country*	*Strategic fit with acquired company*
1	2004	Gemini Industries	U.S.	Growing the peripherals market for consumer electronics business on global scale
2	2002	Intertrust Technologies	U.S.	Securing distribution of digital content to consumers
3	2005	Stentor	U.S.	Providing picture archiving & communication systems (PACS) for health care
4	2006	Intermagnetics	U.S.	Strengthening position in magnetic resonance imaging (MRI) market for health care
5	2006	Lifeline Systems	U.S.	Helping become a global player in home health care solutions market
6	2006	Bodine	U.S.	Facilitating entry into the niche market of emergency lighting
7	2006	Power Sentry	U.S.	Providing entry into the plug-in power surge protector market
8	2006	Avent	U.K.	Consolidating the leading position in European markets in baby care products

(Continued)

Exhibit 3 Continued

ACQUISITIONS				
#	*Year*	*Acquired Company*	*Country*	*Strategic fit with acquired company*
9	2006	Witt Biomedical	U.S.	Securing a position in the growing market for fully integrated catheter laboratories
10	2007	XIMIS	U.S.	Strengthening position in health care informatics
11	2007	Emergin	U.S.	Enhancing performance of patient monitoring systems with new software
12	2007	Digital Lifestyle	U.S.	Helping become a leading player in peripherals for mobile devices
13	2007	Color Kinetics	U.S.	Positioning Philips as a leader in the fast-growing solid state lighting business
14	2007	LTI	U.S.	Gaining access to the growing and profitable entertainment lighting market
15	2007	Genlyte	U.S.	Strengthening leadership position in lighting business
16	2007	Health Watch	U.S.	Consolidating presence in emergency response in health care business
17	2007	Raytel Cardiac Services	U.S.	Enlarging home cardiac monitoring market in health care business
18	2007	Respironics	U.S.	Consolidating presence in the bourgeoning sleep and respiratory markets globally
19	2007	TIR Systems	Canada	Strengthening position in solid state lighting
20	2007	VMI-Sistemas Medicos	Brazil	Securing leadership role in the x-ray market in Brazil
21	2007	PLI	Belgium	Bringing a portfolio of home lighting luminaire products
22	2007	VISICU	U.S.	Gaining entry into telemedicine for intensive care patients

Source: Annual reports.

Exhibit 4
PHILIPS — REVENUES BY SEGMENT

(in € millions)										
Year	Medical Systems	Lighting	Consumer Electronics	Domestic Appliances & Personal care	Components	Semi-conductors	Misc	Others	Innovation/ Emerging Businesses	Total Annual Revenues
1998	1,950	4,453	12,364	1,746	3,814	3,212	1,861	1,059		30,459
1999	2,493	4,548	12,436	1,791	3,754	3,796	1,056	1,585		31,459
2000	3,031	5,052	14,683	2,107	4,562	5,879	1,831	717		37,862
2001	4,834	5,083	10,633	2,224	Divested	5,094	4,471			32,339
2002	6,844	4,845	9,855	2,273		5,032	2,971			31,820
2003	5,990	4,522	9,188	2,131		4,988	2,218			29,037
2004	5,884	4,526	9,919	2,044		Divested		2,482		24,855
2005	6,013	4,775	10,422	2,194				466	1,905	25,775
2006	6,448	5,466	10,576	2,532				167	1,493	26,682
2007	6,470	6,093	10,362	2,968				197	703	26,793

Source: http://www.philips.com/about/investor/financialresults/annualreports/index.page *Annual Report (AR) 2000 p 60; AR 2003 p 10; AR 2006 p 182; and AR 2007 p 37 accessed October 22, 2012*

Exhibit 5
PHILIPS —INCOME FROM OPERATIONS BY SEGMENT

(in € millions)

Year	Medical Systems	Lighting	Consumer Electronics	Domestic Appliances & Personal care	Components	Semi-conductors	Misc	Others	Innovation/ Emerging Businesses	Total Annual Income
1998	(49)	595	(447)	199	44	765	(481)	59		685
1999	181	602	258	220	286	614	(507)	97		1,751
2000	169	668	374	287	569	1,346	(195)	1,063		4,281
2001	(163)	582	(585)	334		(716)	(847)			(1,395)
2002	309	602	208	401		(524)	(576)			420
2003	431	577	248	398		(342)	(824)			488
2004	34	591	361	323		450	(152)			1,607
2005	688	499	404	324				(192)	(165)	1,558
2006	734	577	313	370				(699)	(94)	1,201
2007	743	675	322	510				(297)	(101)	1,852

Source: http://www.philips.com/about/investor/financialresults/annualrepo:ts/index.page *Annual Report (AR)* 2000, p 60; *AR* 2003, p 125; *AR* 2004, p 59; *AR* 2007, p 137t; *AR* 2010, p 151 *accessed* October 22, 2012.

Exhibit 6
PHILIPS — MACROVIEW 2008

Global reach	100 production sites in 29 countries; sales and service outlets in 150 countries and 123,800 employees			
Vision 2010	Launched in January 2008: "To become a truly market-driven, people-centric company with a well-balanced portfolio of professional and consumer businesses with attractive EBITA margins and effective business models"			
Corporate Strategy	• Counter cyclicality with asset-light strategy by outsourcing capacity • Go for higher share of variable costs • Invest in high-growth high-margin businesses • Divest low-growth low-margin businesses • Build leadership positions through acquisitions/partnerships			
Performance Goals	• Double EBITA per share by 2010 from 2007 starting point • Increase the Employee Engagement Index from 64 per cent to 70 per cent • Increase the People Leadership Index from 64 per cent to 70 per cent • Increase the industry leading Net Promoter Score (NPS) of 50 per cent of key businesses to 70 per cent of key businesses (adopted in 2006)			
Strapline	"Sense and simplicity" — Integrating technology and design into people-centric solutions			
Business Line	**Health Care**	**Lighting**	**Consumer Lifestyle**	**Emerging Markets**
Mission	• Provide solutions to meet the needs of patients and doctors at *every* stage of care	• Simply enhancing life with light	• Offer consumers experiences to help them look, feel and live better	-
Strategic drivers	Bridging hospital and home to deliver better patient outcomes and drive down costs	• Applications, not products • Demand for energy efficient solutions • Rise of solid state	• Customers seek experiences rather than products	Ideal for developing future talent
Market segments	• Imaging systems • home health care solutions • clinical care systems • informatics • customer services	• Lamps • luminaires • lighting electronics & controls • special lighting applications • solid state lighting comps • automotive	• Shaving & beauty • audio & video multimedia • domestic appliances • health/wellness • peripherals & accessories	-

(Continued)

Exhibit 6 Continued

Business Line	**Health Care**	**Lighting**	**Consumer Lifestyle**	**Emerging Markets**
Leadership profile	No. 1 or No. 2 position in many product and service categories	No. 1 in lighting globally	No. 1 or No. 2 position in many product and service categories	-
Targeted categories	• Cardiac care • acute care • home health care	• LED	• Personal care products	-
Business Trends	• Remote monitoring on the rise • Chinese health care market rising rapidly • United States the largest market	• Move towards energy efficient sources, solid state technologies and end-user-driven applications	• Consumers want to feel good	• Open innovation • Consumers becoming empowered
Impact of meltdown	Focus on cost reduction	• Fall in infrastructure projects • Low consumer spending	• Credit crunch • Discretionary spending low	• Continuing investments in public infrastructure
Competitors	• GE • Siemens • Johnson & Johnson • Medtronic • Boston Scientific	• GE • Siemens (Osram)	• Samsung • Sony • Mary Kay • Body Shop • Sears • Unilever • P&G	• GE • Siemens • Unilever • P&G • Sony • Samsung

Source: Company annual reports.

Exhibit 7
TOP 10 GLOBAL MEDICAL DEVICES COMPANIES (RANKED ON REVENUES)

#	Company	Country	in ($ millions)			Device sales as % of Total sales
			2007	2006	2005	
1	Johnson & Johnson	U.S.	21,736	20,283	19,100	35.6
2	GE Healthcare	U.S.	16,997	16,562	15,153	10.4
3	Siemens Medical Systems	Germany	14,600	12,600	9,600	13.6
4	Medtronic	U.S.	12,299	11,292	11,292	100.0
5	Philips Medical Systems	Netherlands	9,511	8,511	7,992	24.1
6	Boston Scientific	U.S.	8,357	7,921	6,283	100.0
7	Covidien	U.K.	7,154	6,703	-	70.3
8	Abbott Labs	U.S.	6,894	5,765	-	26.6
9	Becton Dickinson	U.S.	6,360	5,928	5,521	100.0
10	Stryker	U.S.	6,001	5,406	4,872	100.0

Robert Gold, "Industry Surveys: Healthcare Products and Supplies," September 18, 2008, http://www.netadvantage. Standard andpoors.com.proxy1.lib.uwo.ca/NASApp/NetAdvantage/showIndustry Survey PDF.do?task=show Industry Survey&code=hps &type=pdf&date=pdf/hps_0908.pdf, accessed October 29, 2012.

Exhibit 8

MAJOR MARKETS — KEY ECONOMIC INDICATORS

			Actual				Estimate	Forecast				
	UNITED STATES	Unit	2004	2005	2006	2007	2008	2009	2010	2011	2012	2013
	Population	million	293.7	295.7	298.4	301.1	303.9	306.6	309.3	312.1	314.9	317.8
	GDP	$ billion	10,676	10,990	11,295	11,524	11,728	11,790	11,988	12,286	12,618	12,943
1	Domestic Credit Growth	%	4.4	2.3	5.1	3.9	(10.1)	7,2	1.7	4.7	4.8	4.9
	Consumer Price Inflation	%	2.7	3.4	3.2	2.9	4.5	2.4	2.2	2.5	2.4	2.4
	Prime Lending Rate	%	4.3	6.2	8.0	8.1	5.2	4.9	6.7	7.7	7.7	7.7
	Disposable Income Growth	%	3.6	1.4	3.5	2.8	1.5	1.4	2.2	2.3	2.5	2.7
	GERMANY											
	Population	million	82.5	82.5	82.5	82.6	82.7	82.8	83.0	83.0	83.1	83.1
	GDP	$ billion	2,108	2,125	2,188	2,242	2,280	2,305	2,343	2,397	2,456	2,516
2	Domestic Credit Growth	%	0.1	0.1	(0.1)	(0.7)	(1.5)	0.5	0.2	1.0	1.5	2.1
	Consumer Price Inflation	%	1.7	1.5	1.6	2.3	2.9	2.3	1.8	1.6	1.5	1.5
	Prime Lending Rate	%	8.8	8.8	9.2	9.8	10.1	10.2	10.2	10.2	10.2	10.2
	Disposable Income Growth	%	0.5	0.2	0.7	(0.1)	1.9	(0.4)	-	1.4	2.1	2.2
	UNITED KINGDOM											
	Population	million	59.8	60.2	60.6	61.0	61.4	61.9	62.3	62.8	63.2	63.6
	GDP	$ billion	1,201	1,252	1,322	1,401	1,448	1,445	1,469	1,525	1,587	1,663
3	Domestic Credit Growth	%	11.7	10.1	12.3	15.7	10.7	4.4	3.4	4.9	6.0	8.1
	Consumer Price Inflation	%	1.3	2.0	2.3	2.3	3.8	1.9	1.6	2.0	2.3	2.4
	Prime Lending Rate	%	4.8	4.5	5.0	5.5	4.0	2.8	3.3	4.3	4.8	4.8
	Disposable Income Growth	%	1.7	3.0	1.0	1.4	1.1	0.8	1.7	2.6	3.4	3.2

	FRANCE											
	Population	million	60.6	61.0	61.3	61.6	62.0	62.3	62.5	62.8	63.1	63.3
	GDP	$ billion	1,658	1,724	1,809	1,892	1,970	2,015	2,079	2,162	2,258	2,371
4	Domestic Credit Growth	%	5.0	6.6	10.5	11.5	8.1	2.4	3.3	3.6	4.3	4.8
	Consumer Price Inflation	%	2.3	1.9	1.9	1.6	3.7	2.0	2.0	2.1	2.1	2.1
	Prime Lending Rate	%	4.0	3.6	3.7	4.3	4.5	4.0	4.1	4.2	4.3	4.3
	Disposable Income Growth	%	2.4	1.6	2.7	3.4	1.0	0.6	1.2	1.5	1.7	1.8
	THE NETHERLANDS	Unit	2004	2005	2006	2007	2008	2009	2010	2011	2012	2013
	Population	million	16.3	16.3	16.3	16.4	16.4	16.5	16.5	16.6	16.6	16.7
	GDP	$ billion	491.2	513.4	539.9	567.1	605.9	625.6	649.6	679.2	714.6	753.0
5	Domestic Credit Growth	%	9.1	11.0	6.4	16.4	10.9	3.0	2.3	4.3	5.5	5.8
	Consumer Price Inflation	%	1.2	1.7	1.2	1.6	2.5	1.7	1.4	1.6	1.7	1.7
	Prime Lending Rate	%	2.8	2.8	3.5	4.6	4.8	4.6	4.5	4.6	4.7	4.8
	Disposable Income Growth	%	0.6	(1.0)	0.5	3.4	0.6	0.3	1.3	1.5	1.3	1.7
	CHINA											
	Population	million	1,299.9	1,307.6	1,314.5	1,321.3	1,331.1	1,336.7	1,342.5	1,351.0	1,359.6	1,368.3
	GDP	$ billion	16,028	18,869	22,117	24,662	28,905	32,620	36,725	41,260	46,301	51,912
6	Domestic Credit Growth	%	8.8	10.7	16.3	17.6	13.5	9.5	12.7	10.5	9.4	13.6
	Consumer Price Inflation	%	3.8	1.8	1.8	4.8	6.4	4.1	4.0	4.2	4.1	4.1
	Prime Lending Rate	%	5.6	5.6	6.1	7.5	7.2	7.5	7.7	8.1	8.1	8.1
	Disposable Income Growth	%	8.4	8.5	8.5	8.4	6.9	9.3	8.6	8.8	8.8	8.5

Sources: Economic Intelligence Unit Country Forecasts October 2008 accessed November 3, 2012 and http://www.tradingeconomics.com/about-te.aspx/country_forecast accessed November 16, 2012.

Case reflection

The Philips NV case illustrates how a worldwide disruptive force in the form of the global financial crisis impacted the fortunes of a highly internationalized and long-lasting technology company. At the time of the onset of the crisis, the company was making around 27 billion euros in revenue (case Exhibit 2). The vast majority of this revenue was from outside of the home country. Clearly, it had had a winning formula that resulted in a strong global demand for its products. However, the case shows how resilience is not just about satisfying global demand through developing and launching new products, it is also about understanding and navigating global economic conditions. By 2011, the company's revenues globally had dropped to 22.5 billion euros!

Unlike the Tesco's Fresh & Easy case, which centred on the downfall of one of the company's ventures in one market, the Philips case reminds how an entire large company can be affected by external shock across its key markets. The company was divided into three main areas: lighting (the oldest division), consumer lifestyle (including electronics), and healthcare (case Exhibit 6). While lighting was arguably the hardest hit, all these areas were to be affected by the global crisis. Buyers in all areas were more reticent to part with their cash. Also, the company's exposure to the developed world – a result of its previous strategic decisions and heritage – added to the sense of crisis. Developed countries bore the brunt of the global financial crisis. Comparing 2011 with 2010 income we see: healthcare had a reduced profit from 922 million euros to 93 million euros, lighting fell from a 695 million-euro profit to a loss of 362 million euros, and consumer lifestyle from a 595 million-euro to a 392 million-euro profit. Clearly, this trajectory was not sustainable.

The case brings out a number of themes in the literature, especially when one considers the subsequent events. At the time of writing this book in 2020, a little over a decade after the global financial crisis, Philips had divested both its consumer electronics and lighting divisions and was focused solely on healthcare technology provision. It had survived. By spinning off consumer lifestyle and then later (2016) lighting, the company showed that it was able to self-renew at a strategic level (Reinmoeller and van Baardwijk, 2005). It already had some experience of this, spinning off its semi-conductor division in 2004. These moves were consistent with a need to focus strategically. Philips made various 'tuck-in' acquisitions in the 2007–2010 period, right at the height of the financial crisis. Acquisitions would have given it relatively quick ownership over new sources of intellectual property and research-in-progress. They included Respironics and Traxtal in the health care segment, but also acquisitions in lighting and consumer lifestyle. Philips also explored new revenue generation opportunities in services offering finance, turnkey project and managed solutions (MediGo, MediQuip and MediServ in 2009). These new services would build on their already existing market in hospitals. Philips additionally explored new opportunities in developing countries, territories that were generally in growth mode and less affected by the global financial crisis. It surveyed consumers in Brazil, Russia, India and China (BRIC) markets in 2009 and opened eighty Philips-branded lighting stores in China and eight hundred Home Lighting Centres within multi-branded lighting shops. Light Lounges were set up in 28 locations in India showcasing Philips solutions in home decorative lighting. At the same time, the company progressed its expansion (and risk profile) into developing countries. These shorter-term moves underline a strategic search for new entrepreneurial opportunities, mainly within existing lines of business, in new markets. In Reinmoeller and van Baardwijk's (2005) terms, there was a focus on the knowledge base of the firm around venturing in areas that were seen to be potentially fertile for new – and related – opportunities. Overall, there were elements of knowledge management, cooperation, exploration and entrepreneurship in the company's response (Reinmoeller and van Baardwijk, 2005) before the corporate decisions were eventually made to offload consumer lifestyle and lighting.

A major theme in the literature on resilience at a corporate level is the role of internal governance and control, including leadership qualities. It might be argued that leadership and board-level dynamics and decisions contributed to Philips' exposure to the financial crisis. As shown in case Exhibit 3, the company conducted a large number of acquisitions just before the onset of the crisis, many in countries that were affected by the crisis, and many in lighting, a segment with a loss approaching 400 million euros by the end of the crisis. Did this amount to being an ineffectual board, making poor strategic decisions and pursuing over expansion in a desire for power? It might be easy to make these claims with hindsight, but we should tread carefully. Philips was not an Enron, a Kodak or a

Barings Bank. The acquisitions it did make on the run-up to 2007 made sense strategically under normal conditions. The company's immediate response (previous paragraph) included decisions that ultimately helped the company to pull through. Nevertheless, literature does highlight issues at board level that can contribute to corporate failure including imbalanced or inadequate expertise, inferior talent, or disadvantageous social structure (Hambrick and D'Aveni, 1992). We note that Gerald Kleisterlee was replaced as CEO by Frans van Houten in 2011 but that his legacy overall was not defined by the financial crisis. Indeed, he served as CEO at Philips since 2001 and has been credited for much of the company's success prior to the financial crisis. It could be argued that, under his leadership, the company was actually well positioned to respond in the way it did, and, ultimately to survive.

Insight from Nick Waters MBA, pilot, lawyer and aviation expert

Impact of COVID-19 on the aviation sector and issues of resilience

It was May 2020. The global aviation sector was in unprecedented crisis. The COVID-19 'coronavirus' shut down virtually all air passenger traffic as countries closed borders and imposed lockdowns to prevent overload on their healthcare systems. Worldwide flights were down 72%, European traffic down by 90%. Whilst stock markets dropped between 20 and 30%, aviation sector stocks fell much further, in some cases up to 70%. Airlines across the world such as Emirates and EasyJet were forced to ground virtually their entire fleets, Ryanair cancelled 99% of services, IAG 75%, in China two-thirds of the aircraft fleet was grounded.

Support from governments was in most cases rapid and unprecedented, but uncoordinated. Every nation reacted differently, with financial relief packages varying between 5 and 17% of GDP, and measures such as emergency staff furlough schemes to try and prevent job cuts. In the US, a $25bn support deal came with conditions of no job losses for around six months. Some airlines in the Far East that had higher levels of state ownership would likely enjoy some protection, and various countries within the EU were considering airline bailouts for carriers such as Air France/KLM, Lufthansa and Alitalia, most likely in contravention of some EU rules on state subsidy, but that's another discussion altogether in the airline world!

In the middle of this crisis, the path to recovery and what the market would look like on emergence were unclear – as restrictions and quarantines were eased in one location, they were announced in another, making it difficult to reliably plan a service between two points. Longer term there were issues of a 'second wave' of the virus which could reintroduce restrictions. There was the threat of a follow-on global recession due to the drop in economic activity and increase in debt levels. Aviation seemed like a VUCA[30] marketplace on a global scale.

Many airlines were taking the opportunity to restructure for an anticipated reduction in demand. EasyJet announced a potential 30% reduction in staff, British Airways planned to shrink by 25%, representing 12,000 staff, TUI 8,000 staff, Ryanair 3000, the list went on. Norwegian, already in financial trouble before this crisis, rapidly shed 90% of its staff whilst seeking emergency refinancing. Reduction in demand could be driven by economies in recession, or further degradation of the travel experience due to ongoing restrictions slowing transit. Some scenarios threatened to challenge some basic fundamentals of airline business models, such as leaving seats free – the entire low cost airline industry relied on passenger numbers and quick turnaround times. Fewer passengers would likely lead to higher fares and further reduce demand in a vicious circle.

Consider also wider supply chain issues, from oil companies, manufacturers, airports, hotels and tourist destinations. The oil price reportedly went briefly negative for the first time in history, it was cheaper to give it away than shut down production. Boeing, already struggling with the 737 MAX issue, was looking to shed 16,000 staff as orders dried up. Airlines and lease companies cancelled existing orders and sought the return of aircraft deposits. Shares in publicly traded airports dropped by over 50% with no passengers, no landing fees and no duty-free sales, and many regions relied on tourism for a significant portion of their GDP such as Spain, Italy and Greece. Compared to the COVID-19 impact, the three prior significant disruptors to global aviation, the 2008 financial crisis, SARS, and 911 begin to look like minor hiccups.

30 Volatile, uncertain, complex, ambiguous

What could be done to plan and improve resilience for such events?

Some airlines were protected by the state regardless; this was the 'national security' argument which commercial airlines argued supports inefficiency and distorts the market. However, scrutiny will be on those airlines to try to give reasonable value for money to the taxpayer, such as Lufthansa, which was embarking on extensive restructuring after a 9bn euro bailout from the German government.

For the rest, liquidity was the first and primary defence against shock – cash is king. The particular problem encountered by airlines was that they were fundamentally hard work as businesses. Despite enjoying almost 11 years of steady economic growth from world economies and low oil prices, average industry margins were around 5% due mostly to high fixed costs and intense price competition. Airlines that could differentiate with brand or run ultra-low-cost operations could improve margins, but the majority ran much closer to the line, as evidenced by the continued failure of well-known airlines even in relatively good times. IATA[31] estimated that the average world airline had enough cash to cover just two months of revenue, compounding this was that many airlines relied on advance ticket payments for working capital, and airlines were lobbying hard to be allowed dispensations to consumer law, and provide customers with vouchers in lieu of refunds to avoid a run on precious cash reserves.

It had been observed that additional problems could be brought on by the market, the pressure from investors and shareholders to generate paper returns, pay dividends, buy back shares to prop up share prices all erode liquidity. When airlines turned to the state for aid in hard times, even when collapse seemed imminent, there was an understandable political angle to using taxpayer funds when millions had been paid out to high profile shareholders.

It comes back to the basics. Those airlines in the best positions to survive were those with strong brands backed by customer loyalty generated through customer service, having some protectable niche, or those that could operate for the lowest cost. Everything in between was at varying degrees of risk. Liquidity buys the business time to think in the short term, to assess the nature of the crisis as it unfolded and allows adaptable

31 International Air Transport Association

planning as the nature of the market becomes clearer. Restructuring and cost shedding could be appropriate, certainly as an emergency measure, but those with the reserves to keep resources were better placed to take advantage of a surge in recovery demand. The approach of the markets also had a role to play in how companies were valued. Share prices could be based on projected future performance despite an over leveraged balance sheet and few strategic reserves – as we saw here, projections for 2020 [from] 2019 were now worthless.

Implications

The insights from Nick Waters on the impact of COVID-19 on aviation as well as the Philips case serve to remind that global events of a severity one or two orders of magnitude higher than 'normal' day-to-day disruptions sometimes occur. Mercifully, they are relatively infrequent, but when they do occur they have the potential to bring even the largest of organizations to their knees. If Philips did not act in the way it did, it could have gone bankrupt or become a target of a hostile takeover. With global recessions, financial crises that shake the integrity of the world's financial institutions, and, more recently, global pandemics, we see the fundamental logic on which the prior success of large organizations once rested brought into question (Williams and Martinez, 2012). The whole organization becomes threatened and large size does not save it; in fact, being big may even exacerbate collapse in certain situations. A number of thematic implications arise from this chapter.

First, we detect an interesting theme described by Markman and Venzin (2014) as liability of bigness. As the authors note, this "can actually bring about vulnerability that, until the recent financial meltdown, was seen as improbable" (Markman and Venzin, 2014: 1103). This is interesting because, if you recall in chapter 3, we noted how small firms are vulnerable because of their lack of external control, dependence on external actors, lower diversification and lower bargaining power. One would assume that large organizations have many, if not all, of these. But, as Markman and Venzin (2014) pointed out, they don't, especially when the organization is located close to the epicentre of the crisis. The authors also noted how markets are highly globally interconnected. This means a massive shock in one market can travel across borders relatively easily. The traditional view – particularly in the international business literature – that geographic expansion and diversification helps to manage risk (because a problem in one market can be confined to that market) simply does not apply when the shock shows no consideration of national boundaries or, for that matter, demarcation between different lines of business. In the 2020 global pandemic, large well-established airlines with global assets were facing bankruptcy; the virus did not respect borders. The Philips case illustrates how a large and diversified firm active in multiple geographies and product divisions has made itself vulnerable to the crisis' impact on spending, at both a consumer level (consumer electronics) and a governmental level (medical equipment).

Second, there is an interesting thread in the literature relating to the benefits and risks of relatedness of product markets. The risks can be managed and the benefits can be achieved. In the strategy literature, the relationship between diversification and performance has been the subject of a large number of studies. In 2000, Palich, Cardinal and Miller published a meta-analysis based on 55 previous studies. Their review of extant theory at that time yielded three potential scenarios: (1) that there is a positive and linear relationship between diversification and performance; (2) that the relationship is an inverted U-shape and too much unrelated diversification will incur costs (including capability stretch) that will ultimately dampen any performance gains, and (3) that the relationship is positive up to a point, after which it will flat-line. Their meta-analysis provided strong support to the second scenario, the inverted U-shape relationship. They commented: "our findings provide support for the Inverted-U Model. These findings are parallel to increasing anecdotal evidence in the business press that firms diversifying outside of their core businesses or competencies inherit increased costs that interfere with performance" (Palich et al., 2000: 168). So, on the one hand we have the argument that diversification will help the large firm manage risk and be more resilient. On the other hand we have the argument that highlights the possibility of an inflection point after which the firm becomes vulnerable and resilience will be compromised. Similarly, Dundas and Richardson (1980) argued that dominant and related strategies (seen as responses to complexity and uncertainty as sources of market failure) will lead to out-performance and are therefore more resilient approaches. This relatively under-cited work from 1980 may provide some of the answer to the question of diversification and resilience in large firms. A single product design (100% of activities in one product market) or unrelated approach (<70% of revenues from any group of related businesses) will expose the large firm to vulnerabilities; the answer is somewhere in between narrowness and breadth of strategic focus.

Third, there is a massive literature on corporate self-renewal and rejuvenation. Some of this is set in the field of corporate innovation, itself a huge body of literature. While this is too big to summarize here, the selected works that we use have some interesting points to make about building resilience in large organizations. In effect, capacity for resilience comes about through ongoing self-renewal in a large organization. This does not necessarily equate with diversification or growth, which have issues attached to them as mentioned in the previous two points. Instead, it points to how we should consider self-renewal and different forms of corporate innovation (including process and managerial innovation) as ways to boost resilience continually. In the Philips case we see a restructuring and re-focusing at a corporate level involving spin-offs, and some of these changes not taking shape for a few years after initial attempts were made to fend off the crisis. As Bowman and Singh (1993) noted, corporate restructuring can involve a range of different strategic moves, including acquisitions and mergers, divestments, reconfiguring lines of businesses and even large-scale internal changes. They are aimed at helping a firm deal with its changing environment and the large-scale disruptions it faces. As a consequence of one set of disruptions, the firm starts to disrupt itself in order to survive. Arguably, this is what happened in the Tesco's Fresh & Easy case in the previous chapter; although this was positioned in our analysis as being a problem to be dealt with in one part of the organization. The challenge facing Philips (and many others, including in the financial services industry – Markman and Venzin (2014)) during the global financial crisis meant rejuvenation through restructuring had somewhat more at stake. Reinmoeller and van Baardwijk's (2005) study is interesting because it highlighted the fact that organizations can choose from various innovation strategies as part of their attempts at self-renewal in a disruptive environment. The authors identified knowledge management, exploration, cooperation and entrepreneurship based on two dimensions: internal or external resource use, and resources that are already in use or being created. This type of approach for understanding corporate resilience is different to that of the restructuring school and talks more directly to the nature of resources that comprise options for renewal.

Fourth, there is an interesting point made in the literature related to downward spirals in large organizations and the time it takes for a large organization to actually collapse. This serves to remind that it is not just a question of a sudden, unforeseeable shock (such as Nick Leeson's actions at Barings Bank) bringing down a large organization. Sure, this can happen. But in many, if not most, cases, the organization has ample time to do something about the mounting pressures and problems it faces and – perhaps through appropriate re-structuring or balanced innovation – turn itself around. Hambrick and D'Aveni's (1988) study is our anchor for this point about the lingering death of a large organization. It identified the protracted and long-drawn-out nature of decline that ultimately leads to the failure of large corporations. According to Hambrick and D'Aveni's (1988) work, the downward spiral included "early weaknesses in slack and performance, extreme and vacillating strategic actions, and abrupt environmental decline" (Hambrick and D'Aveni's, 1988: 1). The authors focused on external characteristics, meaningful in studies of large corporations that tend to be newsworthy enough to make sufficient secondary data available. Interestingly, no significant result was found for domain initiative, i.e., the extent to which the firm was active in producing new products in its chosen market spaces; inertia did not explain failure. Also, slow environmental decline did not explain failures; it was an abrupt change in the environment's 'carrying capacity' that precipitated failure. Over the long term (up to ten years before collapse), lower levels of slack and financial performance contributed to the likelihood of eventual failure. The sudden change in the environment acted as an 'executioner's sword', terminating the company after many years of lingering weakness.

Finally, we see a strong connection between elements of the corporate governance and internal control of large organizations and their ability to survive in the context of adversity. On the one hand, research highlights how a failure of governance and control can lead directly to collapse. Poor governance itself is the 'disruption' and source of trauma for the whole organization. On the other hand, failure of governance can be seen in terms of its ability to lead, make hard decisions and mobilize resources effectively once a major disruption has been encountered. In the former scenario, scholars use cases such as the one of Enron's collapse to highlight corporate failure as directly caused by ineffectual boards, poor strategic decisions, over-expansion and ill-judged acquisitions, dominant CEOs, greed, hubris and the desire for power, and failure of internal controls. Clark and Demirag (2002) went a little further by putting a spotlight on corporate culture, an informal control mechanism determined by the strategic apex of the organization. An important indicator of this is the public discourse engaged by some CEOs, this sometimes being laden with arrogance and deceit (Craig and Amernic, 2004). In the latter scenario, failure of governance and control can hasten the downfall of a large organization following the onset of a major crisis. One could argue this to be the case with Barings Bank. There were ample opportunities to deal with the problem once it had started in the Singapore office. But the governance structures and internal control systems were not able to detect and deal with the issue. Because of this failure, the problem snowballed completely out of control. These types of control mechanism are extremely dangerous. They are elements of the leadership and control systems for the organization that put the organization in mortal danger either directly or through ineptitude during a recovery phase following a major disruption. The very people that we entrust for the security of the future of a large organization become the ones that live dangerously close to the edge. Conversely, the Philips case provides an example of a smooth change in leadership, from Gerald Kleisterlee to Frans van Houten, another insider who had been in the company since 1986 and had in-depth knowledge of the different divisions. This continuation of transparent corporate governance supported the refocus onto healthcare that subsequently followed, allowing the company to survive and thrive.

Table 5.1 provides a summary of these themes.

Table 5.1 Key themes from the literature on large firm resilience

Theme	*Sub-themes*	*Selected references and examples*
Liability of bigness	Size can bring about the vulnerability in the first place; total asset base can mean the shock is greater should assets become under-utilized and unproductive during crisis; global threats can impact large firms on multiple fronts	Markman and Venzin (2014); Williams and Martinez (2012) Philips case Airline industry

(Continued)

Table 5.1 Continued

Theme	*Sub-themes*	*Selected references and examples*
Managing relatedness	Dominant and related diversification more successful than single-product or unrelated diversification strategy; curvilinear relationship between diversity and performance	Dundas and Richardson (1980); Palich, Cardinal and Miller (2000)
Corporate self-renewal	Self-renewal taking long time frames; the need for balance between different innovation strategies; the need for sustained balance over time; corporate restructuring helping firm to adapt to changing global environment	Reinmoeller and van Baardwijk (2005); Bowman and Singh (1993); Choi and Williams (2014) Philips case
Downward spirals	Long time periods after onset of problems before final bankruptcy; corporate decline is a protracted process	Hambrick and D'Aveni (1988) Kodak
Failure of governance; dangerous control	Corporate governance matters; outsiders may or may not exacerbate problems; upper echelons characteristics, including expertise can worsen resilience; internal works councils boosting resilience in the long run; control is not only internally oriented, external relationships and cronyism matter	Parker, Peters and Turetsky (2002); Hambrick and D'Aveni (1992); Kleinknecht (2015); Clark and Demirag's (2002); Lakshan and Wijekoon (2012) Enron and Barings Bank

Learning points

This chapter provides the following learning points:

- It is not the case that large organizations, by virtue of their size and historical 'winning formulas', are immune to disruption
- Resilience in large firms can be understood through research in the fields of corporate strategy and corporate governance, particularly where researchers examine antecedents of under-performance, decline and collapse

- While much of the work in these fields does not explicitly use the framing of 'resilience', it nevertheless shows how large organizations contribute to either their own demise or their chances of surviving through their decisions and actions
- Relevant studies have been conducted in a number of contexts including: historic accounts, financial services and economic shocks and collapsed companies
- Themes that we can use in our broader understanding of organizing for resilience include: liability of bigness, managing relatedness, corporate self-renewal, downward spirals, failure of governance (internal and external).

Suggested activity and assignment questions

1. Identify a large organization that has faced a major disruption to its entire organizational strategy.
2. What were the main characteristics of the strategy? What were the main characteristics of the disruption? How did the disruption expose inherent weakness in the organization's strategy?
3. Find out what happened in the situation and analyze your findings in order to:

    a. Identify the main variables that helped and/or hindered the organization's actions and responses at a corporate level
    b. Show how these variables are interconnected (with each other and with the outcome).

4. Identify ways in which the literature and examples covered in this chapter resonate with the case you identify.
5. Conduct additional literature review and reflect on academic research into the variables you identify.

6

COMMUNITIES AND ECONOMIES

RESILIENCE AT A COLLECTIVE LEVEL

When shock hits us all

In 2020, the entire world was struck by one of the most infectious and deadly viruses for decades. There was no vaccine and no cure. The only immediate defense was social reorganization: countries were placed in lockdown. People confined to their homes. Schools closed. Some businesses collapsed, others remained on the brink. Central banks pumped trillions into the economy to shore up the welfare of the planet. The shock hit us all.

The previous chapters have journeyed along the spectrum of resilience from an individual level to small firms to parts of large firms and to entire corporations. We now consider an even higher-level analysis; that of a whole economic ecosystem. What we mean by economic ecosystem is a collection of interconnected actors of different types all contributing to – and benefitting from – the vitality of an economy. The view we take here draws from open systems theory (OST) (von Bertalanffy, 1950) as well as work on ecological resilience (Cropp and Gabric, 2002). While each organization has various inter-related components or sub-systems (e.g. procurement, sales, human resources, and accounting), they are also interconnected with various inputs (e.g. materials, labour, capital and information) from their environments or supra-systems. These inputs are transformed into outputs (e.g. finished goods or services) that are eventually transferred back to the environment (Katz and Kahn, 1966). Consider the scenario in which the shock that arises doesn't just impact one organization or a part of it. All actors in one way or another are affected: government and public and policy bodies, firms big and small, and individuals.

One of the interesting features about studying resilience at this level of analysis is the question of control. Who's in charge? Who can we look to in order to guide a response and recovery? Does any one node in the network have complete control of the assets of a vast array of resources, capabilities and knowledge? In most countries of the world, the answer to this last question is no; control and assets are dispersed throughout the economic system. Governments are powerful actors with the ability to impose law and order as might be needed to protect the public in the extreme case of a pandemic, natural disaster such as a volcanic eruption or civil unrest. But even individual governments do not control all resources, capabilities and knowledge, much of which is dispersed and shared across countries. Consequently, we find ourselves delving into a diverse set of literature in this chapter relating to policy (Aiginger, 2009), community resilience (Berkes and Ross, 2013; Sonn and Fisher, 1998; Thornley et al., 2015), social networks and social capital (Poortinga, 2012) and shared innovation and learning (Glover, 2012).

Literature review on resilience in economic ecosystems and communities

Definitional considerations

What is resilience in economic ecosystems and communities?

There are various definitions of resilience in the broad literature that deals with collectives of actors and individuals living and working together.

It's about survival of complex ecosystems. Cropp and Gabric (2002) defined resilience in terms of the time it takes an ecosystem to return to its original state following a perturbation. Aiginger (2009) analyzed resilience at the level of an economy, seeing it as "the ability of an economy to reduce the probability of further deep crises or at least to mitigate the effects of a crisis" (Aiginger, 2009: 310). Aiginger (2009) pointed out that resilience traditionally was seen as a lower-ranked policy goal in Europe, way behind the traditional goals of fighting unemployment, increasing growth and competitiveness, fighting inflation, combating global warming and fighting the effects of the financial crisis. Aiginger saw the key question for Europe at the time of the global financial crisis to be about how to build economic resilience without upsetting any of these goals. He presented 23 individual strategies in five policy areas to do this: (1) resilient economic structures, (2) increasing economic growth, (3) emphasizing long-term goals, (4) regulation to avoid a future crisis, and (5) stabilizing institutions. In essence, resilience of a whole economy should not be treated as an isolated goal, but integrated with the broader goals of growth and well-being.

It's about survival within a territory. Gilly et al. (2014) provided a conception of resilience based on two dimensions: organizational and territorial dimensions. The organizational dimension – consistent with our definitions in previous chapters – refers to the capacity of an organization to manage a disturbance and develop a new pathway for itself. The territorial dimension is interesting for the purposes of this chapter. This stresses the collective capacity of co-located actors (including new forms of cooperation) in responding to external disturbances. This encapsulates aspects such as materializing a common problem, making compromises in order to harmonize strategies, and organizing joint learning processes for innovation. Colovic (2012) discussed the evolution of industrial ecosystems in Japan from the perspective of industry relocation. The phenomenon of industry relocation can be seen as a major form of disruption impinging on a whole collection of firms demarcated by different types of territorial systems: company town, urban industrial zone, regional industrial zone or traditional industry based. Colovic (2012) showed how the adaptive processes and challenges differ depending on the type of territorial system.

It's about community. Berkes and Ross (2013) developed an integrated concept of community resilience. This is integrated in the sense of drawing from the social-ecological systems literature on the one hand and the literature on psychology and mental health on the other. The authors viewed community resilience in terms of multiple community members coming together in times of crisis in order to survive collectively. They drew on Magis' (2010: 410) definition of community resilience: the "existence, development and engagement of community resources by community members to thrive in an environment characterized by change, uncertainty, unpredictability and surprise". This emphasizes community resources, collective action and strategic action (Berkes and Ross, 2013: 7). It is argued that community resilience is "a function of the strengths or characteristics that have been identified as important, leading to agency and self-organization" (Berkes and Ross, 2013: 14). Relatedly, in reviewing the literature on competent communities, Sonn and Fisher (1998) noted: "Competent communities, like resilient individuals, have the capacity and resourcefulness to cope positively with adversity" (Sonn and Fisher, 1998: 459). Adger (2000) defined social resilience as a community or group ability to cope with stresses and disturbance.

Contexts of studies about resilience in economic ecosystems and communities

Various contexts have been used to study resilience at a collective level, including the following.

Rural areas. An important stream of work examines resilience at an economic or community level where the community in question is rural. Glover (2012) investigated resilience of small rural enterprises when faced with adversity, as well as the processes they use to survive. The findings showed that individual enterprises find ways to cope by utilizing various resources and sometimes involving innovation in order to continue operations. Moreover, a resilient culture is created through learning how to cope with adversity, and this also becomes an important aspect of incremental innovations needed for survival. Rockenbauch and Sakdapolrak (2017) provided a conceptual framework for understanding rural communities in the Global South. The Global South refers to low- and middle-income countries in Asia, Africa, Latin America and the Caribbean that are distinct from the rich OECD countries of the Global North (e.g. North America, Japan, European countries). They used an inter-disciplinary approach to understand different views on how social networks in rural communities in the Global South impact resilience. Rockenbauch and Sakdapolrak (2017) drew on literature from three strands: (1) natural resource governance; (2) agricultural innovation; and (3) social support, providing critical points in each of these individual areas and providing a way forward for understanding community resilience in rural areas through the concept of 'translocality'. Translocality refers to a complex movement of people between different locales and different types of places. The diversity of experience gained 'translocally' allows specific rural communities to adapt, transform and survive.

Remote territories. While some of the rural areas included in Glover (2012) and Rockenbauch and Sakdapolrak (2017) will inevitably be remote and inaccessible, this is not always the case. In some studies of resilience of whole communities and economic ecosystems, the researchers have gone to great lengths to analyze extremely remote locations. Williams, You and Joshua (2020) researched resilience in small businesses on one of the world's most remote islands, namely St Helena. As noted in the article, there have been a number of studies in the field of study on small islands and small island developing states (SIDs). Small islands are seen as vulnerable to external shocks adding to their economic marginalization (Encontre, 1999). These shocks include climate change, environmental degradation and natural disasters as well as economic shocks of a non-natural origin, such as changes in commodity prices, changes in exchange rates and decreases in foreign tourist demand (Encontre, 1999). Schwarz et al. (2011) viewed small, remote islands as social-ecological systems in which resilience is underpinned by social processes. Briguglio et al. (2009) pointed out that small island economies also suffer because of fundamental and intrinsic features of their economies, including their economic openness and export concentration. Such features conspire to expose them to external shocks.

Oppressed groups. There is a line of literature that looks at resilience in groups and communities of organizations and individuals that are oppressed by an outside or foreign unwelcomed force. Sonn and Fisher (1998) examined group responses under oppressive systems. They noted that oppressed communities are often viewed as having little resilience. In many cases oppressed groups can resist the oppression they face, this in itself building a sense of community. Sadly, many examples of oppression exist in human history, too many to mention here. Sonn and Fisher (1998) referred to Anglo-Indians and black South Africans during apartheid. Other examples include the Resistance movement during World War 2 in Europe that never capitulated or became assimilated into the Nazi regime. Members shared the same goal of disrupting and eventually defeating the oppressor to liberate their countries. Groups of people that lived under the Stasi surveillance and brutality of the former German Democratic Republic (former East Germany) shared a common interest in fleeing (Funder, 2002). As noted by Sonn and Fisher (1998), many oppressed groups survive and maintain their cultures; they do not give in to the 'stronger' oppressive force. While traditionally it was seen that oppressed communities had their means of natural self-support removed as part of the oppression, leading to negative outcomes such as de-culturization and dysfunction, certain recovery or positive outcomes are also possible. These are influenced by latent processes that include retaining values and practices within the community (Sonn and Fisher, 1998).

Ecological resilience. Scholars of ecological resilience have provided insights that can cross over into organizational studies of resilience. A good example of one such insight is Cropp and Gabric's (2002) simulation model of an ecological ecosystem, and their conclusion that ecosystems will continually evolve to a point that they are most resilient to perturbation. Adger (2000) related concepts from ecological and social resilience, arguing that they relate to each other in important ways. One of the most direct ways is where groups and communities (of humans) depend on ecological resilience and environmental sustainability for their own survival. The two forms of resilience are very much inter-related. Adger (2000) used the case of a resource-dependent community in coastal Vietnam (mangrove conversion) to underscore how institutions (both formal and informal) in human society play a critical role in determining the extent to which natural resources are used in a sustainable way. The case shows how privatization reduced both ecological resilience and the resilience of the human social group. Similarly, Garmestani et al. (2006) pointed out how ecological resilience provides a useful way of interpreting resilience in economic ecosystems. They used concepts from the ecological resilience literature to study how functional richness across firm size influences the survival of industries in the face of economic change. This shows a useful application of logic from ecology; namely, that functional richness of an ecosystem has a positive impact on the survival chances for a species within the ecosystem.

Radical disruptions. When a whole economy or society is affected by disruption, the disruption itself tends to be of a grand scale. It is hardly surprising then, that the nature of disruptions are of an eye-catching order of magnitude in this stream of literature (examples including extreme weather events, natural disasters, global financial crises and global pandemics). For instance, Norris et al. (2009) used two longitudinal datasets collected after the 1999 floods in Mexico and the 9/11 terrorist attacks in New York in their study of psychological stress experienced by individuals in those affected areas. Thornley et al. (2015) examined the consequences of the Canterbury earthquakes in New Zealand. There is a sense of profound trauma in the events characterized in this literature. According to Gilly et al. (2014), external events that trigger resilient responses in economic systems tend to be radical, but they are not necessarily sudden: some are equally profound but incremental in nature. Gilly et al.'s (2014) work conceptualized resilience in organizational and territorial terms. Territorial resilience is important for the theme in this chapter and it comes about through the co-location of networked organizations within an extreme context, even when the disruption they collectively face is creeping by nature. The authors highlighted the role of 'pivot firms' in economic systems confronted with profound disruption; these actors are crucial in bolstering resilience across the territory or economic system.

Ancient history. Studies in areas as diverse as organizational strategy, human ecology and ethnobiology utilize historical data, including rich archaeological evidence, to explore the concept of resilience within economies and communities. Carmeli and Markman (2011) used historical data on the story of the Republic of Rome in their work on resilient strategy. Focusing on the period of its founding and establishment (509 bc to 338 bc), the authors reveal both strategic factors and supporting tactics that allowed the Republic to endure and survive. Rodriguez and Anderson (2013) discussed land use strategy in the Mixteca Alta region of Mexico, showing how the specific technique of 'terracing' has endured to the modern day. Over the course of over 2,000 years, this agricultural technique in this region has withstood a number of large-scale disruptive events, including population growth and changes, site abandonment and destruction, conquest, epidemics, new industries and new crops. The archaeological and historic account shows that Mexican farmers continued to use ancient methods of farming, even after the Spanish conquest and the formation of the Republic of Mexico. They passed on their knowledge of terracing to new generations throughout the centuries. Marston (2015) raised the issue of sustainability of agricultural practices and environmental degradation through a case analysis of the ancient city of Gordion in central Turkey. Over 2,000 years of data on social and environmental change allowed Marston to explore temporal, spatial and organizational dimensions of agricultural practices in communities where cultural and ecological changes co-evolve. The historical account of human-environmental relationships identified concepts of mismatches (social and ecological incompatibility) and thresholds (occurrence of abrupt transformations in time) as central to the question of sustaining agricultural practices over thousands of years.

Understanding resilience at a collective level

Stakeholder relationships. Williams, You and Joshua (2020) researched resilience in small businesses on the remote island of St Helena. As noted in chapter 3, resilience is an important capability to have in small firms; many small businesses struggle, and many fail. But in the context of a small, remote island, this issue is even more profound. Problems of inaccessibility and economic size of the island make it much harder for small businesses to draw on external resources in times of need. The conceptual approach was based on instrumental stakeholder theory (IST) – how a firm's relationships with others within the economic ecosystem can impact the resilience of the small business. Using a fuzzy cognitive mapping (FCM) technique where the authors captured the mental models of small business entrepreneurs on variables of interest, it was found that some aspects of stakeholder theory do apply, such as the importance of having mutually beneficial interaction with partners and nurturing relationships with partners that are valuable. It was also found that there is a cost to managing these relationships that can undermine resilience. The analysis revealed some aspects of government policy to be perceived as directly and indirectly undermining resilience of the small businesses.

Sense of community. Berkes and Ross (2013) noted how community resilience develops through the experience of responding to shocks and stresses as well as socialized learning. Although the characteristics that build resilience may vary from community to community, the authors identified the most important ones: (1) people–place connections; (2) values and beliefs; (3) knowledge, skills and learning; (4) social networks; (5) engaged governance (involving collaborative institutions); (6) a diverse and innovative economy; (7) community infrastructure; (8) leadership and (9) a positive outlook. Chandra et al. (2011) argued that community resilience in the context of health security can be built through identifying and leveraging existing activities and resources that are already in place. The authors identified levers that help to strengthen community resilience through five core components specifically associated with community resilience in health security. The levers include: (1) wellness and access that promote social and economic well-being pre- and post-incident; (2) education in improving effective risk communication; (3) engagement that promotes participatory decision making in planning, response and recover activities; (4) self-sufficiency that enables individuals and communities to assume responsibility for their preparedness; (5) partnership with government and nongovernmental organizations (NGOs); (6) quality that helps to collect and analyze data for resilience building; and (7) efficiency that leverages resources for multiple use and maximum effectiveness.

In their study of the post-Canterbury earthquakes in New Zealand, Thornley et al. (2015) explored resilience from the perspective of six communities and identified a number of factors influencing community resilience. These include: (1) well-being of individuals and communities; (2) community connectedness and infrastructure; (3) community participation in disaster response and recovery; (4) community engagement in official decision-making; (5) external support and (6) exacerbating hardship. They concluded that connected communities with pre-existing community infrastructure can better cope with crises and also find it easier to adapt afterwards. Key strategies suggested include community-led action, supporting and increasing community infrastructure in communities, building strong partnerships between communities and authorities.

Sonn and Fisher (1998) pointed out that existing research on group responses to oppressive systems often neglect the different ways and alternative settings in which groups survive and maintain their cultures and identities. They suggested that by considering the notion of community resilience that involves person-centred factors and setting centred variables in making successful adaptation to adverse situations helps understanding of how groups respond to oppressive contexts. They concluded that oppressed groups do not always capitulate to or assimilate oppressive systems. In different settings (e.g. church groups, sporting clubs, extended family networks) these groups find ways to resist oppression and experience a sense of community for their survival.

Social capital and interconnectedness. Poortinga (2012) explored how social capital builds resilience and health in communities. Adger (2000) viewed social capital as a critical factor in determining the resilience of social groups; it is a crucial mechanism for absorbing political and economic change in the external environment. By employing the social capital framework by Szreter and Woolcock (2004), Poortinga (2012) studied how three types of social capital – namely, bonding, bridging and linking social capital – relate to neighbourhood deprivation and health. These three types of social capital represent different aspects of the social environment in communities. The bonding social capital refers to intra-group social cohesion within the community and civic participation; the bridging social capital refers to inter-group social cohesion and heterogeneous relationships; the linking social capital refers to political participation, activism, efficacy and trust. Those living in deprived areas tended to report poorer health. And all three forms of social capital were negatively related to neighbourhood deprivation; higher levels of social capital was found in less deprived areas. Furthermore, self-reported health was shown to be influenced by bonding social capital (bonding social cohesion and civic participation), bridging social capital (bridging social cohesion and heterogeneous socio-economic relationships) and two aspects of linking social capital (political efficacy and trust). Zhu and Ruth (2013) studied industrial ecosystems by drawing from the concept of resilience in ecological systems and in supply chains. They found that industrial ecosystems are vulnerable to unexpected disruptions; disruptions can quickly permeate through highly connected firms. Industrial ecosystem resilience depends on a number of factors including the density of exchanges between organizations, the level of inter-organizational dependency, and the number of firms in the industrial ecosystem. A large number of firms facilitates more exchanges in industrial ecosystems, increasing latitude and potential for environmental benefit. In the face of severe disruptions, industrial ecosystems withstand adversity by advancing their system's capacity and local adaptability (e.g. better management of inter-firm exchanges, facilitation of trust and early anticipation of disruption).

Policy. Aiginger (2009) argued that economic resilience can be achieved through five policy areas, namely: (1) more resilient economic structures; (2) increasing economic growth; (3) emphasizing longer-term goals; (4) avoiding a crisis; and (5) stabilizing institutions. He presented 23 strategies across these five policy areas and concluded that these strategies should serve as a menu for enlarged cyclical policy, combining demand management with structural policy. However, he acknowledged that not all strategies can foster economic resilience without negative side-effects and costs. The negative effects need to be compensated by integrating special growth strategies into the overall strategy. A strategy that leads to less openness and protectionism should be avoided. Clark, Huang and Walsh (2010) studied relationships between regional resilience and innovation capacity in the UK, the US and Japan. The finding shows that resilience depends not only on endowments (skilled labour, producers and institutions) but also on capacities influenced by policy to leverage innovation in response to changing technology, markets and resource environments. They concluded that policies encouraging small firm innovation have a broad range of benefits for regional economies. Others have noted how resilience can be promoted throughout a community through policies and programmes related to, for instance, emergency and disaster preparedness, public spaces for relaxation or exercise, access to healthcare, affordable housing and food, and employment stability (Southwick et al., 2016).

Understanding trajectories. Norris et al. (2009) examined the notion that resilience can be understood as comprised of a set of trajectories that occur after mass traumatic events. Resilience is not a one-dimensional construct solely about resistance or recovery. The authors explored a number of trajectories including resistance, resilience, recovery, relapsing/remitting, delayed dysfunction and chronic dysfunction paths. Although the results showed that the delayed dysfunction trajectory only appeared in New York post-9/11, all other trajectories were evident in both Mexico and New York, except for: (1) resistance having no or mild and stable symptoms; (2) resilience initially having moderate or severe symptoms followed by a sharp decrease; (3) recovery initially having moderate or severe symptoms followed by a gradual decrease; (4) chronic dysfunction having moderate or severe and stable symptoms.

Case #5 – St Helena: landing a future for a South Atlantic island

IVEY | Publishing

9B18M034

ST HELENA: LANDING A FUTURE FOR A SOUTH ATLANTIC ISLAND

> St. Helena, situated so remote from any continent, in the midst of a great ocean . . . —this little world, within itself,—excites our curiosity.
>
> Charles Darwin, *Voyage of the Beagle*, 1831–1836[1]

On October 14, 2017, the first ever commercial flight landed at the newly built airport on St Helena, one of the world's remotest islands. The journey to reach this point was not easy, with delays in building the airport and a postponement of the initial planned opening date due to unforeseen wind conditions. There were also delays building the island's first hotel. Residents grew frustrated with access issues because it was announced the cheaper sea service to Cape Town, South Africa would be terminated. Safety problems with the runway on neighbouring Ascension Island also limited residents' options for connecting with the outside world. Now that the first commercial flight had successfully landed, how should St Helena's

Economic Development Board approach the next phase of the long-term strategy to boost the island's economy through tourism?

ST HELENA

St Helena Island, along with the islands of Ascension and Tristan da Cunha, formed one of 14 British Overseas Territories (BOTs), having been claimed by the English in 1692. St Helena was created by undersea volcanic activity that was dormant for millions of years. It was one of the most remote, small inhabited islands in the world with a population of 4,534 in the 2016 census, and gross domestic product in 2014–15 estimated at £33.5 million.[2] It was 1,900 kilometres (km) away from the nearest country, Angola, in western Africa, and nearly 4,000 km from the coast of Brazil. It had a landmass of 122 square km (47 square miles).[3]

St Helena's location and mountainous, rugged topography offered a variety of microclimates and distinctive ecosystems. As a tourist destination, the island held multiple attractions, including its biodiversity. However, the economy was almost entirely dependent on receiving aid grants from Her Majesty's Government (the government of the United Kingdom).

Since its discovery in 1502, St Helena had only been accessible by sea. A minimum three-day boat journey was required to reach St Helena from Ascension Island and five days from Cape Town in South Africa. The Royal Mail Ship St Helena (RMS) ran scheduled services between Cape Town, St Helena, and Ascension Island. The RMS was run on behalf of the St Helena government. It carried all imported food and goods to the island and had space for a limited number of fare-paying passengers. Until 2016, all passengers were required to access the island by sea from a variety of vessels (see Exhibit 1 for passenger arrivals between 2010 and 2016); there had never been an airport facility on the island.

LIFE AS A "SAINT"[4]

Life on St Helena was not without challenges. In terms of food supply, almost everything was imported, incurring customs and freight costs. While the island produced some vegetables, it was not self-sufficient and was unable to produce enough food to feed the population. The island was heavily reliant on the RMS for meat, vegetables, fruit, and milk. It took three weeks via Ascension Island before the ship could return with supplies, and there was a capacity limit to the number of containers the RMS could deliver.

It was not uncommon for people to "panic buy" items in fear that the RMS would not arrive on schedule. In one instance, the island ran out of butter, margarine, cheese, potatoes, and onions for three weeks because the RMS had to go into dry dock in Cape Town for maintenance. There were no shopping malls on the island, just small local shops. It was typical to order online items such as clothing, shoes, and household items. Such items would take approximately three months to be delivered.

The island had no tertiary education. What was taught was adapted from the U.K. national curriculum for local use. There was an opportunity for a small number of students to study abroad (mostly on the U.K. mainland). However, this opportunity depended on individuals meeting required criteria and the number of scholarships on offer at any one time. With improvements in St Helena's telecommunications, high school students at Prince Andrew School received tutoring sessions by video conferencing. Another limited opportunity for tertiary education came annually through the Chevening[5] and Commonwealth scholarships. Only one individual at a time could take advantage of this opportunity. Those that aspired to study further through online or distance learning funded themselves, were funded by their employer, or both. It was not uncommon for a student to complete an undergraduate degree course and a postgraduate course such as a master of business administration through distance learning over 10 years.

The island was unable to accommodate or provide medical care services of a serious nature. Patients were often referred overseas. This was done through links with South African and British medical services. The majority of referred patients went to Cape Town, and patients were a common occurrence on RMS sailings. Basic medical services on the island included nursing and community care services, elderly and home care services, pharmacy and laboratory services, dental services, and administrative support services.

For entertainment, there were eight community centres, one in each district. These centres held events throughout the year. There were four local pubs, and clubs that mainly opened on the weekend. The older generation had its familiar haunts, and the younger generation had a choice of three places that they tended to go to. The island was limited in offering entertainment for young children in the 3 to 10-year age group. However, there were special events that took place throughout the year that were family friendly.

St Helena's communication system was dated. The access gateway to the island, although stable, was not sufficiently modern to provide the speed and bandwidth required to meet growing demand. As a result, the island endured limited telecommunications. Mobile phones were only introduced in November 2015, and these were limited in terms of data delivery and service carrier capabilities.

In terms of business climate, the investment environment in St Helena was a constraint for foreign investors. On top of the transportation costs, there were few human resources, expensive and unreliable utilities, high market concentration, weak infrastructure, and a lack of historical evidence on market potential and investment risks. Inward investment had been hesitant. However, just 10 people were registered as unemployed and in receipt of unemployment allowance in February 2016.[6]

In spite of these issues, Saints were known for their resilience and friendliness. Islanders formed a tight-knit community; they knew each other, and it was common for them to wave and greet each other, even passing cars. They supported each other in times of need and were known for being hospitable and generous. However, it was hard to keep things secret, and there was a "grape vine" through which rumours would circulate. One constant rumour related to the building of an airport on the island.

AIRPORT CONSTRUCTION

After a long period of consultation, the U.K. government announced plans to construct an airport on St Helena in March 2005, with an expected completion date of 2010. However, delays ensued, and an approved bidder—Italian group Impregilo (later named Salini Impregilo after a 2014 merger)—was not chosen until 2008. The project was put on hold in November 2008 due to new and unforeseen financial pressures caused by the global financial crisis and credit crunch. In December 2008, the U.K. government announced a pause in the airport contract negotiations. This became known among Saints as "the Pause."

A further consultation took place in 2009 before making a final decision on whether an airport was the most appropriate option for access to St Helena. Three options were considered: Option A—go ahead with the airport at that time; Option B—decide not to build the airport and commission a new ship; and Option C—defer a decision for a period of up to five years.

The consultation period began in April 2009 with the publication of a government consultation paper.[7] The Saints received neither the news of the Pause nor the consultation with open arms. Rather, after the announcement of the Pause, they became increasingly frustrated, perceiving that they were being asked to repeat what had already been said. They doubted that their voice would ever be heard. One of the perspectives respondents shared related to the comparison of funding requirements in the BOTs with those of developing countries; respondents thought the comparison was inappropriate because the issues were different. They pointed to the legal and political rights of St Helena as an Overseas Territory.[8]

Among the younger generation, there was an Option A youth group that promoted the "A campaign."

Consequently, Option A was the preferred choice, with 69 per cent (1,672 individuals) of those who signed the petition, 80 per cent (87 individuals) of those who provided written responses, and no less than 70 per cent of those who responded orally supporting this option.[9]

Eventually, in 2011, an air access memorandum of understanding (MOU) was signed.[10] The MOU recognized that air access would be the catalyst for sustainable economic development for St Helena based on a private sector led tourism industry.[11] Subsequently, the St Helena Sustainable Economic Development Plan (SEDP) was created in 2012.[12] The plan aimed to make St Helena less dependent on British aid by stimulating economic development and growth, specifically through the development of "high-value, low-volume" tourism on the back of air access.[13]

St Helena's economy had been dependent on aid and subsidies, and remittances from migrant labour from the Falkland Islands, Ascension Island, and the United Kingdom.[14] The plan was for such aid to be a thing of the past by opening an international airport that would offer direct flights to Johannesburg, South Africa, and St Helena's neighbouring island Ascension in May 2016.[15] Air access would provide a platform for St Helena to move onto a trajectory of solid economic growth. While air access in itself was no guarantee of economic success, it would offer a chance to reverse years of social and economic decline, and to build a strong, vibrant, self-sufficient, and increasingly confident St Helena.[16] The intention was that tourism would lead the island toward self-sufficiency. To this end, the U.K. government's Department for International Development (DFID) invested £201.5 million in the airport project and allocated £35.1 million for 10 years of operation.[17]

The St Helena government anticipated that despite the lack of an accessible beach and usual tourist facilities, the beauty of the rugged interior, combined with a potentially large hotel investment, would attract 30,000 tourists a year (500–900 visitors per week) to the island by 2021/22.[18] The SEDP provided information on required accommodation for 30,000 annual tourists (assuming low occupancy), expected spread of tourists throughout the year, major goals of the economic development project, and major attractions and sites that tourists would want to see on the island (see Exhibits 2 to 5). A study in 2016 concluded that the continuation of a U.K. subsidy would depend on whether projected estimates of tourism numbers and spend would be exceeded or missed.[19]

The project was set up as a design, build, and operate contract between the St Helena government and South African construction company Basil Read. The scope was to build the airport on Prosperous Bay Plain in the east of the island, as well as build associated infrastructure—including an access road to, and new wharf and bulk fuel installation—in Rupert's Valley, and build an inshore sea rescue facility. Following the construction, Basil Read was to operate the airport for 10 years. Basil Read retained Lanseria International Airport (Pty) Ltd., a private company that also ran airports in South Africa, as a consultant for airport operations. U.K.-based Halcrow Group Limited ran the project management unit (see Exhibit 6 for the key project stakeholders).

With the airport opening imminent, it was recognized by a new development organization called Enterprise Saint Helena, as well as by DFID, that there would be a need for increased accommodation of a suitable hotel standard on the island. With only 30 en-suite bedrooms on the island (18 of which were not available in 2014), additional bedrooms and at least one hotel at or around the airport were required.

In May 2014, South African-based Mantis Development was commissioned to produce outline designs and construction costs for a hotel.

Insufficient tourism accommodation (once the island's air service was operational) carried significant reputational and economic risk to the local tourism industry. The lack of appropriate accommodation would significantly affect the viability of any air service.

UNEXPECTED OUTCOME AND SUBSEQUENT RESPONSE

The St Helena Airport opened and was certified on schedule in 2016, five years after the MOU was signed. It began accepting emergency medical evacuation flights immediately. These flights used a Guardian Air Dassault Falcon 20 jet aircraft from Cape Town, South Africa. On the first flight, an ill baby was able to receive medical treatment in Cape Town in less than a day, compared to what would have been a five-day journey on the RMS. It was not uncommon for very sick patients to die en route to hospital in Cape Town when being evacuated on the RMS.

However, two issues arose in 2016. First, while the airport opened and was deemed to be on schedule, the hotel was not ready for the official opening of the airport in May 2016. Second, the airport itself was not immediately commercially operational, and the official opening date of May 21, 2016 was postponed.[20] The reason for the delay was the result of an "implementation flight" (test flight) in April 2016 using a Comair run Boeing 737–800, which uncovered turbulence and wind shear[21] conditions on approach to the airport. That meant additional work was needed to ensure the safe operation of scheduled passenger flights. The news came as a shock to the Saints.[22]

One year later in April 2017, the people of St Helena remained frustrated because the problem with the airport had not been resolved. Morale was reportedly at an all-time low as they waited to hear when their airport would finally open for scheduled commercial flights. A lack of clarity concerning the deferred opening of the airport continued to surround the future of air access and the livelihood of St Helena's people. Governor Lisa Phillips noted the following in a statement:[23]

> Wind shear is a factor at several airports around the world, including London City Airport, where safe landings happen every day. In the meantime, we are working hard to identify an interim flight solution that can

> land on our second runway (02, from the south). There is no wind shear on this second runway, but there is a tailwind. We have identified aircraft types which can land in these conditions, and airlines that have such planes—and we are now exploring the specific availability of aircraft with these airlines. The Airport is certified and open, as demonstrated by the emergency medevac flight last Saturday when we were able to fly a sick baby to Cape Town. Naturally, we will keep the public informed . . . as we have been doing.

In terms of the northern and southern approach—Runways 20 and 02 respectively (see Exhibit 7)—more data needed to be collected, including weather data and reports of the experience of each of the various flights that had so far operated various approaches into the airport. Specialized equipment was installed at the runway to monitor weather conditions.

The airport launched a new procurement process on December 7, 2016. The tender announced that St Helena government wished to appoint an operator (or operators) using an aircraft type capable of landing on the southern approach (Runway 02), which had a tailwind component. This would be for a period of time while the government continued to explore the potential for scheduled services into the northern approach (Runway 20).[24] The closing date for tenders was January 27, 2017. Relevant data from July 2016 on wind speeds was included in the Information Memorandum for potential operators, and updates were to be provided as they became available. While all dates were provisional and dependent on the outcome of the procurement exercise, the government aimed to award a final contract by the end of May 2017.[25]

In April 2017, St Helena Airport received an open-ended (that is, not time bound) Aerodrome Certificate from Air Safety Support International. At the same time, Air Traffic received certificates of competence for another year of approved operation.

The preferred bidder was announced on June 9, 2017 as SA Airlink Ltd. (Airlink), a privately owned airline registered in South Africa. It was a franchisee to South African Airways and a member of the International Air Transport Association (IATA). As such, it was accredited by the IATA Operational Safety Audit. The St Helena government and Airlink signed an agreement on July 21, 2017 to provide weekly scheduled commercial air services from Johannesburg to St Helena. Airlink would also operate a monthly charter service between St Helena and Ascension Island. This agreement followed a period of contractual negotiations with Airlink. After finalizing the regulatory approvals with the South African Civil Aviation Authority, a successful proving flight occurred on August 22, 2017, using the Airlink Embraer E190-100IGW aircraft.

The government released ticket flight information on September 1, 2017. The hotel was in operation from October 14, 2017, to coincide with the inaugural flight that successfully took place on that date.[26] However, the original plan in the 2012 SEDP to attract 30,000 visitors to St Helena every year was premised on some of those visitors being aircraft passengers and there being daily flights.[27] The second paragraph of the SEDP executive summary stated:

> A significant but relatively modest number of visitors, 30,000 per annum (500–900 visitors per week), is needed to make Saint Helena financially self-sustaining. This requires just two to three cornerstone tourist developments (e.g., Broad Bottom, Ladder Hill Fort and Devil's Punchbowl), serviced by daily flights and an improved island-wide tourism offering. The scale of change, whilst very large in Saint Helena terms, is what is already envisaged and is in absolute terms relatively modest. This is achievable within the 10 years of the Sustainable Economic Development Plan.[28]

EVENTS CONCERNING ASCENSION ISLAND

The Ascension Island Travel Agency (AITA) announced in April 2017 that Royal Air Force (RAF) flights to and from the United Kingdom and the Falkland Islands via Ascension were to be cancelled due to the poor state of repair of the main 3,000 metre runway at Georgetown Wideawake.[29] The Airbus A330 Voyager aircraft were deemed too heavy to land on the runway because it had fallen into disrepair. Given its deteriorated condition, there were safety concerns.

These flights were known as the South Atlantic Airbridge flights. It was possible for civilians, including Saints, to book seats on the flights—where there was availability—through the AITA. Saints would then connect with the RMS to reach St Helena. The flights would land at RAF Brize Norton in the United Kingdom. The announcement indicated that the Airbridge flights would not resume before 2019 or 2020. Official information suggested travellers and residents should use the RMS until further notice.[30] Falkland Islanders had better options and could connect via Cape Town when travelling to the United Kingdom and Europe, and also had options through Latin America. Emergency medical evacuation flights also were not affected.

DECOMMISIONING THE RMS

On October 5, 2017, it was announced that the RMS would continue for only four more months, with its last stop in Cape Town.[31] The announcement stated that, after a quarter of a century service to the island, the RMS would be sold through London shipbrokers C. W. Kellock & Co. Ltd. (part of the Eggar Forrester Group). A new monthly freighter ship would be used instead for cargo and supplies to the island.

Not having the option of boat transport had implications for Saints. The cost to travel by the RMS (on the cheapest deck, the C deck) was cheaper than travelling by air, especially for children under 12 for whom prices were 50 per cent of the adult price on the RMS but 75 per cent for flights. A child seat for the Cape Town return journey by air would be £603 (assuming the ticket was booked enough in advance to get one of the 10 seats allocated at that cheapest price). In contrast, a child return ticket to Cape Town on the RMS would be £429. For families with children, it would work out cheaper to travel by sea. With just a weekly air travel option, Saints were concerned this would take away the option of a more affordable—although longer—alternative. Furthermore, it was anticipated that the new freighter ship would take 3–4 weeks between journeys, extending time between receiving goods and increasing the risk of panic buying.

CHALLENGE FACING THE ECONOMIC DEVELOPMENT BOARD

St Helena's long-held vision was for greater self-sufficiency and sustainable economic development though tourism. The island's Economic Development Board[32] had put the capability of air access to the island at the centre of the vision. There was a 10-year plan for the island (2017–2027)[33] as well as the 2012 SEDP. However, the long-term strategy for the island with a reliance on tourism was brought into question with a series of crises affecting air transport for South Atlantic islands. Other remote islands in the world were able to sustain a tourist-based economy. However, St Helena had seemed to suffer from "one step forward, one step back." What should the island's Economic Development Board now do to maintain recent momentum and create a sustainable future for the Saints of the South Atlantic?

EXHIBIT 1: ALL VISITOR ARRIVALS INTO ST HELENA (2011–2016)

	2010	2011	2012	2013	2014	2015	2016
Total arrivals	3,125	3,262	3,356	3,756	3,839	4,221	3,932

Source: Created by the authors based on St Helena Government, Statistical Bulletin No. 2, 2018, accessed February 6, 2018, www.sainthelena.gov.sh/statistical-bulletin-no-2-2018.

EXHIBIT 2: ACCOMMODATION REQUIREMENTS AS REPORTED IN THE 2012 SUSTAINABLE ECONOMIC DEVELOPMENT PLAN

	Number of Rooms	Bed Nights	Staff	Potential Number of Tourists Supported Per Year
Large hotel and villas	263	596	350	17,484
Medium hotel	48	86	58	2,535
Boutique	20	36	24	1,056
Boutique	20	36	16	1,056
Small hotel*	20	36	16	1,056
Small hotel	20	36	16	1,056
Guest house	10	18	8	528
Guest house	10	18	8	528
Guest house	10	18	8	528
Guest house*	4	7	3	211
Guest house*	7	13	3	370
Guest house*	2	4	1	106
Guest house*	5	9	2	264
Guest house*	5	9	2	264
Self-catering*	28	101	56	2,957
Total	472	1,023	570	30,000
Occupancy rate if 30,000 tourists	56%			
*Already existed on-island, except for self-catering, where 50% existed on-island.				

Source: Created by the authors based on St Helena Government, Sustainable Economic Development Plan, accessed October 23, 2017, www.investinsthelena.com/wp-content/uploads/2015/01/sedp-final-draft.pdf.

EXHIBIT 3: MONTHLY DISTRIBUTION OF TOURISTS AS REPORTED IN THE 2012 SUSTAINABLE ECONOMIC DEVELOPMENT PLAN

	Percentage of Annual Tourists (%)	Number of Tourists at One Time	Capacity (%)
January	12	813	76
February	10	724	68
March	9	610	57
April	8	560	53
May	7	474	45
June	6	420	40
July	6	406	38
August	5	339	32
September	6	420	40
October	7	474	45
November	10	700	66
December	14	948	89
Peak load		948	
Maximum potential load		1,063	
Maximum capacity		89%	

Source: Created by the authors based on St Helena Government, *Sustainable Economic Development Plan*, accessed October 23, 2017, www.investinsthelena.com/wp-content/uploads/2015/01/sedp-final-draft.pdf.

EXHIBIT 4: GOALS AS REPORTED IN THE 2012 SUSTAINABLE ECONOMIC DEVELOPMENT PLAN

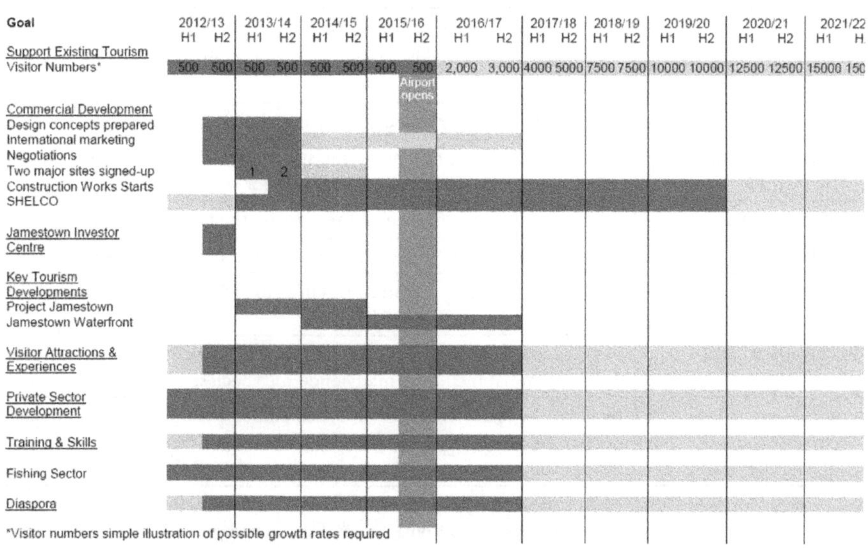

Source: Created by the authors based on St Helena Government, *Sustainable Economic Development Plan*, accessed October 23, 2017, www.investinsthelena.com/wp-content/uploads/2015/01/sedp-final-draft.pdf.

EXHIBIT 5: MAIN TOURIST ATTRACTIONS ON ST HELENA

Attraction/Site	Detail
Napoleonic properties	French Emperor's residence, after exile to St Helena, from 1815 until he died in 1821. The Napoleonic properties include Longwood House, the Briars Pavilion, Napoleon's tomb, and Bertrand's Cottage.
Plantation House (1792) and Jonathan the tortoise (approximately 1832)	Plantation House, built by the East India Company for St Helena's governors. Home to the island's oldest inhabitant (and world's oldest reptile), Jonathan the tortoise.
Jacob's Ladder (1829)	A 699-step inclined plane originally used to haul goods and manure. A route for walking in and out of Jamestown.
St James Church (1674)	The oldest Anglican church in the southern hemisphere.
Museum of St Helena	Dedicated to the history and life of St Helena.
Heart-shaped waterfall	A waterfall located in James Valley.
Ladder Hill Fort	Fort on Ladder Hill with grisly past. Appears in the records of 1733.
High Knoll Fort	Largest military fort on the island, set inland with a view of the island.
Deadwood Plain	Site of the Boer prisoner of war camp and home to St Helena's endemic wirebird.
Halley's Observatory (1676)	Set up by Edmond Halley to study stars from the southern hemisphere.
Boer Cemetery	Cemetery of the Boer War prisoners (1900–1902).
Slavery connection	A slave burial ground uncovered in Rupert's Valley in 2016.
Butcher Graves	The grave of two slaves who worked at Plantation House in the 1700s.
Lot and Lot's Wife	Prominent geological features formed by volcanic activity millions of years ago.
Sandy Bay Beach	A large sandy beach with black volcanic sand; swimming is inadvisable due to dangerous undercurrent.
Shipwrecks	Shipwrecks such as Papanui, Darkdale, Witte Leeuw, Spangeried, Atlantic Rose, Portzic, Frontier, and Bedgellet.
Diving	Clear, warm waters and interesting dive site habitats: rocky reefs with caves and areas ranging from boulders to cobbles and sand. Diverse marine life close to the wharf in Jamestown.
Distillery	The island's only working distillery that makes local spirits such as the tungi.
St Helena's Active Participation in Enterprise (SHAPE)	A non-profit organization providing support for disabled and vulnerable people on St Helena and producing quality crafts for sale.
Mount St Helena Golf Course	9-hole course—one of the most remote on the planet.
Millennium Forest	A 3,000-tree area designated for reforestation in the year 2000.
Walks and hiking	Wide range of hiking opportunities in a rugged landscape, suitable for experienced as well as less able hikers.
Diana's Peak National Park	The highest point on St Helena—823 metres above sea level—containing exotic flora and fauna, including many endemic species.
Birding	Includes the reclusive native moorhen and colonies of noddies, boobies, petrels, and terns on the island's offshore stacks. Viewing can be by boat or coastal walk.
Wildlife	Many unique species and 455 species of invertebrates, including the blushing snail, the spiky woodlouse, the vulturine and golden leafhopper, and Janich's fungus weevil. The island also has a near perfect bee population.

Source: Created by the authors from personal experience on St Helena and from St Helena Tourism, Places to Visit, accessed February 6, 2018, http://sthelenatourism.com/what-to-do/places-to-visit.

EXHIBIT 6: KEY STAKEHOLDERS IN THE ST HELENA AIRPORT PROJECT

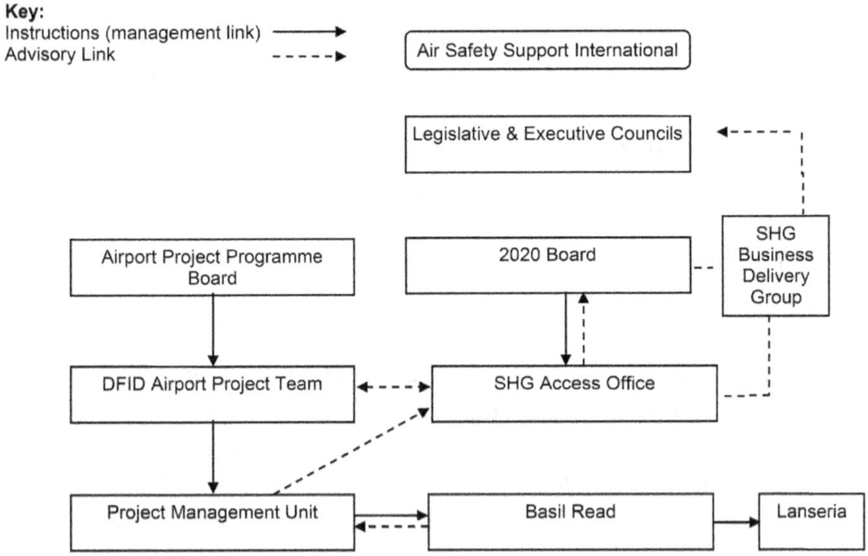

Note: DFID = Department for International Development; SHG = St Helena government.
Source: Reproduced by the authors based on "Frequently Asked Questions," St Helena Government, accessed October 16, 2017, www.sainthelena.gov.sh/frequently-asked-questions.

EXHIBIT 7: RUNWAY CHARACTERISTICS (IN METRES)

	Runway 20	Runway 02
Runway Paved Length	1,950	
Landing Distance Available (LDA)	1,550	1,535
Take Off Run Available (TORA)	1,850	1,635
Take Off Distance Available (TODA)	2,775	2,425
Accelerated Stop Distance Available (ASDA)	1,850	1,635

Source: "Frequently Asked Questions," St Helena Government, accessed October 16, 2017, www.sainthelena.gov.sh/frequently-asked-questions.

ENDNOTES

1 Charles Darwin, *The Voyage of the Beagle* (1839; repr., London, UK: Wordsworth 1996), 538.

2 £ = GBP = British pound; £1 = US$1.25 on March 31, 2017; all currency amounts are in British pounds unless otherwise specified. St Helena Statistics Office, Census 2016, accessed February 3, 2018, www.sainthelena.gov.sh/census-2016-3.

3 Ibid; "The World Factbook: St Helena, Ascension, Tristan da Cunha," Central Intelligence Agency, accessed November 2, 2017, www.cia.gov/library/publications/resources/the-world-factbook/geos/sh.html.

4 The term "Saint" was used to refer to a resident of St Helena.

5 The scholarship was for MBA courses only, and a degree was required.

6 St Helena Statistics Office, op. cit.

7 U.K. Government, Department for National Development, *St Helena Airport Consultation Report*, 2009, accessed November 2, 2017, www.gov.uk/government/uploads/system/uploads/attachment_data/file/67719/St-Helena-airport-consultation-report.pdf.

8 Ibid.

9 Ibid.

10 St Helena Government, *Memorandum of Understanding (MOU) between the Government of St Helena (SHG) and the Department for International Development (DFID) of the Government of the United Kingdom of Great Britain and Northern Ireland, Setting Out St Helena Government's Commitment to Open its Economy to Inward Investment and Increased Tourism in Parallel with the Development of Air Access in St Helena,* 2012, accessed November 2, 2017, www.sainthelena.gov.sh/publications/mou_2012101.

11 Ibid.

12 St Helena Government, *Sustainable Economic Development Plan,* 2012, accessed November 2, 2017, www.investinsthelena.com/wp-content/uploads/2015/01/sedp-final-draft.pdf.

13 Ibid.

14 St Helena Government, *Financial Statements 2015–2016*, accessed November 2, 2017, www.sainthelena.gov.sh/wp-content/uploads/2013/01/Financial-Statements-2015-16-FINAL-signed.pdf.

15 St Helena Government, "St Helena Air Services to be Provided by Comair," press release, March 27, 2015, accessed November 2, 2017, www.sainthelena.gov.sh/wp-content/uploads/2015/03/AIRPORT-St-Helena-Air-Services-to-be-Provided-by-Comair-Aviation-Only-27-March-2015.pdf; "Ascension Air Service to and from St Helena," St Helena Government, October 9, 2015, accessed November 2, 2017, www.sainthelena.gov.sh/ascension-air-service-to-and-from-st-helena.

16 St Helena Government, *Sustainable Economic Development Plan*, op. cit.

17 "Andrew Mitchell MP: Building an Airport for St Helena," Department for International Development, U.K. Government, November 3, 2011,

accessed November 2, 2017, www.gov.uk/government/speeches/andrew-mitchell-building-an-airport-for-st-helena.

18 St Helena Government, *Sustainable Economic Development Plan*, op. cit.

19 National Audit Office, *Realising the Benefits of the St Helena Airport Project,* July 7, 2016, accessed November 2, 2017, https://www.nao.org.uk/wp-content/uploads/2016/06/Realising-the-benefits-of-the-St-Helena-Airport.amended.pdf.

20 St Helena Government, "Airport Opening Ceremony Postponed," press release, April 26, 2016, accessed November 2, 2017, www.sainthelena.gov.sh/airport-opening-ceremony-postponed.

21 Wind shear was a dangerous atmospheric condition occurring when wind speed changes dramatically over short distances.

22 St Helena Government, "Airport Opening Ceremony Postponed," op. cit.

23 "Statement from Governor Lisa Phillips," St Helena Airport Project, June 10, 2016, accessed November 2, 2017, www.sainthelenaaccess.com/news/2016/06/15/st-helena-airport-statement-from-governor-lisa-phillips.

24 St Helena Government, "Air Service Tender Launched," press release, December 7, 2016, accessed November 2, 2017, www.sainthelena.gov.sh/wp-content/uploads/2016/12/AIRPORT-AS-Tender-Launched-7-December-2016-F.pdf.

25 Ibid.

26 "First Commercial Flight Lands on Remote St Helena," BBC News, October 14, 2017, accessed November 2, 2017, www.bbc.co.uk/news/world-africa-41620003.

27 St Helena Government, *Sustainable Economic Development Plan*, op. cit.

28 Ibid.

29 "Important Announcement Regarding Travel to and from Ascension Island," Ascension Island Government, April 28, 2017, accessed November 2, 2017, www.ascension-island.gov.ac/important-announcement-regarding-travel-to-and-from-ascension-island.

30 "Ascension Island Closed to Heavy Aircraft until 2019/2020," ch-aviation News, May 18, 2017, accessed November 2, 2017, www.ch-aviation.com/portal/news/55978-ascension-island-closed-to-heavy-aircraft-until-20192020.

31 "St Helena Line to Withdraw RMS St Helena from Service and Seeks Buyer for Vessel," Royal Mail Ship St Helena, October 5, 2017, accessed November 2, 2017, http://rms-st-helena.com/2017/10/05/st-helena-line-withdraw-rms-st-helena-service-seeks-buyer-vessel.

32 The board included the island's governor, chief secretary, financial secretary, and members of the DFID.

33 St Helena Government, *St Helena Island 10 Year Plan 2017–2027*, 2016, accessed February 3, 2018, www.sainthelena.gov.sh/wp-content/uploads/2012/08/10-Year-Plan-20-January-2017.pdf.

Case reflection

The St Helena case centres on the issues surrounding the construction and delayed opening of the first-ever airport on the island. The islanders ('Saints') wanted the airport, and they wanted the economic boost that would come from an inflow of tourists at levels not experienced before on St Helena. Given the extreme remoteness and isolation of the island, it was never plausible that 30,000 tourists per year could ever visit the island using the RMS boat service, cruise ships or private yachts. Two features in the case, however, resulted in a growing realization in the years after the airport was built that 30,000 tourists were not going to materialize any time soon even with a fully equipped international airport. The first was that the airport opening was delayed due to wind shear effects only discovered after the airport was built (while it was being tested). Second, the outcome of this was a smaller plane running much less frequently (weekly not daily) from Johannesburg. There was little chance that 30,000 tourists would appear in this revised solution. As reported in Williams, You and Joshua (2020): "Half-year numbers for 2019 indicated 2,091 passenger arrivals by air, of which only 811 were non-St Helenian tourists. Tourists arriving by sea (yachts) remained broadly unchanged following the airport construction (*St Helena Independent*, 2019)" (Williams, You and Joshua, 2020: 6). On reflection, many Saints observed an economic stimulus *during* the construction of the airport, i.e., while airport construction workers were stationed on the island, but saw this economic boost deteriorate once the construction workers left.

The case brings us full circle to our opening case in chapter 2 on Giselle Richards and her G-Unique Designs jewellery business on St Helena. The sentiment of entrepreneurs and small businesses on St Helena – of which there were around 300, many with fewer than five staff – is a barometer for the health of the island's economy. It is noteworthy that in 2020 some of the younger generation on the island had already left to seek opportunities on the UK mainland or, like Richards and her young family, were considering relocating to the Falkland Islands. Our first reflective point, then, is supportive of writers such as Welsh (2014) and Berkes and Ross (2013) in the sense that there is both a systems-level component to community resilience at a time of crisis and an individual-level one that rests on the mindsets, psychology and mental health of individuals in the community.

We see this quite strongly in the St Helena case, albeit with a 'bitter-sweet' twist. While resilience of the small business community on the island can only be a good thing as far as the overall economic development plan for the island is concerned (Williams, You and Joshua, 2020), if talented and creative small business owners and entrepreneurs end up leaving the island, this will reduce the supply of quality services to tourists as and when the numbers pick up to a higher level.

There is some evidence of sharing and leveraging of resources on the island in order to cope with the lack of tourists. This provides support to some – but not all – of the levers described by Chandra et al. (2011). One that stands out is engagement that promotes participatory decision-making in planning, response and recover activities – this continues to be an area of activity on the island and is one that is often reported on in the island's weekly newspaper, the *St Helena Independent*. Another is self-sufficiency that enables individuals and communities to assume responsibility for their preparedness: there is a level of self-sufficiency on the island, for instance in maintaining and running automobiles that might well in other countries be sold for scrap or spare parts, and in the G-Unique Designs case, utilizing glass washed up on the shoreline as material for jewellery products. Another area is the community spirit and activities within the community that broadly follow a tradition supportive of wellness and social well-being. This is in line with the concept of resilient culture described by Glover (2012). Perhaps more questionable would be the extent to which the government agencies explicitly collect and analyze data for resilience building and the degree to which small businesses and individuals work in partnership with government and NGOs; this also might be somewhat mixed (the Williams, You and Joshua (2000) study revealed perceptions of a negative impact of government decision-making on the resilience of small businesses on the island).

Studies of resilience at community level often touch on the construct of identity (e.g. Sonn and Fisher, 1998). Saints do have a strong sense of identity. Those who have resettled on the UK mainland gather for an annual community sporting event in Reading, UK. This started in 1979 and has been going ever since. This sense of identity dovetails into the theory of bonding social capital and strong ties also mentioned in the literature on community resilience (Poortinga, 2012). This underpins a social cohesion both within and outside of the island and is manifested in civic participation and the heterogeneous socio-economic relationships described by Poortinga (2012).

The case also raises questions about how the types of policies described by Aiginger (2009) in the context of Europe's recovery from the global financial crisis could be (or should have been) used by government policymakers. This would have involved not only the Saint Helena Government (SHG) but also representatives of the UK Government and in particular the Department for International Development (DFID). Aiginger (2009) argued that economic resilience can be achieved through a combination of 23 different strategies that fall into five policy areas (noted above). The key point is that resilience 'thinking' can be synthesized with economic developmental 'thinking'; resilience should not play second fiddle. A read of the original 'sustainable economic development plan' before the airport construction (SEDP, 2012) would indicate a preponderantly traditional policy mind-set. Aiginger (2009) lists: fighting unemployment, increasing growth and competitiveness, fighting inflation, combating global warming and fighting the effects of the financial crisis. The tone of the SEDP (2012) document very much relates to growth and competitiveness. An interesting feature of St Helena is that the island's level of unemployment is extremely low. The global financial crisis did cause an earlier 'pause' in the project to construct the airport. And the price of goods relative to average wages is a commonly discussed issue among Saints. The main focus of the SEDP (2012) was the growth and competitiveness of the island as a tourist destination.

Insight into an initiative to produce hand sanitizer on St Helena under lockdown

Community spirit in action

Following the onset of the global coronavirus pandemic the whole world went into lockdown. There were very few parts of the planet that were not affected by the virus and by the economic and social damage caused by the lockdown. However, at the time of writing, St Helena had not reported any cases and there were no deaths. Flights to St Helena out of South Africa had stopped, and a strict quarantine was put in place for any new arrivals on the island. It seemed the relative isolation of St Helena was turned to its advantage. Nevertheless, the island was in short supply of key equipment that could help it fight the virus should an outbreak occur. This included alcohol-based hand sanitizer. The close relationship capabilities of small business people on the island came to the fore in what happened next. Vlad Cucuiu, the island's resident pharmacist, and Paul Hickling, owner of the island's only distillery, combined forces to produce hand sanitizer for the local community. According to the *St Helena Independent* (Volume XV, Issue 18, 9 April 2020), Hickling had the ethanol and Cucuiu the chemistry books. They followed the exact formulation given by the World Health Organisation's Guide to Local Production of WHO-recommended Handrub Formulations. They needed to wait one full week for their mix to sit for quality-control reasons. The hand sanitizer was to be supplied by the entrepreneurs to the island's Health Directorate at no cost.

It is interesting to see the following comment in the message by St Helena governor, Philip Rushbrook, in the *St Helena Independent* on 15 May 2020. After one year in the governor's job, and dealing with multiple challenges relating to the economic development of the island, especially acute at the time because of the COVID-19 pandemic, the governor noted:

> If there is anything I have learnt over the past year, it is that the community spirit and looking out for one another is a precious character of Island life. More than ever in the potentially difficult times ahead we need that sense of community.[1]

Implications

When numerous individuals and organizations are highly interconnected and bound together in a common economic destiny, they can end up being exposed to the same disruption together. As Zhu and Ruth (2013) noted, vulnerability arises at the collective level through interconnectedness between actors; disruptions then permeate, sometimes very fast. We can learn a lot from the St Helena case where the nature of the various disruptions

1 "One year on: Governor's message to St Helena, Ascension and Tristan da Cunha", *St Helena Independent*, Volume XV, Issue 23, Friday 15 May 2020, www.independent.sh/wp-content/uploads/2020/05/St-Helena-Independent-20200515.pdf, accessed 19 May 2020

(delay in airport construction, discovery of wind shear problems, lower than expected tourist numbers) impinged on all islanders. They were all 'in it together' as a consequence of the island's remoteness and inaccessibility, as well as its economic heritage and level of development. One of the things that makes this collective level of analysis particularly interesting is that, while this interconnectedness and common interest are definitional in the meaning of a disruption, they are also characteristics that can determine the response in both reactive and proactive terms. We see this in Cucuiu and Hickling's effort to provide hand sanitizer during the global pandemic at no cost. A number of themes arise here.

First, there is the issue of scale. If a disruption ends up affecting a whole economy, ecosystem or community, its scale is large. Many different types of actors are likely to be affected, from both private and public sectors, not-for-profit and religious organizations, and, of course many individuals in the general population as well. Studies of the effects of natural disasters highlight the widespread damage and disruption caused across whole societies and economies. Natural disasters can be devastating, bringing on hardship especially to those already struggling to survive (Thornley et al., 2015). Victims can be dispersed across large areas, with whole families needing to be relocated (Norris et al., 2009). Damage is not measured in terms of the stress levels of one individual, the exit from a single market by one part of an organization, or even the collapse of one organization. And damage is not only measured in financial terms. Here, damage is measured in terms of the financial, physical and psychological well-being of many countless individuals and enterprises. Another feature is that the scale of these types of disruption are felt for many years. They are not transient, short-term blips. Homes, businesses and careers have to be rebuilt. Individuals may need continued health care for life. An example is the austerity measures enacted in the UK and other countries as a consequence of the recession and credit crunch caused by the global financial crisis. While the crisis started in 2007, the end of austerity was only formally announced in the UK by the British government in 2019.[2] Another example is the evacuation

2 "Chancellor Sajid David declares end of austerity", BBC News Online, 4 September 2019, www.bbc.co.uk/news/business-49577250, accessed 22nd April 2020

of the complete population of 264 people on the remote South Atlantic island of Tristan da Cunha in 1961 due to the island's erupting volcano. The residents were relocated back to the UK for two years before deciding to return to the island to resettle in 1963.[3] While these two examples are very different, they both speak to the long-term and enduring effect on a whole population within an economic system.

Second, in this chapter, perhaps more so than the others, we encounter the trauma and tragedy of man-made suffering. Much of this form of suffering is also large in scale, but it does not arise because of natural disasters. Here we see the effects of global or regional wars, terrorist attacks such as 9/11 (Norris et al., 2009), as well as the sad phenomenon of oppression (Funder, 2002; Sonn and Fisher, 1998). Again, the literature here is vast, and we have only scraped the surface of this theme in this chapter. History has shown how humans working in organized ideological groups oppress other groups of humans in order to claim victory in their battle for supremacy and power. Sonn and Fisher's (1998) study is especially interesting because it highlights how oppression meets resistance by – and resilience of – those being oppressed. Important for this chapter, then, is that this ugly phenomenon is experienced by groups of people, not just individuals. Groups may be defined in many ways, for instance along the lines of gender, race, religion, nationality, social class etc. Certain mechanisms and dynamics within oppressed groups show that they actually can be highly resilient, despite their temporary relinquishing (to varying extents) of freedom, power and control. Sonn and Fisher (1998) showed how oppressed groups can find ways to protect their values and identities. Man-made suffering, while being omnipresent in human existence, can bring out the strengths of communities of people bound together with the same aim, goals, or cultural norms. Often, members of the oppressed group are willing to make the ultimate sacrifice in defense of their culture and purpose.

Third, in many situations the economic ecosystems and communities that we analyze at a collective level can be demarcated physically. Quite literally, it is possible to put a geographic boundary around the territory

3 "Tristan da Cunha Volcanic Eruption – October 8, 1961", Devastating Disasters, https://devastatingdisasters.com/tristan-da-cunha-volcanic-eruption-october-8-1961/, accessed 22nd April 2020

affected by a disruption (Gilly et al., 2014; Williams, You and Joshua, 2020). At one end of the spectrum we have the societal and human problems caused by regional natural disasters, such as the eruption of Eyjafjallajökull in Iceland in 2010 that brought air traffic in Western Europe to a standstill. At the end other end of the spectrum we have global catastrophe such as COVID-19; here we can draw the boundary around the whole world. The case of St Helena involves a remote volcanic rock measuring 16 km by 8 km in the South Atlantic. Similar arguments can be made for earthquakes (Thornley et al., 2015) and, sadly, terrorist attacks (Norris et al., 2009). This notwithstanding, we need to be cognizant of the fact that some communities affected by shock and adversity are not delineated by geography. This could be the case, for instance, with religious communities, sub-cultures that span countries, and even online communities. Nevertheless, many collectives affected by disaster and shock, whether natural or man-made, are ones that we can draw a dotted line around on a map.

What is the relevance of this? The main point relates to proximity and attachment to 'place'. We saw the beneficial effect of proximity to resilience in chapter 4 when we reviewed studies of subsidiary survival in conflict zones. There is also the disrupting nature of distance (such as the CAGE distances – Ghemawat, 2001) in the field of international business. As geographic distance from the epicentre of an adverse event increases, so might the cultural, institutional and linguistic distances, especially as the pointer moves across national boundaries. These distances will increase the delays and coordination costs of those trying to help the community in distress. Related to this is the attachment to 'place' that many communities feel. Although some have noted how place-based communities have been in decline over the decades (Bridger and Alter, 2006), we argue that the trust and reciprocity that underpin social capital in communities do provide for a sense of community and belonging around place. Community members attached to one place share the same cultural norms and institutions. Place is not irrelevant because many natural and man-made traumas are place-demarcated. When these happen repeatedly over many years (such is in the oppression of a particular people in a geographic zone, or natural disasters that repeatedly occur in the same region because of geo-climatic conditions), learning and knowledge about how to resist, cope, recover and survive resides with survivors at that place (Glover, 2012).

Fourth, we uncover insights from the field of formal policy and regulations. The thrust here is that governments at regional, national and international levels can make decisions about allocating resources throughout the economic system in such a way that the system can buffer against shocks. Regulations in financial services (or lack thereof) were demonstrated to be wholly inadequate in the run-up to the global financial crisis; scholars refer to this type of phenomenon as 'regulatory failure' (Breyer, 1979). Changes that ensued included those coming about through state intervention as well as those generated through the financial sector's own regulatory bodies (Young and Park, 2013). But these regulatory responses did differ from country to country (Young and Park, 2013). As Aiginger's (2009) work demonstrated, policy for resilience can be seen as a menu of options; policy-makers are able to choose from this menu across the economic cycle. This approach is important because it spotlights the importance of proactive stances at national and international levels, not just reactive responses and wholesale changes following a post-mortem. Similarly, communities within and across economies can self-regulate, for instance with environmental legislation relating to agriculture (Glover, 2012) and localized idiosyncratic institutions that maintain and protect standards in a territorial brand such as in the Champagne area of France (Spielmann and Williams, 2016). In response to the COVID-19 outbreak we see countries across the world establishing policies for lockdown, social distancing and quarantining, although there have been some differences in terms of the exact nature of these enforcements and their timing. It is interesting to note how many of these types of policy and regulatory interventions come about following the onset of a large-scale crisis and also how some of the very biggest crises are brought about by regulatory failure.

Finally, the literature on resilience at a collective level contains a substantial volume of work related to informal norms, behaviours and social cohesion and support. This is very much in the opposite corner to the previous point on formal policy and regulation to enhance collective resilience. A democratic government cannot force a population to engage socially under threat of law enforcement and punishment, although it may have a role in nudging its members to participate in community action, for instance asking for volunteers in times of national emergency. Cucuiu and Hickling's response to the threat of coronavirus reaching St Helena was not mandated by government. It came about through their own volition and sense of duty of care for those around them. This emphasis on community relations and mutual cooperation among and between all types of actors (some affected, some unaffected) exists as a socialized action to help the broader collective deal with the disruption or shock. Here we see concepts such as sense of community (Sonn and Fisher, 1998), social capital and bonding (Berkes and Ross, 2013; Poortinga, 2012; Szreter and Woolock, 2004), as well as trust and cooperation between individuals and different types of organization. We can group these together under the banner of close relationship capabilities, a central thrust of instrumental stakeholder theory (Jones et al., 2018). Williams, You and Joshua (2020) used this theory in their exploration of how close relationship capabilities between small firms on St Helena contribute to their resilience. The findings showed that many aspects of close relationship capabilities help boost resilience, with the strongest effects being supportive coordination, knowledge sharing between actors, and partnerships that are respectful, trustworthy and long term. The study also identified aspects not captured by Jones et al. (2018), including a negative effect of government policy on the island on the perceived resilience of small firms. This is evidence that counters the previous point on the role of formal policy and regulation on resilience. There is a strong implication for resilience at the collective level, especially given the importance of small businesses to the espoused economic development plan for the island.

Table 6.1 provides a summary of these themes.

Table 6.1 Key themes from the literature on resilience at a collective level

Theme	*Sub-themes*	*Selected references and examples*
Grand scale	Many different types of actors are affected by the disruption or shock; natural disasters often inflicting widespread damage and disruption; effects felt by many people over a long time frame	Norris et al. (2009); Thornley et al. (2015) COVID-19
Man-made suffering	Oppressed groups; man's afflicting of suffering on fellow man	Funder (2002); Sonn and Fisher (1998) Apartheid

(Continued)

Table 6.1 Continued

Theme	*Sub-themes*	*Selected references and examples*
Territorial demarcation	Affected actors physically and economically co-located; co-location allows actors to come together to respond; issues of remoteness, inaccessibility and rural settings; territorial systems for innovation	Gilly et al. (2014); Williams, You and Joshua (2020); Rockenbauch and Sakdapolrak (2017); Glover (2012); Bridger and Alter (2006); Colovic (2012) St Helena case
Policy failure	Regulatory failure; different responses across countries	Young and Park (2013); Breyer (1979)
Policy entrepreneurship	Conceptualizing policy for resilience as a menu; building resilient economic structures; policy to promote innovation in firms	Aiginger (2009); Clark, Huang and Walsh (2010)
Close relationship capabilities	Range of concepts under the umbrella of instrumental stakeholder theory (IST); importance of physical exchange between actors; different forms of social capital (bridging, bonding); sense of community	Williams, You and Joshua (2020); Zhu and Ruth (2013); Szreter and Woolock (2004); Berkes and Ross (2013); Sonn and Fisher (1998) St Helena case St Helena hand sanitizer initiative

Learning points

This chapter provides the following learning points:

- Resilience in economic ecosystems and communities has received considerable attention from scholars
- The contexts of studies in this area are diverse and include: rural areas, remote territories, oppressed groups, human interaction with ecology, radical events and ancient history
- There are various aspects to resilience at this level, including the importance of stakeholder relationships, having a sense of community, social capital and interconnectedness between actors, and policy and formal institutions

- Implications that we can use in our broader understanding of organizing for resilience include the following: grand scale, man-made suffering, territorial demarcation, policy failure, policy entrepreneurship, close relationship capabilities.

Suggested activity and assignment questions

1. Identify an example of an entire economy or community that has faced a major disruption to its economic security and survival – feel free to examine cases as far back in history as data availability allows.
2. Find out what happened and analyze your findings in order to:
    a. Identify the main variables that helped and/or hindered how the crisis was dealt with
    b. Show how these variables are interconnected (with each other and with the outcome).
3. Identify ways in which the literature and examples covered in this chapter resonate with your case.
4. Conduct additional literature review and reflect on extant academic research into the variables you identify in your case example.

PART II

LOOKING FORWARD

RESILIENCE IN AND FOR THE FUTURE

7

SYNTHESIS

THE RESILIENCE LANDSCAPE

Part 2 of this book reflects on the insights from prior literature and cases in order to form a basis for new ideas about organizing for resilience in the future. Obviously, prior literature and cases all happened in the past. One looks into history when examining any academic article in the field of business and management. The problems and solutions embodied in both the studies and the cases of resilience all happened in the past. Some of those disruptions might occur again, but they might be slightly transposed, different in terms of character or severity. Some of the solutions and factors shown in the past to underpin resilience might work again in the future. But they might not. There might be slight contextual and environmental differences meaning that a solution that worked in the past is no longer valid. It could even make the problem worse. Past research in the field of resilience shows significant inroads across different levels, summarized in various themes at the end of the previous five chapters in Part 1. What can we learn from this that will shape new thinking and new approaches for the future and the unknowns that lie ahead?

Learning from disruption per se

First and foremost, past research and stories of adversity across the spectrum of resilience provide an opportunity to look beyond the character of resilience and towards the character of disruption. Part 1 of the book has only touched the surface of the world of disruption and adversity. It is by no means a complete map of the suffering and trauma that affect people and organizations. But it reveals one very important insight: it is not possible to fully appreciate the organizational imperatives for resilience without understanding the nature of disruption per se. In plain speak, organizations need the right tools for the job, and for this they need to understand the nature of the job. The following is highly pertinent for understanding the nature of disruption per se.

Volition. As we moved through the spectrum of resilience (from individual to collective communities and economies) there are a wide range of disruptions and different ways in which researchers have analyzed them. We also see a certain amount of subjectivity and chance[1]: depending on the hilltop on which one stands, an event may negatively affect our ability to survive and compete, or it may be completely irrelevant to us. Assuming that any given event does represent a disruption that negatively affects an organization (or has the potential to), there are also different ways of looking at that disruption. On the one hand there is the type of disruption that is not our fault, where we had no choice (Ungar, 2008; Winfield, 1991). Through no fault of our own, we find ourselves in an adverse situation. Perhaps through birth, the geographical location on the planet where we happen to be raised, our social and economic setting, perhaps through genetic inheritance, perhaps through decisions taken by predecessor managers, perhaps through past policy and actions of governments and powerful bodies; the consequence could be negative and counter to goals, interests and the need to survive and compete. On the other hand there is the type of disruption that we expect to encounter because we made explicit decisions, including career choices, to put ourselves in a vulnerable position, in harm's way (Bonanno et al., 2012; Cornum et al., 2011). We may have chosen a specific career in the military or front-line health services, we may have chosen to

1 E.g. personalized reality in chapter 2

enter a foreign market with a new product format that had never been tried or tested anywhere before, or we may have succumbed to the temptation to behave unethically, hubristically, arrogantly and greedily at board level. We may have made such decisions, and assuming at least a modicum of prior insight into what we might be letting ourselves in for, we should have seen the disruption coming.

Evolution. There is also a complex and dynamic evolution of disruption and adversity over time (Carmeli and Markman, 2011; Colovic, 2012; Kahn et al., 2018; King et al., 2016; Marston, 2015; Williams et al., 2017). One thing leads to another; disruption can build on disruption, especially if left unattended. As noted by Cunha, Clegg and Kamoche (2006), sometimes anticipated issues in organizations take an unexpected shape. These might go unnoticed by a manager. While McFarlane and Norris (2006: 4) pointed out that "a potentially traumatic event . . . has an acute onset, and is time delimited", one can also argue there is no such thing as a *single* disruptive event! The causes of many crises are not well understood (Van der Vegt et al., 2015). Many major crises emerge from a chain of events and the consequences at each part of the chain are hard to predict. Any evidence of an event that negatively impacts the operational strategy of the organization is only one link in a much longer chain of disruptive events that never had a beginning and will never have an end. The sub-prime mortgage scandal in the US led to a credit crunch in the Eurozone. The lack of tourists arriving on St Helena after the delay to the new airport led ultimately to some key people and entrepreneurs leaving the island, further weakening its stock of human capital. The initial failure to address the publicized union protests outside Tesco Fresh & Easy stores in the US led to more protests and stunts, many of which were publicized in the local communities. The willingness of key actors to sustain the culture within Enron's leadership team and accounting practices led ultimately to the demise of the organization, and also to the demise of its main accountant. What the literature at different levels of analysis tells is that disruptions are often interlinked, highly complex and not unitary or isolated events. Often, the failure of the human-led organizational system to deal effectively with them leads to their effects being hard felt the next time they occur. Think of the failure of a local government to invest in flood water prevention systems following damaging floods, only for those floods to return. Or unconvincing political viewpoints on the very essence of climate change and its effects and doubters undermining efforts to change human behaviour to become more respectful of the planet. Multiple disruptions over time are interlinked and interconnected.

Cross-level effects. The literature across the different levels also describes the complex nature of the effects that can be felt as a consequence of the disruption. Morgeson, Mitchell and Liu (2015) pointed out that events can originate at a specific location on any hierarchical level and the dispersion or direction of its effects can be vertical (upward or downward), or horizontal within the same level, or both. Clearly, this point can be illustrated by looking at each of the different levels. Individuals might lose jobs and incomes, suffer health consequences or sadly face death. Organizations of all sizes may haemorrhage cash, become devalued, or go out of business. Communities and economies may suffer collectively from economic and social hardships. But there is more to it than myopic views at singular levels. The effects of disruptions are often interlinked across the levels. Individuals who decide to migrate for personal economic reasons (i.e. who had adverse experiences due to prior disruption at an individual level) can contribute, through their actions, to the undermining of the economy in which they originated. A small firm highly dependent as a supplier on a large firm that suffers from a crisis is also in a highly vulnerable position. Organizations of all shapes and sizes that go out of business will negatively impact both individual employees and their families and the health and well-being of the overall economy. This point is particularly relevant to our concept of the 'Resilience Landscape' introduced below, and finds reinforcement in much of the resilience literature that emphasizes cross-level effects (Fleming and Ledogar, 2008; Kimhi, 2016; Linnenluecke, 2017; Liu et al., 2017; Obrist et al., 2010; Southwick et al., 2014). However, the point here concerns specifically the cross-level interlinkage of disruption and the need to appreciate how disruption at one level can very quickly lead to disruption at other levels. This is aligned with the previous point of disruption being an eternal evolution of interconnected adverse forces, but differs in terms of putting an explicit emphasis on evolution back and forth across levels.

While we discern these three attributes of disruption per se (volition, evolution and cross-level impact) there are likely to be many other ways of describing the sources and consequences of adverse affects on individuals, organizations and ecosystems. The key point here, and one that we shall return to in the next chapter, is that organizational leaders wishing to make their organizations more resilient will need to pay due care and attention to the nature of disruption and learn from an appreciation of its intrinsic attributes. This is essential in order to disarm and stop in its tracks not only an immediate disruption but also many others in the future.

Learning from actions in relation to disruptions

The second big area of learning that one can consider from the past literature and cases on resilience concerns the consequences of individuals', organizations' and communities' actions as they relate to disruptions. In each of the chapters in Part 1 we find literature that clearly identifies proactive actions and factors that explain resilience in advance of any specific disruption. An example from chapter 2 is Moenkemeyer, Hoegl and Weiss' (2012) factors for helping cope with innovation project failure, including having hope and optimism. Another example, also from chapter 2, is Cornum, Matthews and Seligman's (2011) emphasis on emotional and spiritual fitness assessment as well as individualized training. There are many examples of reactive actions and responses that were taken as a direct consequence of specific disruptions. An example here is Mark Welling's response to the tragic death of his business partner, Antoine van Veldhuizen, and how he approached the leadership of the company following this dreadful event (chapter 3). Philips' reaction to the onset of the global financial crisis (chapter 5) and how Giselle Richards was prepared to move away from St Helena (chapter 2, but also chapter 6) are relevant reactive actions.

Proportionality. A first point here is the need to learn about how these types of actions in relation to the nature of specific disruptions lead to certain outcomes. In some cases, reactive responses were effective. In others, proactive preparations were more suitable. In other instances, the actions and responses (reactive or proactive) were not effective, as in the Tesco's Fresh & Easy case (chapter 4). The responses to under-performance highlighted in the case – such as adaptation of the marketing mix and grocery shopping experience – were not sufficient to avoid eventual exit. Overall, in terms of these different types of outcomes, it is vitally important to learn from the 'not effective' category as well as from the 'effective' category. A key point here is the need to understand the extent to which the action was proportionate to the nature of disruption. Simply put, low levels of preparedness or little by way of response might work for disruptions that do not have much of an impact. But these actions would fail as soon as the disruption hits an inflection point that leads to increased suffering for which the action is ineffective. Conversely, over-preparedness or a massive 'knee jerk' reaction in relation to a threat or an actual disruption may deflect attention and resources (and incur costs) that are not justified. So there is an issue of using learning of action in relation to disruption as a basis of improving an organization's ability to be proportionate.

People. Reflecting on the chapters in Part 1, effective organizing for resilience puts people squarely in the middle of the picture. This is clearly the case in terms of the phenomenon at an individual level. But moving through the organizational levels, front-line workers, middle-ranking managers and strategic leaders of organizations have key roles to play in how proactive and reactive forms of resilience unfold in the wider organizational setting. In small firms, the central entrepreneurial figure (or figures) is (are) key (chapter 3). In parts of large organizations (chapter 4), the way individual employees on the ground in specific locations are managed, resourced, trained and incentivized over varying forms of distance from the organization's headquarters is critical (Williams et al., 2017). They are crucial to the organization's ability to predict or detect disruptions that may occur only locally to that part of the organization. Due to distance and information asymmetry, headquarters' managers will not be able to accurately and consistently perform this prediction and detection function as well as people 'on the ground'. But if these people do not have the means, the tools and the commitment to carry out these functions, then the ability of the wider organization to implement the quarantining effect, as discussed in chapter 4, is called into question. High performance work systems in parts of large organizations matter to how knowledge flows into and out of those organizational parts (Williams and Lee, 2016). And when we move along the spectrum to the issue of large firms and enterprise-wide shocks (chapter 5), the role of the strategic apex and the personalities within that relative small but powerful unit becomes critical. The cases of Enron, Barings, Olympus and others where governance failure and a culture of greed and arrogance – as opposed to honesty and integrity – are the norm demonstrate this point. The character of people at the strategic apex becomes part of the disruption that culminates in the failure of the entire organization. At the level of collectives in communities and economies (chapter 6) we also see people very much at play. Here it is both the sharing of norms and values between people regardless of position or status within a social hierarchy and the role of individual leaders and those that can affect policy decisions. Within and across all the levels one sees time and time again the role of people in enabling the relationship between action and disruption. Our learning of the phenomenon, then, is intrinsically connected to our understanding and insight into the human condition.

More cross-level effects. In much the same way that we can learn from disruptions that span different levels of analysis, we can also learn from human actions in relation to disruptions across levels of analysis. Indeed, there is a profound need to appreciate the relationship between action and disruption as it manifests itself in and among individuals on their own, in organizations of different sizes, and in collectives of individuals and organizations. There are two interesting points here. First, the nature of the relationship between disruption and action can be different across the levels. For instance, positive coping, behavioural control and altruism (Meredith et al., 2011) are examples that encourage resilience in individuals, while wage freezes and reducing employee numbers (Smallbone et al., 2012) are decisions that apply at a small firm level. Learning about cross-level effects needs to acknowledge that there are some multivariate relationships where the nature of the variable in question is specific to that level of analysis. Nevertheless, and second, a better learning of the phenomenon can be achieved by relaxing this rather compartmentalized approach and acknowledging relationships between action and disruption at all levels. For example, Colovic and Mehrotra (2020) explain how a social movement union organization in India (called SEWA) advances conditions of self-employed women and women entrepreneurs in India. This is perhaps typical of the work of NGOs the world over; they tend to have a social purpose targeted at a sub-section of the population in need. In this case an organization at the broader community level is dedicated to support resilience at an individual and small firm level. Another example could be one of a wage freeze that may be effective at the small firm level (Smallbone et al., 2012). But we might also be aware of the positive coping, behavioural control and altruistic mentalities among our staff that will amplify the positive effect of wage freezes in dealing with the disruption. The story of Vlad Cucuiu and Paul Hickling's social enterprise to produce hand sanitizer on St Helena during the COVID-19 pandemic (chapter 6) is a case in hand. Here we see an example of two *individuals* combining knowledge and resources from their *small firms* in order to boost the resilience of the *community*. The relationship between human action and disruption has spanned multiple levels and the pre-awareness and foresight behind the venture would have – at least tacitly – taken consideration of this relationship at various levels.

Overall, the relation between human action (proactive and reactive) and disruption (of different forms) provides a fertile ground for learning about organizing for resilience. The three points – proportionality, people and (more) cross-level effects – can help guide this learning. Similar to the points made about learning from disruption per se (above), there may be other salient points one can distil from the literature and historical cases. Identifying and discussing these will be crucial for the development of knowledge in this field. Nevertheless, learning from disruption per se as well as from action in relation to disruption provides a basis for defining the Resilience Landscape that all organizations are part of.

The Resilience Landscape

Few would dispute understanding the nature of risk to be essential for promoting resilience. While it is impossible to identify all potential risks (Van de Vegt et al., 2015), undertaking best efforts to identify them based on current knowledge, categorizing them in terms of severity and putting plans in place to deal with them if they occur is widely seen as valuable strategic practice for any organization. Our purpose is not to describe or repeat the essence of this process; it has been covered in the literature. We think the metaphor of landscape is particularly useful.

It is not uncommon to see metaphors in the business and management literature; they create a way of illustrating features and processes involved in strategy and learning (Bürgi et al., 2005). Interesting metaphors in the literature see strategy in military terms (Kolar and Toporišič, 2007), as a toolbox with different tools to use in different conditions (Bröder and Newell, 2008), and even as a river (Lamberg and Parvinen, 2003). In terms of resilience, Norris et al. (2008) noted how the field of resilience has "metaphorical origins" (p. 128) in the natural sciences and engineering, and even suggest the theory of relativity to be metaphorical to resilience theory (p. 146)!

A landscape is normally defined in terms of a view, or a picture, that one looks at. The view is typically over land and water; it shows scenery, sometimes natural, sometimes man-made, often a mix of both. It is also a word that connotes backdrop, a stage on which events take place. Think of the great European landscape artists of the 18th and 19th centuries such as Turner, Constable, Van Gogh, Monet, Cézanne. Our use of the word landscape is not physical. Instead, we use it to represent a mental image that is internal to the person looking on. There is a scene, a depiction of detail, in the mind of someone who is concerned with how to organize for resilience.

What is the essence of the Resilience Landscape metaphor?

Based on the previous points concerning (1) learning from disruption per se and (2) learning from action in relation to disruption, we believe the metaphor of landscape goes beyond a mechanistic risk analysis and needs to encompass both disruption per se as well as action in relation to disruption. The key detail on the landscape concerns disruptions and actions. Neither are singular, there are plentiful disruptions and plentiful actions. The disruptions in the Resilience Landscape can be seen in terms of volition, evolution and cross-level effects. Actions in relation to disruption can be seen in terms of proportionality, people and (more) cross-level effects. Importantly, four properties of the landscape metaphor assist analysts of organizing for resilience in the future.

- *360-degree view*: The person looking on[2] (the 'onlooker') is standing on a particular hilltop and has a maximum 360 degree view. If you are into hiking or mountain climbing you will recognize this feeling. You will also obtain it at the top of the Eiffel Tower in Paris, the Burj Khalifa in Dubai or at the top of a Ferris Wheel. The reality, however, is our view is often obstructed, perhaps by the weather, perhaps by a building in the foreground, perhaps because we are sitting in an office looking at a

2 In principle this could be anybody. For the purposes of this book we can imagine the entrepreneur, the organizational manager, the leader, the key decision-maker in the organization to be the onlooker. This individual is normally surrounded by others in a social network; each has a view of the Resilience Landscape and can influence the focal person by sharing their knowledge and opinions.

screen containing information we can't interpret effectively. However, our aim must be for a 360-degree view.

- *Depth of field (foreground, middle ground, background).* The person looking on ideally does not have eyesight problems that restrict their ability to distinguish objects close up from those that are further away. A pair of binoculars or a telescope might be needed. So might an opticians' test. The Resilience Landscape includes disruptions that are close by as well as ones that are further away. It also includes actions in relation to disruptions that are close by, as well as those that are further away. All may be relevant.
- *Horizon.* There is a point past which the onlooker cannot see. In a real-world landscape, the land meets the sky. The curvature of the Earth means the onlooker has to physically move in order to see what is beyond the horizon. There is a cost attached to finding out what is beyond the horizon. Sometimes it is necessary to go there to find out about it and/or to work with partners who can go there or have been there.
- *Evolution.* If the onlooker stays in one position long enough, they will observe changes to the detail in the landscape. The landscape is constantly changing. New objects will come, some will disappear. In some settings, the seasons may mean the fall of leaves make it more possible to see further. However, the onlooker is part of the landscape. Their actions, movement and travel through the landscape will make it change.

Figure 7.1 schematizes this concept. The onlooker is travelling through time (evolution), perceiving disruptions and actions related to disruptions in what is only possible to perceive (horizon). Some disruptions are perceived as more pressing and relevant than others (depth of field), while the onlooker aims for a complete view (360 degrees). Disruptions are denoted by a cloud shape – the larger the shape, the closer the object. Actions in relation to disruption are denoted by black boxes.

These properties of the Resilience Landscape can be useful to understand how organizations address the challenge of how to organize for resilience. They need to see as much as they can (360 degree view), they need to appreciate what is imminent versus what is not (depth of field), they need to have some idea of what is over the horizon before it comes into

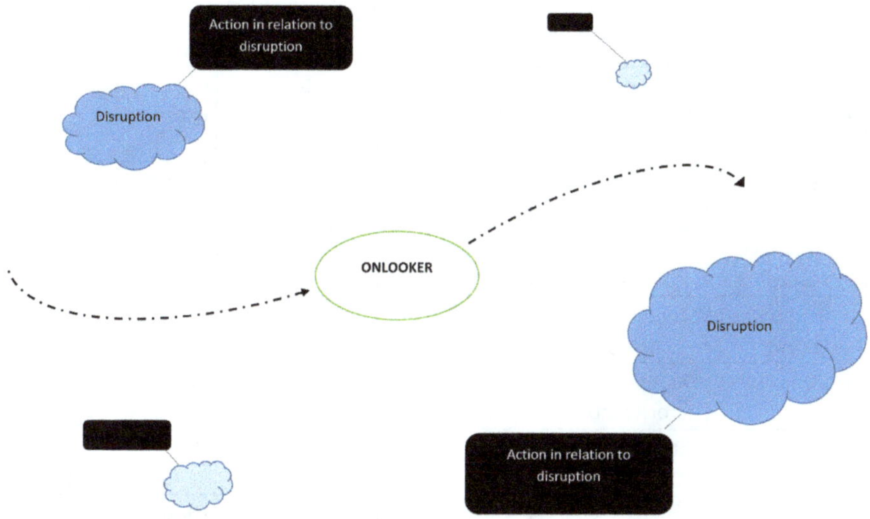

Figure 7.1 The Resilience Landscape

view, and they need to be able to appreciate the evolution of the picture they are looking at while recognizing they are part of it. And all the while the onlooker needs to be cognizant of a wide range of disruptions of different characterizations as well as a wide range of actions in relation to those disruptions.

Table 7.1 shows a summary of the main themes identified in chapters 2–6. There are 27 items in all. As noted earlier, there are some similarities across the levels. For instance, the construct of communal schemas identified in the discussion on resilience in small firms (chapter 3) has conceptual overlap with the close relationship capabilities of chapter 6, an item categorized at the collective level, especially in terms of shared sense of community. And the policy entrepreneurship identified at the collective level may conceptually overlap with the process of corporative self-renewal, especially as it relates to changes in the administrative and governance systems that regulate how people behave. Nevertheless, many of the items in Table 7.1 are specific to the assigned level. Personalized reality at the individual level is an example of this.

Another way of looking at these implications is to map them onto the broad categories describing the nature of: (1) vulnerabilities that can give

Table 7.1 Summary of key themes from chapters 2–6: objects in the Resilience Landscape

Resilience at an individual level	*Small-firms, big shocks*	*Big firms, isolated shocks*	*Big firms, enterprise-wide shocks*	*Communities and economies*
Complex sources	Size-related vulnerability	Collateral damage	Liability of bigness	Grand scale
Personalized reality	Communal schemas	Collective effort	Managing relatedness	Man-made suffering
Individualized coping	Muddling through	Managing distance	Corporate self-renewal	Territorial demarcation
Self-awareness	Disruption orientation	Establishment mistakes	Downward spirals	Policy failure
Evaluative capacity	Intermittent resilience	Quarantining	Failure of governance	Policy entrepreneurship
Reciprocity				Close relationship capabilities

rise to specific disruptions and (2) classes of actions that can be used to counter disruptions. In other words, some of the 27 items in Table 7.1 amount to vulnerabilities in the landscape, aspects that make the landscape a dangerous place to be. They are essentially higher-order attributes of specific instances of disruptions. On the other hand, some of them amount to means of addressing vulnerabilities, things that make the landscape less dangerous and worth journeying through. These can be seen as actions in relation to disruptions. Included here are the psychologically oriented items such as communal schemas, disruption orientation and self-awareness. At face value they might not sound like actions. However, the utilization of them amounts to a way of influencing and guiding action. Table 7.2 shows a transposition of the 27 items in this way. Returning to the metaphor of a Resilience Landscape, we can view these items as objects visible to an onlooker within the landscape.

To operationalize the Resilience Landscape, we need to map the specific objects from Table 7.2 onto new variants of Figure 7.1. We do this through the use of worked examples. Consider the following situations facing organizations in Examples A, B and C. In Example A, the disruption in the spotlight was purely hypothetical; it was a concern amongst managers,

Table 7.2 Categorizing objects in the Resilience Landscape

Level of analysis	*The nature of disruption*	*Actions in relation to disruption*
Communities and economies	Grand scale Man-made suffering Territorial demarcation Policy failure	Close relationship capabilities Policy entrepreneurship
Big firms	Liability of bigness Downward spirals Failure of governance	Corporate self-renewal Managing relatedness
Parts of big firms	Establishment mistakes Collateral damage	Managing distance Quarantining Collective effort
Small firms	Size-related vulnerability	Communal schemas Disruption orientation Muddling through Intermittent resilience
Individuals	Complex sources Personalized reality	Self-awareness Individualized coping Evaluative capacity Reciprocity

albeit a very real one. The question therefore, is how to be proactive and prepare for the possibility of disruption. In Example B, the organization in question is caught right in the middle of a disruption. In this case, it was not well prepared and the disruption had come as a surprise. The key question is how to react. In Example C, the main disruption is in the rear-view mirror. It seems to have passed. However, there had been ample warnings about a resurgence of the disruption – a 2nd wave – and the question is how the previous reactive actions from a recent period of time can provide knowledge that will help with how to be proactive ahead of a potential 2nd wave.

Example A – a foreign subsidiary's worry that its joint venture partner will steal its IP

Situation. Imagine an overseas operation of a large, international company facing a potential issue that could threaten its position in a given host country. Its parent company had set it up as a joint venture (JV) but there were concerns that its JV partner could behave opportunistically and steal its IP. There was no evidence that this had happened yet, but the threat was real. The rules and regulations in the host country were not particularly strong vis-à-vis IP rights, and other companies had faced similar issues in the past. Imagine the parent company had broader performance issues and had underperformed at a corporate level for a number of years. As a consequence of this, its top managers had not been paying sufficient attention to the subsidiary, or helping it with organizational mechanisms or practices to help it manage its JV and protect its IP.

Analysis. The potential disruption affecting the subsidiary is comprised of a combination of various vulnerabilities in the resilience landscape: (1) establishment mistake (unit level) that opened it up to JV opportunism,[3] (2) policy failure in the host country (collective level) that could fail to protect the subsidiary, (3) a downward spiral of the parent (large firm level) that hinders practice transfer and help for the subsidiary, and (4) the potential for collateral damage (to the corporation) if its IP falls into the wrong hands. However, also imagine that similar instances were encountered by the parent in the past in other countries, leading to: lobbying for policy change (policy entrepreneurship), bringing in lawyers from corporate headquarters to deal with the issue (collective effort) and new administrative processes and HR systems to prevent leakage of intellectual property implemented elsewhere (corporate self-renewal). The corporation was also making serious attempts at self-renewal in response to the downward spiral. The Resilience Landscape in this case would look somewhat like the schematic in Figure 7.2.

As a part of a large firm potentially sailing into a crisis in its particular setting, the subsidiary is no longer an onlooker. It has journeyed straight into a specific disruptive context and could soon be engulfed by it. Importantly, it can learn from vulnerabilities and actions in relation to disruptions within its horizon in order to cope with the context. The extent to which corporate self-renewal on the one hand and collective effort and policy entrepreneurship on the other are useful in dealing with the situation will need to be evaluated by managers in the subsidiary working collaboratively with others within the international firm and local agencies.

3 Not all JVs end this way and not all should be seen as 'mistakes'. We use this expression in this instance as a connotation for the initial conditions that led to the potential issue arising.

Perhaps it is a combination of all three actions that will be most useful. Perhaps only one of them makes sense, or they should be staged over time. The key point is that without an awareness of the Resilience Landscape, the subsidiary would be restricted in terms of its identification and use of actions, and it would suffer more than it needed to.

Example B – a small firm suddenly losing its single biggest client

Situation. Imagine the case of a small firm that has been highly dependent on one client for the majority of its revenue. Despite making attempts to diversify into a larger client base, it has not managed to achieve more than 15% of its sales from other clients. The main client, a large public sector organization, had been its main client at inception and remained so after five years of operation. Indeed, the entrepreneur who founded the small firm used to work at the organization in question and therefore had knowledge of its needs as well as social connections among its managers. Due to a combination of government cuts, changes within the client's organizational structure and competitive forces, the client suddenly decided to streamline its supplier base. It decided not to use the small firm anymore and gave the firm two months' notice that it would not be renewing its contract. The loss of the single biggest client was an immediate issue because the ability to cover costs and pay bank loans were dependent on the renewal of the client contract as growth in sales to other clients had not materialized.

Analysis. The disruption facing the small firm in question consists primarily of size-related vulnerability. The firm had not reached a point of maturation in which it had broad offerings that would appeal to more than one client at sufficient scale. The small firm had been heavily embedded in the one client, with the entrepreneur-owner relying on his previous contacts within the organization for contract renewal. However, these contacts had now moved on and a new management team had been under pressure to make the client more efficient through reducing the number of small firm suppliers. The disruption to the small firm is also a consequence of the subjectivity and personalized reality of its founder. This person had viewed the relationship with the client as solid and enduring. He had not been sufficiently critical of it and had not challenged his own assumptions. He did not appreciate that the relationship was something that could end so easily.

The Resilience Landscape for the small firm is schematized in Figure 7.3. Size-related vulnerability is a critical area of vulnerability. The entrepreneur had experienced difficult phases with the client in the past and this had led to periods of wage freeze and reduction of workforce. He had experience of muddling through and intermittent resilience at the firm level. But there is also a personal aspect in this example at the individual level. The problem with complacency surrounding the comfortable relationship with the client is something that he should have shown greater awareness of. It is also something that he could have dealt with through developing reciprocity in relationships with the new management team in the client organization. The Resilience Landscape for Example B allows a reflection on how actions in relation to disruptions can be used to deal with the new situation in order to avoid the firm suffering more than it needs to.

Example C – a remote community reeling from a first wave of COVID-19

Situation. Imagine the case of a remote rural community in an economically challenged part of the world, thousands of miles from the nearest major city. The local economy was mainly agriculture-based, GDP per capita in the community was lower than the world's average, and health facilities were not at developed country levels. The community had been hit hard by the global COVID-19 pandemic but the numbers of new cases and deaths had now fallen. In line with the data at national level, the experts had indicated that the first wave was almost over, but a second wave could still be just around the corner and winter was only a few months away. There was no vaccine in place yet. The lockdown had meant that transport links to the community were reduced and there was a lack of personal protective equipment and ventilators for the small hospital in the community. Nevertheless, the community had pulled through and things were returning to what was being dubbed the 'new normal'. Schools were back in operation but there were still some social distancing measures in place.

Analysis. Figure 7.4 shows a schematic of the Resilience Landscape for this community. As the community moves through time, as indicated by the arrows denoting its trajectory, the crisis of the first wave is now behind. However, it is not possible to see over the horizon, and it is not known if a second wave will come, and if it did come, how serious it would be. Maybe there would be a new, more virulent strain of the virus. This is clearly a situation in which the community has a short period of time to prepare and to be proactive in getting ready should a second wave hit the community before a vaccine is ready. There was little time to prepare for the first wave, but now a lot more knowledge was available, locally, nationally and globally, that could be used to guide preparations.

What objects are relevant and how can these be incorporated into the Resilience Landscape? Two aspects of disruption per se are pertinent and shown on Figure 7.4. The first is the issue of grand scale. The nature of adversity is broad, affecting the whole planet, and it affects all parts of the focal community, both directly in terms of infected individuals and indirectly in terms of people disadvantaged through the lockdown and social distancing measures. The second is a disruptive object from the individual level: personalized reality. This is relevant in this situation because of the different ways in which individuals were affected by the pandemic. Some avoided the virus. Others caught the virus but had no or minor symptoms. Others sadly passed away. There had been two areas of action in relation to the first disruption. Policy entrepreneurship had taken place at a national level to conduct testing among the population, and this testing capability was now reaching the remote community in question. There was also ample evidence of close relationship capabilities, including members of society volunteering to help vulnerable quarantined individuals by transporting food and medicines to them. At the individual level, people had become more aware of their potential vulnerability to the disease through both their demographic grouping and their job and life-style. Relatedly, there had been a high degree of reciprocity, especially in the area of volunteering; this having a strong overlap with the close relationship capabilities at a community level. Planning for a potential second wave should consider how these elements can be brought forward. Testing can be continued and the data from testing utilized appropriately, following the evolving national guidelines. Meanwhile, individuals who had made important contributions during the first wave can be rewarded with recognition within the community, this providing an incentive for community cohesion ahead of the second wave.

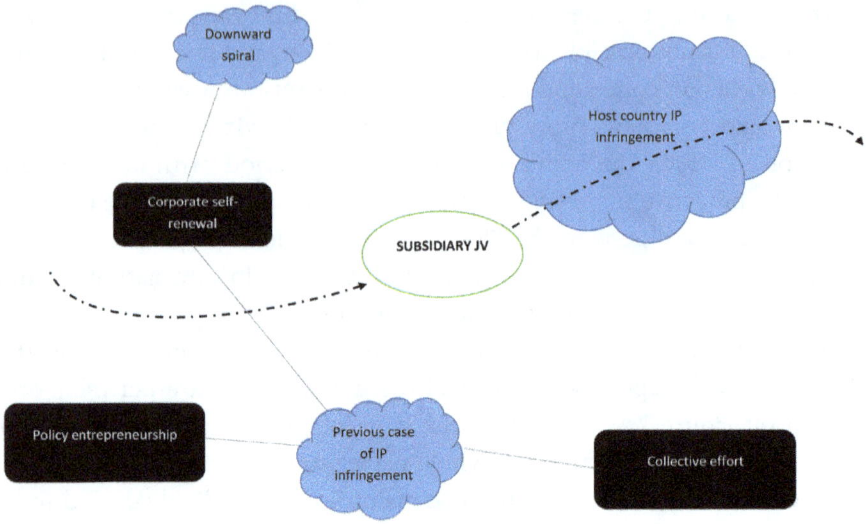

Figure 7.2 The Resilience Landscape in action – Example A

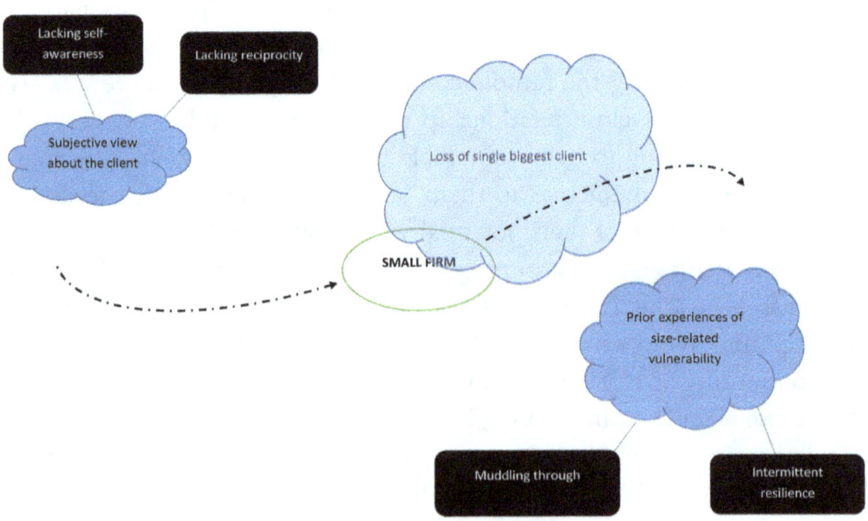

Figure 7.3 The Resilience Landscape in action – Example B

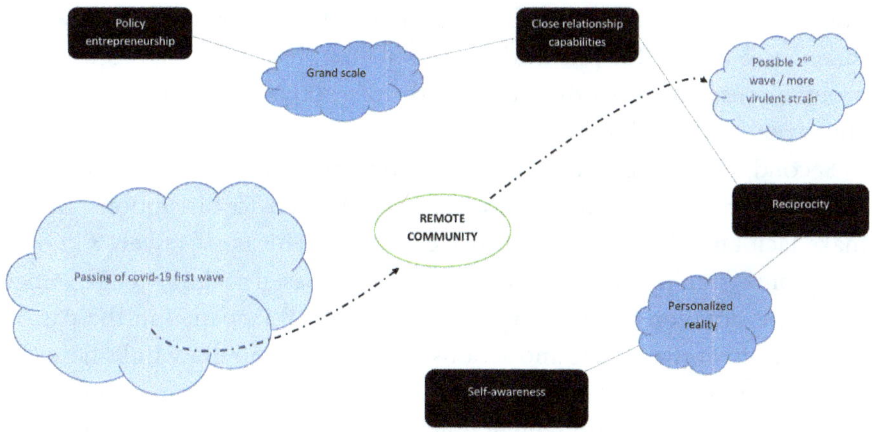

Figure 7.4 The Resilience Landscape in action – Example C

The value (and problem) of synthesis using the Resilience Landscape

The spectrum of resilience (chapters 2–6) yielded a wide array of concepts, ideas and frameworks relating to how individuals and organizations cope with adversity. These range from internal psychological state and skills of individuals (Liu et al., 2017) to the way economies are managed through policy (Aiginger, 2009). The synthesis in the current chapter can be valuable for academic researchers or practitioners when analyzing resilience in future scenarios. In particular, the Resilience Landscape can be a useful tool that encourages the analyst to reflect on and ask questions about the situation while also generating one or more diagrams as schematic representations of the knowledge the analyst has gained about the situation.

First, the Resilience Landscape is useful because it does not constrain the view taken by an 'onlooker'. It allows the analyst to include only what is relevant to the situation. The property of depth of field means that less relevant objects can be ignored or can be drawn as small in size (i.e. distant in relevance) and more relevant objects can be enlarged, with more detail annotated. The property of evolution means that the onlooker can be positioned before, during or after a focal disruption; the passage of time is captured in relation to a given disruption and the analyst is free to make this positioning as they see fit. A Resilience Landscape can be drawn to schematize a view for practically any situation. It can be used to facilitate group discussions about the nature of the disruptive environment in which any given individual, organization or collective finds itself.

Second, the Resilience Landscape allows the analyst to make connections between disruptions and actions in relation to disruptions and to make tacit knowledge of these linkages explicit. This is effectively a knowledge conversion process (Nonaka et al., 2000). Based on knowledge gained about the situation in question – and about what happened in the past in terms of disruptive events and actions – the analyst can draw links between disruptions and related actions and make notes on why those actions were taken and also on the subsequent outcomes. This stock of knowledge about historical events can be used to guide actions in the future. These connections are important. Some of these connections may be robust, enduring across different Resilience Landscapes, others might be specific to a given situation. Making explicit knowledge about what worked well and what worked less well in the past will be crucial as onlookers become engulfed in new traumas and seek to justify new solutions.

Third, the objects that an analyst can put on the Resilience Landscape are not limited to the main themes highlighted in chapters 2–6 – i.e., those listed in tables 7.1 and 7.2 Any number of sub-themes (see the middle columns in tables 2.2, 3.1, 4.1, 5.1 and 6.1) can be included, as can any other construct that makes sense to the analyst. Our literature reviews and case examples in chapters 2–6 were limited for space reasons, and other research is likely to come to light allowing an analyst to add to these lists and derive their own higher-order themes. There is merit in maintaining the distinction between disruptions and related actions as it is through these links that the analyst is able to learn and justify a response to a new potential or actual disruption. The definitions and wordings used can be different to those presented here, they can be a combination or decomposition of the ones we use, or they can be entirely original and specific to the analyst's own reading of the literature, case material and actual situation.

Fourth, the Resilience Landscape can be used in a proactive (anticipating a potential event) or reactive (responding to a real and known event) manner. In Example B, the storm cloud had already engulfed the small firm. What was initially sought was a reactive response. In Example A, the subsidiary was worried about IP theft from the JV partner and wanted to develop ways of 'heading it off at the pass'. This was a proactive position. The juxtaposition of the onlooker to the disruptive cloud (see figures 7.2 and 7.3 as examples) can be used to represent this.

When used in this reflective way, the Resilience Landscape can help to build consensus around the nature of vulnerability in the environment and how to deal with it. This is particularly the case in groups where different members bring different perspectives and experiences on the situation to construct an integrated or combined view. This kind of attempt to allow an analyst to bring together such a diverse range of constructs across so many different levels of analysis must be qualified. There are likely to be shortcomings that analysts and practitioners need to be aware of as they approach new scenarios in the future. These may include the following.

First, there might be a tendency for over-simplification and reductionism in the process of reflection and analysis for producing a schematized Resilience Landscape. Clearly, there is only a limited amount of space on a piece of paper or a document on a computer. There is no way that all the detail for every single disruption and action in relation to disruption that ever happened can be captured. For this reason we would encourage the use of qualitative data structures (Gioia et al., 2013) or fuzzy cognitive maps (Özesmi and Özesmi, 2004; Williams, You and Joshua, 2020) to provide the additional detail, in either hierarchical form or network form for each disruption – action pairing on the Resilience Landscape. In this way the final schematic is merely a top-level or summary representation, with knowledge justifying the main objects being articulated in other exhibits or documents.

Second, the production of a Resilience Landscape diagram does not actually mean the onlooker has managed (proactively or reactively) to deal with a traumatic situation. The assessment of the knowledge used to produce a Resilience Landscape still needs to be agreed and acted upon. This is likely to require agreement among senior managers (in a large-sized organization), agreement among key stakeholders (in a community or economic ecosystem), and subsequent changes in the deployment of scarce resources. We know from the field of strategy how difficult it is to implement new ideas and initiatives and how implementation can often be the reason for strategic failure. Just producing a Resilience Landscape and conducting the analysis behind its production is not enough. Careful thought and attention still needs to be paid to the implementation of actions to be proactive and/

or reactive in the face of potential and/or real disruption. We will refer to this point in the next chapter.

Third, the Resilience Landscape may be biased towards the views and experiences of those that generate it. While they may have taken steps to ensure a broad base of knowledge is brought to bear, there remains the possibility that this knowledge is biased, for instance through sampling issues or political brinksmanship, or that certain key elements of knowledge are withheld. Those contributing or being asked to contribute must be incentivized to do so; there must be no impediment to their sharing of knowledge relevant to the situation. This point is considered in the next chapter, especially with respect to the need for leaders to build a resilient mind-set across the organization, an informal control mechanism aimed at encouraging effective knowledge sharing during the process of generating a Resilience Landscape.

Learning points

This chapter provides the following learning points:

- Lessons from prior research on – and cases of – disruptions and resilience can be identified and used as a basis for future analysis and managerial action
- Some prior research and cases may not have used the vocabulary of resilience but nevertheless provide a useful basis for learning: the resilience analyst needs to look at the nature of the phenomenon when drawing conclusions rather than the labels used by any given researcher
- It is possible to group themes from prior literature and cases into two main categories – (1) disruptions per se and (2) actions in relation to disruptions – and to use these as the basis for analysis and guiding managerial action in the future
- While disruptions per se and actions in relation to disruptions have distinct properties, they also share certain properties, such as being cross-level phenomena
- The Resilience Landscape provides a way of reflecting on the situation facing a given organization in a given disruptive setting, producing a high-level schematic of the path of the organization juxtaposed against relevant disruptions and actions in relation to disruptions

- Every person and every organization journeys through a Resilience Landscape over time, each journey is unique and each perspective distinct
- The Resilience Landscape can be used by analysts working in groups and sharing knowledge
- The Resilience Landscape should be reinforced through articulation of other supporting analysis at lower levels.

Suggested activity and assignment questions

1. Working individually or in a small group:
   a. Identify a specific organization that is currently facing – or could face in the future – an uncertain and disruptive problem
   b. Research the background to the organization and its strategic setting in order to identify prior examples of disruptions and actions in relation to disruptions that are relevant
   c. Produce a Resilience Landscape schematic for the case, supported by additional analysis as appropriate
   d. Conclude with recommended actions for the case.
2. Take some time out to reflect and write up your reflective thoughts and lessons learnt.

8

LEADERSHIP IMPLICATIONS

ORGANIZING WITH A RESILIENCE MIND-SET

> Do not judge me by my successes, judge me by how many times I fell down and got back up again.
>
> Nelson Mandela

This famous quote from Nelson Mandela is a fitting point to open the final chapter of this book. Coming from someone who personally experienced a brutal form of adversity and hardship for a large part of his life under the South African apartheid regime – including 27 years in prison – the quote is perhaps apt. Mandela is a good example of a leader who was seen to guide change with a resilience mind-set. He has been widely credited with bringing about an end to apartheid and making democracy a reality for the whole population of South Africa.

This chapter explores leadership implications arising out of the ideas and topics in this book. A central theme is the notion of a 'resilience mind-set' in an organization and how leaders can influence the psychology of a wider set of people in such a way that the organization is able to navigate the

Resilience Landscape successfully. However, when we broaden our view like this we may ask: what do we mean by leadership in a disruptive context? Who really are the key actors that have the ability to influence the development, maintenance and deployment of a resilience mind-set throughout an organization? What role do other organizations that interface with a focal organization play, and how do the relationships that develop between these organizations matter? We will therefore cast the net somewhat wider than a traditional view of hierarchical control from the strategic apex of an org chart and towards other ways in which organized systems of people are influenced to become more resilient. This opens up the construct of 'relational resilience' for discussion and allows an examination of how external consultants can advise and support a client organization with resilience in mind. We also consider the role of academic research in providing scientific evidence and insight that, if communicated effectively, can have an impact in guiding an organization through the Resilience Landscape.

The judging of leaders by others

Not all leaders bring about positive change in the world around them. Some have led with a disruptive mind-set rather than a resilience mind-set, many hell bent on their own greedy gain over the interests of those they purport to lead. In the corporate world, Sajko et al.'s (2020) work showed how greedy CEOs were associated with firms that did not recover following the global financial crisis of 2008. The stock market was the judge in this case. But we also see the damaging effects of greed by leaders in the geo-political arena. For instance, the continent of Africa underwent dramatic transformation in the years following the end of World War II as country after country assumed independence from European colonial powers. Many of the leaders of African countries post-independence became despotic tyrants (Meredith, 2013). These tyrants repressed their own peoples and pursued self-interest over the interests of others, often using brutal and barbaric methods. Corruption and economic mismanagement put many African countries at a global disadvantage. This has been a problem elsewhere in the world too, a problem on a grand scale and very much in line with the theme of man-made suffering noted in chapter 6. History has shown how humanity has a habit of allowing bad leaders to come to the fore. Some are elected to their position, others assume power through unconstitutional means, as in Pinochet's military coup d'état in Chile in 1973 (Kornbluh, 2016) or the 1962 coup d'état in Burma (Perry, 2007). While they may not last for ever, such leaders can be around long enough to be the cause of severe trauma for others' freedoms, health and prosperity. Idi Amin, the tyrannical leader of Uganda in the 1970s, was widely believed to have been clinically insane as he unleashed a reign of terror on his own countrymen and women.

Mandela's words are a reminder of how leaders are judged by their actions and behaviours and, importantly, how good leaders are aware they are being judged by their thoughts, words and deeds. Leaders constantly come under scrutiny (Boin et al., 2016; Meister et al., 2017). They are in the spotlight by virtue of their positions of power and influence. Their ability to hold sway over the fortunes and welfare of others means that others will inevitably appraise the utility and value of their leaders' decisions and actions. While bad leaders might even be oblivious to this, the world around them rarely is. Many years after the fall of Idi Amin's regime, a former British Government foreign secretary, David Owen, admitted suggesting having Amin assassinated in the late 1970s, such was the disgust with events in Uganda at the time.[1]

Many other contexts exist where leaders face intense scrutiny and judgment. An interesting one is football (soccer) management. Using a sample from the Dutch top flight, Bruinshoofd and Ter Weel (2003) showed that sacking a football manager due to the team's poor performance does not necessarily help the club. The study showed that sacking does not improve the seasonal average of either old or new managers, and it does not lead to more rapid improvement compared to situations in which the manager was not forced to resign. Flint, Plumley and Wilson (2016) raised ethical and legal considerations relating to the ability of clubs to instantly sack managers in the English Premier League. They observed an instability in football management, a volatility in the hiring and firing of leaders that does not reward loyalty and can even exacerbate performance problems.

1 "UK considered killing Idi Amin", BBC News website, 16 August 2003, http://news.bbc.co.uk/1/hi/world/africa/3157101.stm, accessed 24 May 2020; to the best of our knowledge this suggestion was dismissed at the time and was never sanctioned by the British Government

Brian Clough, who managed Nottingham Forest FC in England for 18 years from 1975 to 1993, led the club to numerous trophies including two European Cups and was labelled the 15th greatest manager of all time by France Football, once said: "If a chairman sacks the manager he initially appointed, he should go as well."[2]

The key point from these rather different fields is that leaders will face pressure and scrutiny from many different stakeholders (shareholders, employees, the public, governments and even sports fans!) and that this pressure will be especially focused in times of disruption and crisis. Their styles, approaches and decisions and the subsequent outcomes linked to those decisions are continually questioned, and they constantly face pressures that can lead to their own demise and removal.

Instilling a resilience mindset throughout the organization

One key lesson from these insights into leadership in the very different fields of geo-politics and football management is that leaders clearly do not have all the answers. However, they are in a position to inspire others to contribute to a shared understanding of the Resilience Landscape. As shown in the previous chapter, the nature of the Resilience Landscape is complex, multi-layered and continually evolving. A successful leader in a disruptive environment is one who can inspire others, such as Nelson Mandela, not force their brutal will over others, such as the many tyrants from history. Quoting the Oxford English Dictionary, Thrash and Elliot (2003: 871) noted that inspiration refers to: "A breathing in or infusion of some idea, purpose, etc. into the mind; the suggestion, awakening, or creation of some feeling or impulse, especially of an exalted kind." According to Thrash and Elliot (2003), inspiration involves motivation (an energizing effect on an individual), it is evoked (induced by one entity towards another), and it involves transcendence (the individual gains clarity and has access to novel ideas and insights beyond their normal view). As far as

2 "Brian Clough on Sport in Question 1995", YouTube clip, https://youtu.be/MYpA6XCoi2Y, accessed 4 February 2021

the Resilience Landscape is concerned, no single person will have all the knowledge necessary to accurately construct a view of it, let alone chart an appropriate course through it. Inspiration can act as a way of energizing others to be perceptive to the Resilience Landscape and contribute to its shared understanding.

Another lesson is that those judging leaders are also capable of sometimes getting it wrong. A football manager may be abruptly sacked due to poor team performance, then the team performs even worse. A CEO may be sacked by shareholders, but the firm still continues its long downward spiral. A military coup d'état may lead to the complete economic collapse of a country despite the country's valuable resources (Meredith, 2013; Perry, 2007). Again, those judging the leaders do not have all the knowledge needed to accurately predict the future. How they were inspired to make the decision to intervene in the formal leadership of the organizational system can be brought into question. Perhaps there was an issue with their motivation; perhaps it was about how they were induced to believe what they did; perhaps they were unable to transcend their existing world view (Thrash and Elliot, 2003).

Organizations need to think and act as a collective whole if they are to navigate the Resilience Landscape in a coherent way. The alternative, especially in larger organizations, is for different parts of the same organization to take their own distinct journeys through the Resilience Landscape. While this can undoubtedly happen because of knowledge asymmetry between units and the headquarters (as in the Tesco's Fresh & Easy case), if the paths are so distinct that a unit becomes completely isolated, the organization has effectively begun to disintegrate. Coherence and reducing knowledge asymmetry should be considered with disruption in mind. Building on the concept of the previous chapter, the whole organization needs to be psychologically tuned in to the Resilience Landscape and be able to interpret threats to – and ways of protecting – organizational survival. Weick and Roberts (1993) argued that reliable performance in a complex organizational system is achieved through a collective mind and heedful interrelating. A strong and commonly shared culture within the organization (Deal and Kennedy, 1982; Eisenhardt, 1985) matters. Claire Agutter (chapter 3) mentioned this in terms of the agile mind-set in her small firm. Strong and shared cultures have been described in the literature as ways in which employees can be controlled such that they agree to the norms and values of the organization. They are particularly useful in situations where trust is important, where learning and tacit knowledge flows are needed, and where innovation and creativity are valued (Williams, 2018). Instilling a resilience mind-set should be part of a shared cultural environment across the organization, one that allows the whole organization to navigate through the Resilience Landscape over time without disintegrating.

Literature acknowledges that leaders play an important role in determining the shared cultural norms of an organization (Fairholm, 1994). In Colovic and Williams' (2020) operationalization of group culture (based on Henri, 2006), leaders are mentors and facilitators of shared group norms, and this then has a positive impact on innovativeness. Everly (2011) contended that an organization's ability to develop a culture of resilience has parallels with how an individual learns to cope with disaster and bounce back; it is essentially a learning issue for the organization. According to Avery and Bergsteiner (2011), an enabling, widely shared culture is an important higher-order attribute (the authors describe this in terms of 'practices') of an organization that underpins a stakeholder-centric sustainable leadership approach, which in turn provides more resilience over the longer term. Stephens et al. (2013) found that the ability to express emotions (positive and negative) within an organizational culture has a net benefit on resilience at individual and team level. Leaders can influence resilience by allowing and encouraging individuals and teams to share their emotions with each other in normal times as well as during adversity.

Leaders can also embrace the concept of mindfulness as a way of dealing with a disruptive environment. Organizational theorists have discussed the links between mindfulness and resilience, including in 'high-reliability organizations' that are sensitive to the sources of threats facing them and attentive to the need to respond to those threats (Levinthal and Rerup, 2006; Weick and Sutcliffe, 2001, 2006). Such a 'mindful organization' spends more time on understanding the nature of disruption and building capabilities for resilience than a less mindful one. They devote more of their available attention to the Resilience Landscape. According to Weick and Sutcliffe (2006), one key aspect of mindfulness that matters is the vividness of attention on the environment[3]; in our terms the vividness of perception within the Resilience Landscape. They argued vividness is a means

3 Others being focus, stability, sustainability and filtering (Weick and Sutcliffe, 2006: 518)

to achieve commitment to resilience in the organization. Vividness occurs in organizations that "expend more effort to see things clearly" (Weick and Sutcliffe, 2006: 519). Similarly, You, Vu and Williams (2021) drew on the Buddhist concept of skillful means and developed the concept of skillful resilience, which highlights three core capabilities for organizations in managing an uncertain environment. These are: (1) context flexibility; (2) emotional intelligence; and (3) the ability to visualize and deconstruct complex situations. Having more routinized ways of perceiving and dealing with disruptions in the environment to the detriment of vividness amounts to becoming more mindless. Mindfulness – with its concomitant capabilities for vivid perceptions of (1) disruptions and (2) actions in relation to disruptions – across the organization can be instilled by leaders in their organizational approaches, and in particular in how they establish cultural norms in the organization.

The developing and maintaining of a shared culture that has been inspired with resilience in mind is not only the responsibility of those at the top. It is also influenced laterally throughout the organizational system. The development of a mindful organization is not solely the purview and responsibility of the owner-founder (in the case of a small-sized firm), CEO (in the case of a larger firm) or community leader. Clearly, the people at the strategic apex of the organizational system have an important role to play; they are in the limelight and their thoughts and decisions are judged by others. But just as information, knowledge and power can flow laterally in an organization and between organizations, so too will forms of inspiring that stem from human ingenuity, creativity and individual-level mindfulness. Author and mental health practitioner Keith McCoy mentioned how he was inspired by a theatre production of Arthur Miller's *Death of a Salesman* and how this opened up new directions by first encouraging him to self-reflect and accept aspects of himself (chapter 2). The online programme at a large university (chapter 4) showing its resilient characteristics during the global pandemic meant that it was also a source of inspiration for other programmes, particularly in terms of capabilities and know-how for enhancing student engagement online. We also see this very clearly in the example of hand sanitizer on the Island of St Helena during the global COVID-19 pandemic (chapter 6). The initiative came from two individuals on the island, each with part of the knowledge and skill needed to produce a product locally that could benefit the wider health system on the island.

Vividness and clarity of perception were not attributes handed down by the governor or government officials. They were co-created collaboratively between individuals with expert knowledge gained by operating their small businesses. In all these examples, inspiration is seen to come from many sources, some of which are in other parts of the same organization, some of which are in nearby organizations, and some further afield, including sports, the creative industries and the arts.

Deployment of the resilience mindset

When a mind-set for resilience is instilled across an organization there will be benefits in three key areas. It will mean that all employees and associates: (1) will be encouraged to be sensitive to disruptions as they arise, and even before they arise; (2) have a common ground when working together to determine if and how intervention is required, and (3) collaborate constructively on implementation of changes in order to address the nature of the disruption. These three aspects are supported by connective thinking among disparate groups and will be efficient when there is a common belief in the need to navigate the Resilience Landscape. Importantly, it must be a mind-set that allows divergent thinking to take place. All individuals must be allowed to express their views at each step, and views might be different. Indeed, researchers have shown how the closing down of divergent views can be dangerous for problem-solving and creativity (Post et al., 2009).

The first aspect relates to the characteristic of the 'mindful organization' in terms of being alert. It is about perception and detecting danger within the Resilience Landscape in the first place. The second point relates to utilizing a group culture in which people with different views can socially connect in a trustworthy way to share knowledge. A key output from this is a common view of how the Resilience Landscape is changing and what the response might be. This resultant view is annotated by multiple inputs and is not necessarily the myopic view of any single person. The third point relates to implementation decisions and how implementation is then carried out; how resources are reallocated and how time is to be re-utilized in order to avoid a catastrophic demise for the organization as a consequence of disruption. In all three fundamental processes a resilience mind-set matters. It legitimizes the being alert to disruption, the talking about disruption and its consequences, and the co-creation of solutions. Individuals will be less inclined to ignore disruption, however seemingly small and insignificant. They will be motivated to seek out intelligence related to disruptions – including from each other. And they will even be encouraged to look beyond the horizon in the Resilience Landscape (i.e. a 'horizon-stretching' role) for potential disruptions and actions in relation to disruptions which otherwise would not be visible.

The second aspect relates to transforming the collective understanding of the Resilience Landscape into evaluative knowledge. Does the organization need to act? If so, how? Are we clear about the reasons? Having a resilience mind-set throughout the organization will mean the answers to these questions will be generated more effectively compared to a situation where there was no shared attentiveness to the Resilience Landscape. There will be common ground and a focal point, similar to Lee and Williams' (2007) depiction of an entrepreneurial community in a large firm context, that brings diverse opinions to the fore in order to make decisions aimed at helping the organization to survive. In Lee and Williams' (2007) model, the purpose of the entrepreneurial community is to help rejuvenate the organization, the community being transient and leaving behind a legacy in terms of new practices and routines. In terms of organizing for resilience, the evaluative knowledge that will be generated through a shared resilience mind-set will be dynamic, it will be replenished over time. But the mind-set itself should not be transient, it is the key factor that will facilitate replenishment. Unlike notions of entrepreneurial communities and communities of practice (Lave and Wenger, 1991), and especially ones that may come and go, the resilience mind-set needs to be enduring if it is to allow evaluative knowledge to be continually generated and updated. We see this in action at an individual level in the Giselle Richards case in chapter 2. At the time of writing the case she was clear about her options but had not implemented any of them yet. At a higher level we see it in action in the Tesco's Fresh & Easy case (chapter 4) at the point in time before the decision was made to exit the US. In essence there were two top-level options, each with pros and cons: (1) stay, fix the problems and seek profitability; (2) exit and cut the losses. And in the case of St Helena (chapter 6), the community on the island was deeply involved in the decision to build an airport on the island – there had been in-depth consultation in the community and even a vote on the matter. Option A was to build the airport, Option B was to not build the airport but commission a new ship, and Option C was to defer the decision for up to five years. While there was some dissatisfaction within the community to be consulted on a matter that they had already voiced an opinion on, they did indeed choose Option A. It is interesting that there was no option to build an airport and retain the passenger-carrying ship service. These examples are signs of a wider resilience mind-set and its role in allowing the evaluation of options across a wider body of people.

The third aspect relates to implementing new decisions in response to changes observed in the Resilience Landscape. The literature shows there is a wide array of mechanisms at play here. At an individual level we see this in the form of coaching and mentoring of employees as noted in chapter 2 (Green et al., 2007). Without the luxury of time and in the face of a sudden life-threatening situation such as a natural disaster, individuals need to act to protect themselves and their property quickly (Lowe et al., 2015). If intervention is required then early intervention has been shown to have greater benefits (Back et al., 2016). One also sees this in the situation confronting Mark Welling at Expatica Communications (chapter 3); with little time to act and under a great deal of pressure, decisions have to be implemented. It is sometimes very difficult – or even impossible – to consider a 'do nothing' response. With larger firms we see decisions related to entry modes in foreign countries adopted in order to minimize risk (Delios and Beamish, 2001; Gaur and Lu, 2007) or seek new innovative competences (Williams and Vrabie, 2018), and exit decisions followed through, even if they are associated with a loss (as with Tesco's Fresh & Easy) (chapter 4). Implementation decisions are made at a strategic level for ongoing corporate self-renewal (Reinmoeller and van Baardwijk, 2005; Williams, 2018), and the Philips case (chapter 5) shows how a large well-established company was able to fend off the impacts of the global financial crisis by making some hard decisions related to the business areas it wanted to focus on. In chapter 6 the airport construction project on St Helena gave the local economy an immediate boost (chapter 6). A resilience mind-set pays dividends during implementation of actions in relation to disruptions, keeping those involved in the implementation focused on delivering the changes needed while allowing those affected by the implementation process to understand why the changes are needed.

Deploying a resilience mind-set is a primary leadership concern. Having this cultural norm infused into the rituals, practices and behaviours of individuals within the organization will allow the organization to navigate the Resilience Landscape effectively. It will allow the organization to get the better of the Resilience Landscape and not the other way round.

The leadership of relational resilience

As noted by Olekalns, Caza and Vogus (2020), the quality of relationships in organizational life plays an important role for the success of the organization. In times of disruption, the relational capability of an organization becomes critical to its resilience: managing disruption is a coordinative social process involving a variety of entities (e.g. individuals, teams, organizations). As Kahn et al. (2018) noted, relationships between parts of an organization influence the overall resilience of the organization. Kahn et al. (2018) identified integration, disavowal and reclamation as key relational processes, albeit on an internal basis.

Leaders do not only have a role in setting the internal organizational climate in a way that is conducive to enduring resilience. They also have an important role to play in developing and managing strategic relationships with other organizations and stakeholders such that those relationships can be brought to bear in times of adversity and trauma (Chandra and Paras, 2020; Sajko et al., 2020; Wieland and Wallenburg, 2013). A wide range of actor types are possible: business partners in the supply and distribution chains, formal institutions in government, industrial functions and R&D, public sector organizations including universities, and social entrepreneurs, social enterprises and NGOs.

With a focus on business partners, Wieland and Wallenburg (2013) studied supply chain resilience in manufacturing firms and found that communicative and cooperative relationships with suppliers and customers had a positive impact on resilience. In their study, communication had a positive impact on both agility (a reactive form of resilience) and robustness (a proactive form) while cooperation only had a positive impact on agility. Communication within inter-organizational relationships with suppliers and customers relates to helpful and timely exchange of information, feedback about performance and keeping each other informed about events that may affect the other party. Chandra and Paras (2020) explored how social entrepreneurs helped in the recovery of the Philippines following the super-typhoon Haiyan in 2013 when over 6,300 people died.

The social entrepreneurs were found to create public value in part through stakeholder relations following the crisis, using selective partnerships during periods of internal uncertainty (dealing with internal organizational issues) and open partnerships when there was external uncertainty (such as a lack of coordination in relief efforts).

These points resonate strongly with our depiction of the resilience mind-set above, as well as the sense of community (Pietrantoni and Prati, 2008), openness (Stephens et al., 2013) and reciprocity (Williams, You and Joshua, 2020) identified in chapters 2 and 6. Cooperation in Wieland and Wallenburg's (2013) study was operationalized in terms of problems being joint responsibilities, one partner not taking advantage of another, willingness to make cooperative changes and accepting owing other partners a favour. This also aligns with openness and reciprocity but it also puts a stronger emphasis on trusting norms and being able to tolerate a position of vulnerability in a relationship (Blatt, 2009; Hedner et al., 2011; Poortinga, 2012). Interestingly, the third variable of interest in Wieland and Wallenburg's (2013) study, integration with suppliers and customers, did not have any significant effect on either agility or robustness. Integration related to joint use of planning systems, synchronizing production plans, sharing data electronically and sharing knowledge of inventories. This impotent effect of formal (systemized) integration between organizations on resilience is interesting because it helps to underscore the importance of tacit over explicit knowledge and relational norms between humans over integration between computers.

Darnhofer et al. (2016) proposed a relational approach to study resilience in rural farms in Europe. They pointed out that farms and farmers cannot be separated from their place or their past, and that "resilience is not a character or attribute of the farm, nor seen as primarily located in the capability of the farmer to navigate change, but in relations that are never stable, that must be enacted, performed every day" (Darnhofer et al., 2016: 117).

The authors provided examples including organic farmers in Austria collaborating with each other in joint initiatives and relations with supermarkets for distribution of organic milk. They also pointed to shared experimentation, such as with different varieties or production methods, and the fact that they often do this in "partially intersecting informal networks" (Darnhofer et al., 2016: 116).

Afifi, Merrill and Davis (2016) put forward a theory of resilience and relational load. While this is set at an individual level (i.e. couples in relationships) and not between organizations, the concept of relational load is particularly interesting and could be utilized at an organizational level. Relational load occurs when relationships become fatigued. There is a depletion of relational resources and individuals will be less likely to want to continue to relate to each other. At an organizational level, this could mean organizations no longer want to collaborate. According to Afifi et al. (2016), positive communication helps to avoid relational load – there are particular *communicative maintenance strategies* that can be identified and used, including efforts to uplift the other partner. When relational load and depletion are avoided, couples will turn towards each other in times of crisis, not away from each other.

Sajko et al. (2020) examined the effect of CEO greed on the ability of their firm to bounce back from the global financial crisis of 2008. They argued that investment in CSR is an indication of a general stakeholder concern, a long-term mentality for others that will be associated with organizational resilience. Their findings showed support for a negative effect of CEO greed on a firm's recovery to pre-crisis levels (measured by stock market price). Strong stakeholder relations (as measured through investment in CSR) were found to be linked to positive recovery outcomes.

These selected studies and insights show how resilience has been seen in relational terms, and how relationships (rather than systems integration) between organizations can boost an organization's chances of surviving and thriving. Williams, You and Joshua's (2020) study of SME resilience on St Helena clearly identified aspects of close relationship capabilities that were perceived by the small business owners as being vital for their resilience (chapter 6). And the hand sanitizer example in chapter 6 could also be examined from a relational load perspective (Afifi et al., 2016) – there was enough goodwill, social capital and positive energy in the relationship that this initiative could be conceived and implemented to the benefit of the island's community.

Establishing and maintaining relational resilience at a strategic level is a leadership priority. Leaders should be continually engaged with a wide range of actors to generate positive social capital and trust, efficient and open communication channels, and they should make attempts to avoid the problem of relational load with other actors who are able to help the focal organization navigate the Resilience Landscape.

The role of external advice

The consulting industry is one that is full of disruption and adversity (Williams, 2019). While the industry has broadly been expanding for nearly a century, consultancy firms – as well as individual consultants – can suffer from many sources of setback and shock. Some professional services firms go out of business completely following major trauma, as we saw in the Enron-Andersen case in chapter 5 (Clark and Demirag, 2002). Others may find their positions weakened through competitive pressures and are subject to outflows of human capital or takeover. Many attempt to be sources of disruption themselves, aiming to shake up the basis of competing in the industry (Christensen et al., 2013). In this respect, individual consultants and consultancy firms are subject to disruptive forces in much the same way that individuals in other professions and other types organizations are. The foregoing synthesis of ideas about resilience and the leadership implications above can apply in consultancy as much as it can elsewhere. Nevertheless, there is an interesting attribute of the consultancy industry vis-à-vis the topic of resilience. This relates to the influence that consultants have over resilience in their client organizations.

The following is taken from our article in *Management Consulting Journal*, published by the Institute of Consulting in the UK in 2018.[4] The premise of the article is that consultants have a duty of care for their clients in supporting them with their ability to cope with disruptions. When we pursue this line of logic we find some interesting dilemmas and questions. For instance, if a client firm suffers – either as a consequence of a consultant's advice or for some other reason – this could be an opportunity for the consultant to help. However, it may also mean the client has less financial capacity to enlist the help of external advisors. Also, if the consultant

4 Williams, C., and You, J. (2018). "Building resilience in client organizations: The consultant's challenge", Management Consulting Journal, Volume 2: 10–12.

perceives an issue with the client's ability to cope with a given disruption but the area in question is outside of the scope of the contract with the client, how does the consultant proceed? The article introduced the concept of the Resilience Landscape, used in a specific way with respect to the consultant–client relationship.

THE CHALLENGE FACING CONSULTANTS IN DEALING WITH RESILIENCE IN CLIENT ORGANISATIONS

When we consider the issue of resilience within client organisations in a consultant-client relationship, there are two basic scenarios. On the one hand, a consultant may be engaged by a client organisation in order to advise on how to deal with a problem that has been **explicitly** recognised as relating to the client's resilience. In other words, the client itself has framed their issue in terms of problems they are having dealing with disruptions. Perhaps there have been recurring disruptions that have been inadequately dealt with and that have adversely impacted the performance of the client. On the other hand, there is a scenario in which a consultant is engaged by a client organisation to work on a non-resilience-related problem or a broader strategy issue where resilience is *implicitly* – not explicitly – mentioned by the client as being the central concern. An example could be to help develop a new growth strategy for a firm considering entering new markets. This distinction is important. Strategy is a much broader concept than resilience alone. Following Hambrick & Fredrickson's (2005) strategy framework, consulting in strategy requires the consultant to provide guidance on (1) the arenas in which the organisation should participate, (2) the vehicles for achieving this objective, (3) the differentiators which should represent the organisation's belief in how it will achieve its objective, (4) the staging of moves to be made by the organisation over time, and (5) the economic logic of how the organisation will obtain returns. Consulting for resilience, on the other hand, is about how the organisation – once it has adopted a strategy and set out to fulfil its strategy – will be able to deal with (often unanticipated) disruptions along the way. The point is that some client problems will be framed to the consultant as being explicitly about resilience.

We argue that in both of the scenarios (implicit and explicit) the consultant's ability to engage with the client on the issue of their overall resilience is both (1) necessary and (2) not straightforward. In the first scenario, the assignment brief will necessitate an explicit focus on the capabilities to deal with disruptions. In the second scenario, the consultant has a duty of care obligation to the client; the consultant should not provide any advice or guidance on a particular issue that might have a side-effect of lowering the client's resilience (i.e., increasing the client's vulnerability to disruptions) in other areas. This latter point is especially interesting because there is much pressure on consultants themselves to act as disruptive forces in – and for – their client organisations (Bessant & Davies, 2007; Christensen et al., 2013). In their good faith attempts at being disruptive, are consultants actually an accident waiting to happen?

Firstly, we think it is important in both explicit and implicit scenarios for management consultants to make deliberate attempts to *understand the client's resilience landscape*. We do not mean here the strategic or competitive landscape; we mean the resilience landscape. As noted above, there are multiple levels to consider as regards the issue of resilience: the individual, the organisation, and the wider network level (National Research Council, 2011). The literature also explains there are two sides to the question of resilience at each level: it is not just about a client's capabilities for dealing with disruptions, there is also the nature of the disruptions themselves. Consultants, therefore, need to gain understanding in various areas in order to be able to contribute to the client's resilience. Consultants need to understand the nature of past, present and even possible future disruptions. Are they internally or externally arising? Do they impact on the whole value chain, the client organisation only, or just one part of the client organisation? Do they occur suddenly or do they build up over time? This means that there is the issue of understanding the client's broader organisational system. For large and interconnected client organisations, we might expect that there could be a dispersion of disruptive events across these dimensions. Sometimes, disruptions might be felt most acutely in sub-units of the organisation; sometimes, they might impact on the client's position in its external network.

Consultants need to understand what it is about the client's resources and capabilities that allow the client to deal with disruptions or prevent it from dealing with them. Again, this is not about the classic view of resources and capabilities to enact a broader strategy. It is about resources and capabilities specifically for resilience. Are certain individuals (including leaders) supportive of – or inhibiting of – resilience? Are all of the client's external partners contributing adequately to the resilience capability of the client organisation? Again, there is likely to be variance across the landscape on the question of resilience capabilities.

It will also be necessary for consultants to understand why the client's prior responses to disruptions have been successful or possibly unsuccessful; in other words, identifying the causal mechanisms. It will be necessary to ask questions about what kind of response was made, in particular, whether it was a response based on rigidity and robustness (Ponomarov and Holcomb, 2009) or one based on adaptability, agility and flexibility (Lengnick-Hall et al., 2011).

Gaining this knowledge about the *resilience landscape* in a client organisation is likely to be a non-trivial and potentially problematic task. It will be a costly and time-consuming exercise, especially in large client organisations and/or when the consultant is operating alone as an independent consultant (i.e., not in a large engagement team). It will be necessary to connect with a large number of stakeholders who have been involved in the client's organisational ecosystem to identify and interpret perturbations that have occurred. A consultant may only ever obtain a narrow view of the resilience landscape working on their own. Their data collection may also be restricted because of project scope and commitment made to the client regarding project costs and deadlines. Going outside the scope of agreed assignments might annoy the client, particularly if the consultant seeks to interview a range of individuals and external partners who seemingly have little connection with the assignment at hand. And making sense of the knowledge obtained will be tricky. Just because a certain individual interviewed by the consultant provides attribution for an inability to deal with a disruptive event does not necessarily mean that the attribution is correct. Others may disagree. A highly politicised discussion around 'who was to blame' could follow. In international client organisations a political arena could develop, leading to new complexities in the managerial environment of the firm (Williams & Lee, 2009).

Secondly, we also think that it is necessary in both explicit and implicit scenarios for the consultant to be proactive in their advice and guidance to a client on the question of the client's resilience. Gaining understanding of the client's resilience is one thing. Turning this knowledge into sound advice and delivering it so that this will help the client to become more resilient is quite another. Again, the literature is informative in that it points to areas where a consultant may want to offer advice. The consultant will need to decide if advice specifically related to resilience (not overall strategy) is to be directed at certain individuals (including leaders), at the organisation as a whole (e.g., structure, systems and culture), at the client's network partners (in supply and distribution chains), or at a combination of these. The consultant will need to demonstrate evidence for any 'resilience capability' gaps at these different levels in order to be credible with the client. A participatory approach that promotes the client's capacity for learning could be useful. It could act as a facilitating mechanism to enhance client resilience through the sharing of experiences or jointly developing innovative solutions.

Possibly the trickiest aspect will be that of thought leadership and the fundamental framing of the problem in resilience terms. The consultant will need to decide which 'stance' to recommend and to articulate this clearly and confidently to the client: should the mind-set be based on rigidity and robustness, or should it be based on adaptability, flexibility and change, or should there be a combination of the two (if so, how)?

These aspects of advice-giving also represent challenges to management consultants. If the consultant chooses to adopt an advisory approach based on compartmentalisation of the problem (e.g., a *narrow focus* on one part of the organisation and one specific area of capability such as IT), there is a chance that the client ends up devoting resources to boosting its resilience within that 'compartment', only for another disruptive event to suddenly have a devastating impact elsewhere. Such narrow advice might appear to have blindsided the client, annoying them and weakening the consultant's credibility. On the other hand, a *broad scope* approach where the consultant seeks to guide the client to address large-scale resilience capabilities at all levels and all parts of its ecosystem might be seen as too ambitious and possibly unrealistic. Implementing the solution in an acceptable timeframe could be fraught with difficulties.

The literature also suggests that giving advice on client resilience is a challenge because of the question of 'stance'. Recommending a rigidity stance might be seen as a direction that the client might have conceived without outside help, thus weakening the consultant's perceived value. Although management consultants often fulfil a useful role in validating a client's own approach, some – especially those promoting an innovative agenda within the client – may question why an external consultant should be required to recommend a rather un-innovative solution. Conversely, suggesting an adaptability/agility stance is also fraught with challenge. Brusset (2016) pointed out that instilling agility in an organisation is a multi-faceted and cross-enterprise problem, including operations, strategy, information systems, marketing and human resources. The consultant is also challenged with the decision of whether to recommend a Tan Xing approach, or a Ren Xing approach; in other words, within the concept of agility there are more nuanced forms that will have implications for how operations, strategy, information systems, marketing and human resources are reconfigured. In addition, there could be severe consequences for a consultant in recommending an adaptability/agility approach where the outcome leaves the client exposed to new disruptive events in other areas.

In summary, there are some fundamental choices facing a management consultant when it comes to using their knowledge of the client's resilience landscape in order to develop and profit from the client relationship. Given that the issue of resilience strikes at the core of the client's operational performance, any error by the consultant that misdirects the client will lead to low client satisfaction, a lower chance of repeat business, and possibly legal action.

SIX SUGGESTIONS FOR CONSULTANTS WHEN ADVISING CLIENTS ON HOW TO DEVELOP RESILIENCE

We suggest six areas for management consultants to consider when dealing with the issue of resilience in a client organisation. We believe that these suggestions are relevant for both explicit and implicit resilience contracts and our first suggestion speaks directly to this point.

1. **Answer the question: Am I working on an explicit or an implicit resilience assignment?**

Management consultants need to be clear about whether a current or proposed assignment explicitly relates to resilience, i.e., has the client formally recognised the problem it faces as a resilience issue and has it framed it as such? If it has, there is perhaps a stronger case to be made for broadening the scope of the project to conducting an audit of the client's resilience landscape. If the assignment is of an implicit resilience nature, in our line of thinking the consultant will need to tread carefully. They will need to take extra precautions to ensure there will be no adverse side-effects in terms of weakening the client's ability to deal with new disruptions as a consequence of any advice that is forthcoming.

2. **Build a holistic understanding of the client's resilience landscape during the ongoing relationship with the client and keep this knowledge up to date**

Clients contain individuals (employees) working in units (teams). They execute strategy (as an organisation) and often they are part of large and complex value chains (networks). Management consultants need to understand individual, team, organisational and network effects *as a collective whole*, not as individual parts. It is essential for a consultant to have a holistic view of how different actors or stakeholders within the client's ecosystem interpret and understand issues or problems when faced with disruptive events. Complex adaptive systems (CAS) thinking can help in building a mental model or a cognitive map of the client's resilience landscape in terms of what they know, how they perceive disruption and what they do when disruptions occur. This knowledge should include insight into how the various levels inter-relate, and cases illustrating how the client has dealt with major disruptions in the past. Such knowledge development will take time and should be a core feature of the ongoing consultant-client relationship. Eventually, this knowledge will help the consultant to identify the client's weak spots and areas of vulnerability in terms of overall resilience. It will also help the consultant to build legitimacy and credibility with strategic leaders in the client organisation.

3. **Produce a compelling pitch to conduct a 360-degree resilience audit for the client**

Conducting a 360-degree audit of resilience in a client organisation would be an explicit project. It would require an acknowledgement and sign-off by senior-level budget holders. It would be highly visible and would need a sanctioning and sponsorship within the client organisation for the consultant to collect data from all parts of the client's organisational system. Depending on the size and complexity of the client, it is likely to be a non-trivial and time-consuming exercise. Particularly in situations where the client has not requested an explicit assignment on resilience, there may be some hesitation or resistance: "Why do we need this?" Nevertheless, consultants should not wait for the client to approach them. They will gain credibility by being proactive and recommending a broad-scope resilience audit for the client.

4. Nudge the client towards a resilience mind-set

Especially when working on implicit resilience assignments, the consultant can introduce the language of resilience into day-to-day communications with the client, and particularly with senior managers and decision-makers within the client organisation. Being sensitive to the issue of resilience in the client organisation, even when working on other assignments for the client, will act to nudge the client towards thinking more about resilience at a strategic level. It may also act to boost the trustworthiness of the consultant in the eyes of the client. The client will feel that this consultant 'really cares about us'. Nudging the client towards a resilience mind-set may pay dividends for the consultant in the long run as the client starts to think about explicit resilience projects and how they might use the consultant to assist them in such new projects.

5. Work with academics who understand the theory of resilience

Consultants may benefit by linking with academics and researchers who have an in-depth understanding of resilience in multiple contexts. The organisational resilience literature has become quite well established; there are multiple competing books in the market and a growing base of scholarly research in business and management. Consultants may not have studied resilience in an overt form on their MBAs or other formal education programs. Working with academics at the cutting edge of organisational resilience research (much of which is based on primary data and cases – forms which will be accessible to – and interpretable for – consultants) will help to develop the consultant's heuristics in the field of resilience. This can take various forms, ranging from attending conferences and workshops, seeking out the latest publications and new work from academics, engaging in joint research projects and case development, participating in informal knowledge sharing meetings, inviting academics to speak at consultancy forums and so forth.

6. Be on call for key clients

Quite often, episodes of disruption for clients occur suddenly and they can also be highly sporadic. We think that the best time to learn from them is while they are actually taking place. Interviewing people about events and responses that might have occurred months or years in the past can be troublesome because of recall bias and other time-lag effects on the quality of the data. Gaining an insight into resilience capabilities in real-time and as they are utilised can be highly beneficial for the consultant. This will likely entail the consultant offering to be on call and prepared to travel to client locations to personally experience and work with clients through specific episodes of disruption.

The role of science: Implications for theory, research and ethics

The field of scientific research can play an impactful role in helping leaders of organizations understand and navigate the Resilience Landscape. Linnenluecke's review of the literature on resilience showed an exponential growth in the number of publications on resilience in the business and management field (2017, Figure 1). Between 2006 and 2013 the rate of growth was over sixfold. Our examination of articles using a Web of Science search and the terms 'resilience', 'disruption' and 'strategy' between 2013 and 2019 also shows a growth, with a rate of over threefold. With all this up to date research, the question is how this body of knowledge can help those with decision-making authority in organizations. As the academic output continues to multiply, how can leaders keep track of what the scientific evidence is saying? As noted above, there will be a role for educated and capable consultants in translating the output from the scientific community into a form that is meaningful and relevant to organizations so that it can be comprehended and utilized alongside other sources of knowledge. The science must be understandable by organizational leaders. And as more and more senior managers and leaders in organizations have experience of studying academic works (for instance on MBA and DBA programmes), they themselves should be able to make sense of academic output.

Nevertheless, the task of translating the growing academic output on organizational resilience into a form that can be understood and acted upon in practice is not trivial. First, many executives do not have the time to regularly trawl through academic works. Second, the use of consultants for this purpose will be costly, and only as effective as the skills of the consultant. Third, academics themselves sometimes get it wrong and findings often encounter contradiction and refutation within the academic community itself. Fourth, the academics are often 'behind the curve', with studies only conducted after disruptive events have taken place and after the long journey of article development and peer-review has been completed. For instance, the work by Sajko, Boone and Buyl (2020) is a highly interesting and useful work, but it appeared in press 12 years after the onset of the disruptive event that it focused on.

Can theory in academia help leaders in practice?

One challenging area relates to how leaders of organizations develop cognition of resilience, how they form opinions on the relationships between constructs related to resilience and how they justify these relationships in their minds. On the one hand, much of this cognition may stem from their prior experience in the organizational world, their background, as well as any education and study they undertake. Senior managers will have ingrained beliefs about the environment that determine how the environment is scanned and how strategic responses are formulated by their organization (Daft and Weick, 1984).

On the other hand, academics are still in the process of developing theory around resilience in organizations. As noted by Afifi, Merrill and Davis (2016), the field of resilience is largely atheoretical. Their response was to develop a new theory of resilience and relational load (TRRL), a useful approach at the individual level. Others shed light on how capability-based theory (resource-based view/dynamic capabilities view) is useful to explain resilience in organizations (Lindbom et al., 2015). Linnenluecke's (2017) review identified a number of theories in use in the field, ranging from evolutionary theory (Staw et al., 1981) to normal accident theory (Perrow, 1984) and high reliability organizations (Roberts, 1990). However, she also called for more work on integrating theory across streams. In the literature covered in this book there is a broader range of relevant theory, especially when one considers works concerning organizational performance and survival that have not explicitly used a resilience framing; such works are ultimately very much about resilience. An example is the study of survival and governance of foreign subsidiaries of international firms in disruptive environments. Here there is a much broader array of theory at play, such as institutional theory (Gaur and Lu, 2007), transaction cost logic and internalization (Williams and Martinez, 2012) and learning theory (Delios and Beamish, 2001; Sousa and Tan, 2015). Furthermore, one can ask the question about whether existing theory needs to be developed and utilized in new ways in the field of organizational resilience. Instrumental stakeholder theory (Jones et al., 2018) was used as the base theory in Williams, You and Joshua's (2020) exploration of close relationship capabilities involving small firms on St Helena. The result was support for many of the aspects of this theory, although not in equal proportion, while also revealing some new variables (such as a negative effect of government policy on small firm resilience) that could be used to annotate the theory in the future.

There is a wide range of theory at play to explain the resilience of organizations; different researchers have used different approaches at different times. This can be confusing for leaders in practice and also for the consultants that guide them. There is no single unifying theory that academics have come up with that can explain how organizations can navigate the Resilience Landscape. On top of this, there is also the consideration of multi-level theorizing in the field (Bhamra et al., 2011; Linnenluecke, 2017; Kimhi, 2016; Obrist et al., 2010; Southwick et al., 2014). While some theoretical advances are specifically at certain levels (Afifi et al., 2016; Williams, You and Joshua, 2020), many have stressed the need for multi-level theorizing, and some have developed frameworks with this goal in mind. Carmeli and Markman (2011), for instance, argued that the study of the strategy for resilience for a complete economic and military ecosystem (in their case it was the history of the Republic of Rome) will lead to implications that can be applied to organizations of all types, including small firms. If leaders in organizations are to take the time out to engage in academic work – and to bear the costs of using consultants to assist in this task – then they must be convinced that it is a worthwhile exercise that will not confuse or muddle their thinking. The theoretical choices and the multi-level challenges may need to be condensed into formats that executives can access with limited time and possibly limited academic training.

This is not an impossible task, and it is certainly do-able for academics to both develop theory of organizational resilience and engage with the practitioner community in order to balance rigour with relevance. This may need the proper incentives being in place for academics to devote time to developing readable depictions of the state of the art of theory in the field, and to find time to share this in practice settings. There is a role too for the learning and teaching of organizational resilience in business schools. Very rarely – if at all – will you find a module called 'organizational resilience'. The topic might be partially covered in operations or supply chain management, or it might be indirectly covered in strategy or strategic management. However, as we have seen in this book, the topic also covers leadership, psychology, economic governance and ethical behaviour. We would contest that the time has come for business school programme design teams to consider designing organizational resilience modules to tie in with – and complement – the more traditional modules that can be found in strategy, leadership, marketing, operations management and finance.

Ideas for future empirical research

In parallel to these points about how theory in academia can be bridged to resilience in practice, there is also an opportunity to push back the boundaries of *empirical* study of organizational resilience. Empirical work can of course contribute to theoretical debate. It can also be translated into formats that are readily understandable by organizational leaders. A leader in an organization grappling with a specific Resilience Landscape might be turned off by high-brow theoretical debate among academics. But empirical work can have a legitimizing effect, especially if the work provides lessons from contexts that are identical, similar or analogous to those of the practitioner.

First, there is an opportunity to conduct empirical work on resilience in new and evolving contexts (Linnenluecke, 2017). The contexts identified in chapters 2–6 serve as illustrations of where established work has already been conducted. These examples are by no means exhaustive. Future work could consider resilience in: (1) newly emerging industries and sectors (such as Fintech or where organizations are built around blockchain technology), (2) in locations where new organization systems and forms of governance emerge (such as in a transition economy), and (3) in the context of the evolving world of work (including modes where there is more remote working and virtualization than ever before). Other contexts are likely to spring up in the future (or may already exist but are relatively hidden) that can be useful as 'natural laboratories' for examining organizational resilience. For instance, the issue of small firm resilience on a small remote island (Williams, You and Joshua, 2020) illustrates how certain contexts might be seen as ideal natural laboratories in which to examine resilience. Natural laboratories are locations that have unique properties rarely found anywhere else that allow the research to be conducted without contaminating effects. Guridi, Pertuze and Pfotenhauer (2020), for instance, showed how the natural laboratory of the astronomical cluster in the Atacama Desert in Chile had a policy domain with spill-overs between institutions, knowledge, technological infrastructure, the economy and social capital. Such settings are also likely to spring up over time conducive for generating knowledge regarding organizational resilience, especially as the world's economy changes with migration, FDI flows, changes in regulation and institutions as well as post-COVID-19.

Second, and related to point (3) in the previous paragraph is the future opportunity to conduct more empirical work on the inter-relationship between organizational resilience and the way the internet is used by organizations. Internet usage is very much an organizational issue as leaders harness social networks on the internet in order to underpin their organizations' broader strategic learning and endeavours (Williams, Du and Zhang, 2020). Research in the field of information management has shown how different individuals use social networking sites on the internet in different ways, and that the harnessing of social capital over the internet differs from culture to culture (Chang and Zhu, 2012; Chu and Choi, 2010). The context of the internet is an interesting one for resilience, not only as internet diffusion and usage spreads but also because of new ways in which it is used. The extent to which social capital on the internet can help an organization in its proactive and reactive capabilities to deal with disruptions is a question that has not been answered by researchers. Another intriguing angle here is the extent to which the internet itself poses a threat and whether organizations might 'cut off their noses to spite their faces' by actively encouraging internet-based social networking as a basis for developing a resilience mind-set and resilience capabilities. Is this context for resilience a double-edged sword that can both undermine and boost an organization's resilience? If so, the contingencies under which these effects occur need to be established.

Third, there will be new empirical possibilities for synthesizing the field of organizational resilience with more traditional themes in strategy and international business. The field of strategy fundamentally concerns itself with understanding the drivers of performance in organizations. While much of the classic and widely cited works have not explicitly framed these drivers in terms of resilience and bouncing back from adversity, this does not mean the variables and approaches used in the organizational resilience field cannot be seen in conjunction with the field of strategy. Indeed some works reviewed in this book, such as Markman and Venzin (2014) and Carmeli and Markman (2011), showed how this has already been achieved. In chapter 4, for instance, we used the proxy of survival to frame discussion about resilience in parts of large firms. There is an opportunity for future empirical fieldwork to more explicitly incorporate measures of resilience and integrate them with measures of strategy. Survey designs are one area of empirical research where this could be done as there is now a plethora of established scales tapping into various aspects of resilience and that could be used in combination with more traditional strategic variables. These include resilience in supply chains (Chowdhury and Quaddus, 2017), resource reconfiguration, disruption severity and resilience (Ambulkar et al., 2015), innovativeness and resilience (Golgeci and Ponomarov, 2013), and disruption orientation (Parker and Ameen, 2018). While these scales appeared originally in operations management/supply chain management and general management journals, there is an opportunity to combine them more tightly with strategy work in the future. Similarly, the emerging research on global value chains highlights opacity in international networks, with many 'hidden' firms that, despite their camouflaged status, have an important influence on the operation of the value chain, including its performance in terms of CSR (Serdijn et al., 2020). Resilience of entire international value chains can be examined by digging deeper into areas where such firms lurk, uncovering their roles and functions.

Fourth, there have been ample suggestions and recommendations in prior work on organizational resilience for where to focus in future work, especially in terms of measurement and empirical approaches. Linnenluecke (2017) provided a table of future research directions in the field that included a whole sub-section on measurement. This posed questions such as "How can/should resilience be operationalized?", how to detect the presence or absence of resilience, and whether it is possible to learn about resilience by comparing case studies across different contexts (Linnenluecke, 2017, Table 9, pp. 26–27). Similarly, in their review, Bhamra, Dani and Burnard (2011) called for more case study and survey designs to validate theory. There are numerous recommendations at specific levels too. For instance, Hill, Wial and Wolman (2008) argued that to understand economic resilience, both large sample size quantitative analysis and in-depth case studies that allow deeper understanding of path-dependence and systemic resilience should be used. The emphasis is on engagement of the researcher with the real world, and the need for the researcher to embrace a phenomenological approach. Coming from a systems modelling perspective, Fiksel (2006) recommended development of new approaches for modelling complexity and dynamic systems. Perhaps this can also be adapted into the broader organizational and managerial research on resilience in organizations; greater use of systems thinking for which in-depth case studies can be beneficial. As shown in chapter 7, the Resilience Landscape can be seen in terms of systems thinking: it is complex, relies on experience of the dependency between various objects, and is a dynamic schematic. The cases included in this book have demonstrated the usefulness of detailed story-telling relating to situations of disruption and adversity facing organizations. As noted at the end of each of the chapters 2–6, as well as in chapter 7, a range of themes and variables arise through case detail and comparison. Fiksel (2006: 20) also made interesting points in terms of fostering transdisciplinary collaborations, improving communications to educators and the media, and developing integrated dialogue across multiple types of stakeholders. Including these outreach and networking aspects to research projects on resilience will bring multiple fresh insights across different domains useful to organizational leaders.

Ethics in future research on resilience

Ethics should be a prime consideration in future research on the Resilience Landscape. Ethical decision-making concerns the choices confronting managers and how these can be framed from the perspective of 'what is right and what is wrong?' In many cases these choices are not clear-cut; they are not black and white and there is a whole spectrum of grey (Holian, 2002). One sees ethical decision-making at the root of many of the famous cases of disaster, disruption and collapse in organizations. These include the examples given at the opening of this book: BP's Deepwater Horizon, Nick Leeson and Barings Bank, the Olympus corporate scandal in Japan. One also sees ethical issues at the core of corporate decline through governance issues, such as in the Enron case (chapter 5) and in research showing how greedy CEOs were more likely to be associated with less resilient firms (Sajko et al., 2020). Viewing an organization as existing within a complex Resilience Landscape means appreciating the continual pressure to make decisions about the development and deployment of capabilities to avert decline in the face of disruption. These decisions are commonly made by the upper echelon of the organization, although a wide body of related stakeholders can exert influence on these leadership processes. Nevertheless, as an important information-processing unit, the strategic apex needs to effectively process knowledge of disruptions and actions in relation to disruptions at a strategic level. This task has been characterized as a complex one with multiple interacting agents and a governance challenge of maintaining function amidst uncertainty (Welsh, 2014). Furthermore, unethical mind-sets and irresponsible behaviours can hinder the effectiveness of the challenge of this knowledge conversion process (Clark and Demirbag, 2002; Sajko et al., 2020). Future research can utilize the concept of the Resilience Landscape to explore ethical decision-making (Holian, 2002) in light of the dynamic nature of knowledge and perception. Ethical decision-making can be seen as a characteristic of action within the Resilience Landscape. Unethical decision-making can be seen as a disruptive force. Decisions are made about which knowledge is important to guide future postures for resilience. Mind-sets will influence how knowledge is selected and utilized, and value systems will guide this process. Future work can build on Doorn's (2017) ideas on how social justice indicators can be included in resilience research. Social justice comprises both distributive justice (where goods are allocated justly) and procedural justice (where the process is seen to be fair). Doorn (2017) suggested more work on how systems views (similar to our Resilience Landscape concept) impact justice for individuals. In this sense, the Resilience Landscape concept can be used to frame research on ethical decision-making as it pertains to values, knowledge and capabilities for resilience.

Learning points

This chapter provides the following learning points:

- It is a key function – if not duty – for any leader to guide their organization through the Resilience Landscape
- Greedy, hubristic and self-oriented leaders are likely to be ineffective in this process
- Given there is no one 'right or wrong' organizational form for resilience, it is vital that leaders instill a resilience mind-set throughout their organization
- A resilience mind-set will facilitate perception within the Resilience Landscape, interpretation and evaluation of disruptions and actions in relation to disruptions, as well as implementation of decisions related to navigation
- Leaders should be tuned in to the issue of relational resilience and have capabilities in developing it strategically in order to navigate the Resilience Landscape
- There are important considerations for consultants to address around the theme of resilience in client organizations
- There is a role for science and academic endeavour to assist and influence leaders in their quest to build more resilient organizations, although there are challenges with this process given the lack of coherent theory and bias in empirical studies.

Suggested assignment questions

1. Working individually or in a small group:
    a. Identify a leader that has succeeded in guiding an organization or wider collective of people through a disruptive time
    b. Identify a leader that has failed to guide an organization or wider collective of people through a disruptive time
    c. Produce a high-level schematic of the Resilience Landscape for each case
    d. Compare and contrast the characteristics of the leaders and identify the traits associated with successful navigation of the Resilience Landscape
    e. Decide to what extent was a resilience mind-set instilled in each case and what were the influences behind this.

2. Identify an example of when external consultants attempted to help a client organization become more resilient:

    a. Gain as much information about the situation as you can
    b. What was the nature of the disruption facing the client and what was the nature of the advice given?
    c. How effective was the advice given?
    d. How did the client evaluate the quality of the advice given?

3. Choose one of the academic articles featured in this book, or one related to the theme of *Organizing for Resilience* that is not mentioned here but which you have come across:

    a. Read the article carefully
    b. Write an impact essay explaining how the knowledge generated from the article can be utilized by managers
    c. Include an awareness of the weakness and strengths of the article.

4. Take some time out to reflect and write up your reflective thoughts and lessons learnt from these activities.

9

CONCLUDING COMMENT

At the outset of this book we commented on the perceived imbalance between strategic thinking on the one hand and resilience thinking on the other. For instance, there are more hits in search engines when one searches for 'strategy' compared to when one searches for 'resilience'. If such an imbalance exists it is troublesome. Many strategies are impeded or fail completely because of creeping or unexpected sudden disruptions that strategists did not account for. It is vital that resilience thinking is incorporated into the process of strategic decision-making and its implementation in reality. And it is vital that researchers account for resilience when investigating the role of strategy in organizational life and performance. To understand strategy fully should entail thoughtful consideration of how strategy is protected during its deployment.

But neither the imperative for strategy in reality to embody a resilience component nor the study of strategy to account for resilience by researchers is straightforward. The function of strategy is to serve the needs of an organization at its particular stage of development. At the start-up stage, a strategy may focus on how to attract investment and become established in the market. And if fortune prevails and the organization becomes established as a global corporation, strategy for exploiting opportunities in new markets while rejuvenating competitive capabilities becomes essential. Understanding strategy given the nature of the organization has to involve the nature of resilience at that stage of development. Where the organization is positioned on the spectrum of resilience matters.

However, the difficulty of the challenge is not because of a lack of prior knowledge in the broad domain of organizational resilience. Indeed, there are many examples in past research and cases, particularly in firm- and organization-level analyses, where the research was not framed with a resilience lens despite being concerned with performance degradation or survival issues in organizational units and entire organizations. Meanwhile, there is a lot to be learnt from scientific academic studies – both conceptual and empirical ones – that do tackle resilience head on. Furthermore, there is arguably even more to be gleaned by scrutinizing cases and real-world examples of past under-performance and survival issues in organizations and framing the analysis explicitly in terms of resilience. Armed with this knowledge, strategists will be able to succeed in their quests for successful outcomes in organizations. For academics, learning and understanding from the field of resilience can enrich the field of strategy and indeed help bring the fields into sync.

Part 1 of the book shows how organizational resilience can be analyzed along a spectrum, starting with the individual person and ending with a broad collective of a whole economy or community. This means there is a wide range of disparate literature from different disciplines to consider (including psychology, social studies, ecology, general management, economics). At each point in the spectrum there is a different literature, different contexts in which research has been conducted, and different factors and frameworks that have been identified and developed by researchers to explain resilience at that point in the spectrum. There are also different types of traumatic events and disruptions that impinge on strategic intentions, as well as differences in the nature and scale of responses and outcomes. The cases show a temporal aspect, stories of suffering and trauma in organizational settings unfolding over time. They also show a boundaryless aspect in the sense of events spilling over from one level to another. And they highlight the role of organizational leadership in exposing the organization to vulnerability and/or healing the organization when restoration is needed. In essence, Part 1 shows how diverse and heterogeneous the field of resilience has been in the past.

In taking more of a future orientation, Part 2 of the book brings together the broad array of themes emerging from the reflection on past research and cases. It shows that these can be categorized in terms of disruptions and actions in relation to disruptions. These can be seen as objects that populate the Resilience Landscape for a given individual or organization. Any future situation that an individual, organization or broader collective finds itself in on its strategic path can be analyzed and described in terms of disruptions and actions in relation to disruptions within a dynamic Resilience Landscape. Understanding where these objects fit within the Resilience Landscape and how they relate to the given focal entity will be critical for successfully organizing for resilience. Collectively, the objects embody knowledge that, once articulated and transformed into a form that strategists can internalize, allow ongoing organizational decisions to be made to protect the central strategy from demise and defeat.

Leaders play a key role in establishing an organizational mind-set that supports this knowledge transformation process. There are a number of features to this including the need to be mindful at a strategic level, the need to develop and maintain strategic capabilities in relational resilience, the need to utilize advice from external sources such as consultants and the scientific community in an appropriate way, and the need to make decisions ethically. This resilience mind-set of the future might well be different to the past in the sense that it empowers resilience capabilities (sensitivity to disruptions, cooperation in evaluating disruptions, and collaboration in implementing responses) throughout the organization. It is one in which openness to relating to outsiders is seen across the organization as being just as important as it is on an internal basis.

It starts and ends with the person

At the beginning of the spectrum of resilience in chapter 2 we used the expression "It starts with the person" as the first subject header. The book then illustrates how, at all points along the spectrum, the nature, attitudes and capabilities of people are crucial to how resilience is developed and maintained at the higher levels. Often times this is in the form of recognized leaders, CEOs and government agencies that have organizational and economic responsibility. But it also relates to those at other levels behaving inappropriately (and in so doing exacerbating the suffering) or, conversely, behaving with a resilience mind-set (such as taking initiatives to solve problems in a more entrepreneurial manner). The behaviours of individuals appear to be centre stage in the fight to avoid suffering of organizations.

If there was an ideal person that every organization would want to have in its employee base in order to execute a strategy with maximum protection from disruption, that person would likely be the stuff of fiction or cartoon-land. Nevertheless, we see copious examples of best practice in the people mentioned in the cases and examples of the book, as well as examples of characteristics of people that have brought organizations to their knees. It goes without saying that the perfect organizational person for resilience is a hybridization of all of the good and none of the bad. Given that none of us are clones or robots, that we all have good sides and bad, building the resilient organization is not without a margin of error. We need to expect that all organizations will be vulnerable because of the proneness for humans to err in their behaviour. However, leadership through the future Resilience Landscape can reduce the uncertainty of human fallibility in organizations and allow organizing for resilience to be a lethal weapon in the strategists arsenal that will help to protect strategy from the inevitable suffering that the world will throw at it.

REFERENCES

Acquaah, M., Amoako-Gyampah, K., & Jayaram, J. (2011). Resilience in family and nonfamily firms: An examination of the relationships between manufacturing strategy, competitive strategy and firm performance. *International Journal of Production Research*, 49(18), 5527–5544.

Adger, W.N. (2000). Social and ecological resilience: Are they related? *Progress in Human Geography*, 24(3), 347–364.

Afifi, T.D., Merrill, A.F., & Davis, S. (2016). The theory of resilience and relational load. *Personal Relationships*, 23(4), 663–683.

Aiginger, K. (2009). Strengthening the resilience of an economy. *Intereconomics*, 44(5), 309–316.

Aiken, M., & Hage, J. (1971). The organic organization and innovation. *Sociology*, 5(1), 63–82.

Alliger, G.M., Cerasoli, C.P., Tannenbaum, S.I., & Vessey, W.B. (2015). Team resilience: How teams flourish under pressure. *Organizational Dynamics*, 44, 176–184.

Ambulkar, S., Blackhurst, J., & Grawe, S. (2015). Firm's resilience to supply chain disruptions: Scale development and empirical examination. *Journal of Operations Management*, 33, 111–122.

American Psychological Association (APA). (2010). The road to resilience: Resilience factors & strategies. Available at: www.apa.org/helpcenter/road-resilience (accessed 28 August, 2019).

Avery, G.C., & Bergsteiner, H. (2011). Sustainable leadership practices for enhancing business resilience and performance. *Strategy & Leadership*, 39(3), 5–15.

Back, A.L., Steinhauser, K.E., Kamal, A.H., & Jackson, V.A. (2016). Building resilience for palliative care clinicians: An approach to burnout prevention based on individual skills and workplace factors. *Journal of Pain and Symptom Management*, 52(2), 284–291.

Bass, B.M., & Bass, R. (2009). *The Bass handbook of leadership: Theory, research, and managerial applications*. New York: Simon & Schuster.

Berkes, F., & Ross, H. (2013). Community resilience: Toward an integrated approach. *Society & Natural Resources*, 26(1), 5–20.

Bessant, J., & Davies, A. (2007). Managing service innovation. *Innovation in Services*, 21(2), 139–161.

Bethel, J. E., & Liebeskind, J. (1993). The effects of ownership structure on corporate restructuring. *Strategic Management Journal*, 14(S1), 15–31.

Bhamra, R., Dani, S., & Burnard, K. (2011). Resilience: The concept, a literature review and future directions. *International Journal of Production Research*, 49(18), 5375–5393.

Biggs, D., Hall, C.M., & Stoeckl, N. (2012). The resilience of formal and informal tourism enterprises to disasters: Reef tourism in Phuket, Thailand. *Journal of Sustainable Tourism*, 20(5), 645–665.

Blatt, R. (2009). Resilience in entrepreneurial teams: Developing the capacity to pull through. *Frontiers of Entrepreneurship Research*, 29(11), 1–14.

Boin, A., Stern, E., & Sundelius, B. (2016). *The politics of crisis management: Public leadership under pressure*. Cambridge: Cambridge University Press.

Bonanno, G.A., Mancini, A.D., Horton, J.L., Powell, T.M., LeardMann, C.A., Boyko, E.J., . . . & Millennium Cohort Study Team. (2012). Trajectories of trauma symptoms and resilience in deployed US military service members: Prospective cohort study. *British Journal of Psychiatry*, 200(4), 317–323.

Botes, A., Niemann, W., & Kotzé, T. (2017). Buyer-supplier collaboration and supply chain resilience: A case study in the petrochemical industry. *South African Journal of Industrial Engineering*, 28(4), 183–199.

Bottrell, D. (2009). Understanding 'marginal'perspectives: Towards a social theory of resilience. *Qualitative Social Work*, 8(3), 321–339

Bowman, E.H., & Singh, H. (1993). Corporate restructuring: Reconfiguring the firm. *Strategic Management Journal*, 14(S1), 5–14.

Branicki, L.J., Sullivan-Taylor, B., & Livschitz, S. R. (2018). How entrepreneurial resilience generates resilient SMEs. *International Journal of Entrepreneurial Behavior & Research*, 24(7), 1244–1263.

Braunscheidel, M.J., & Suresh, N.C. (2009). The organizational antecedents of a firm's supply chain agility for risk mitigation and response. *Journal of Operations Management*, 27(2), 119–140.

Breyer, S. (1979). Analyzing regulatory failure: Mismatches, less restrictive alternatives, and reform. *Harvard Law Review*, 547–609.

Bridger, J.C., & Alter, T.R. (2006). Place, community development, and social capital. *Community Development*, 37(1), 5–18.

Briguglio, L., Cordina, G., Farrugia, N., & Vella, S. (2009) Economic vulnerability and resilience: concepts and measurements. *Oxford Development Studies*, 37(3), 229–247.

Brœder, A., & Newell, B. (2008). Challenging some common beliefs: Empirical work within the adaptive toolbox metaphor. *Judgment and Decision Making*, 3(3), 205.

Bruinshoofd, A., & Ter Weel, B. (2003). Manager to go? Performance dips reconsidered with evidence from Dutch football. *European Journal of Operational Research*, 148(2), 233–246.

Brusset, X. (2016) Does supply chain visibility enhance agility? *International Journal of Production Economics*, 171(1), 46–59.

Bullough, A., Renko, M., & Myatt, T. (2014). Danger zone entrepreneurs: The importance of resilience and self–efficacy for entrepreneurial intentions. *Entrepreneurship Theory and Practice*, 38(3), 473–499.

Bµrgi, P.T., Jacobs, C.D., & Roos, J. (2005). From metaphor to practice: In the crafting of strategy. *Journal of Management Inquiry*, 14(1), 78–94.

Burns, T., & Stalker, M. (1961). *The Management of Innovation*. London: Tavistock.

Carmeli, A., & Markman, G.D. (2011). Capture, governance, and resilience: Strategy implications from the history of Rome. *Strategic Management Journal*, 32(3), 322–341.

Chakravarthy, B.S. (1982). Adaptation: A promising metaphor for strategic management. *Academy of Management Review*, 7(1), 35–44.

Chandra, A., Acosta, J., Howard, S., Uscher-Pines, L., Williams, M., Yeung, D., . . . & Meredith, L.S. (2011). Building community resilience to disasters: A way forward to enhance national health security. *Rand Health Quarterly*, 1(1), 6.

Chandra, Y., & Paras, A. (2020). Social entrepreneurship in the context of disaster recovery: Organizing for public value creation. *Public Management Review*, 1–22. https://doi.org/10.1080/14719037.2020.1775282

Chandrasekhar, R., & Williams, C. (2014). Tesco PLC: Strategy for India. Ivey Publishing (product ID: 9B14M096).

Chang, Y.P., & Zhu, D.H. (2012). The role of perceived social capital and flow experience in building users' continuance intention to social networking sites in China. *Computers in Human Behavior*, 28(3), 995–1001.

Choi, S.B., & Williams, C. (2014). The impact of innovation intensity, scope and spillovers on sales growth in Chinese firms. *Asia Pacific Journal of Management*, 31(1), 25–46.

Choi, S.B., Lee, S.H., & Williams, C. (2011). Ownership and firm innovation in a transition economy: Evidence from China. *Research Policy*, 40(3): 441–452.

Chowdhury, M.M.H., & Quaddus, M. (2017). Supply chain resilience: Conceptualization and scale development using dynamic capability theory. *International Journal of Production Economics*, 188, 185–204.

Chrisman, J.J., Chua, J. H., & Steier, L.P. (2011). Resilience of family firms: An introduction. *Entrepreneurship Theory and Practice*, 35(6), 1107–1119.

Christensen, C.M., Wang, D., & Van Bever, D. (2013). Consulting on the cusp of disruption. *Harvard Business Review*, 91(10), 106–114.

Christopher, M., & Peck, H. (2004). Building the resilient supply chain. *International Journal of Logistics Management*, 15(2), 1–13.Chu, S.C., & Choi, S.M. (2010). Social capital and self-presentation on social networking sites: a comparative study of Chinese and American young generations. *Chinese Journal of Communication*, 3(4), 402–420.

Clark, J., Huang, H.I., & Walsh, J.P. (2010). A typology of 'innovation districts': What it means for regional resilience. *Cambridge Journal of Regions, Economy and Society*, 3(1), 121–137.

Clark, W.W., & Demirag, I. (2002). Enron: The failure of corporate governance. *Journal of Corporate Citizenship*, 8, 105–122.

Colovic, A. (2012). Territorial systems and relocation: Insights from eight cases in Japan. *Entrepreneurship & Regional Development*, 24(7/8), 589–617.

Colovic, A., & Henneron, S. (2018). Corporate social responsibility and SME internationalization: Insights from the food industry. *Management international/International Management/Gestiòn Internacional*, 22, 30–41.

Colovic, A., & Mehrotra, S. (2020). Lifelong activism and women's entrepreneurship: How a social movement organization improves conditions for self-employed women in India. *European Business Review*. https://doi.org/10.1108/EBR-09-2019-0215.

Colovic, A., & Williams, C. (2020). Group culture, gender diversity and organizational innovativeness: Evidence from Serbia. *Journal of Business Research*, 110, 282–291.

Cornum, R., Matthews, M.D., & Seligman, M.E. (2011). Comprehensive soldier fitness: building resilience in a challenging institutional context. *American Psychologist*, 66(1), 4–9.

Craig, R.J., & Amernic, J.H. (2004). Enron discourse: the rhetoric of a resilient capitalism. *Critical Perspectives on Accounting*, 15(6/7), 813–852.

Cropp, R., & Gabric, A. (2002). Ecosystem adaptation: do ecosystems maximize resilience?. *Ecology*, 83(7), 2019–2026.

Cunha, M.P.E., Clegg, S.R., & Kamoche, K. (2006). Surprises in management and organization: Concept, sources and a typology. *British Journal of Management*, 17(4), 317–329.

Cuthbertson, R., Furseth, P.I., & Ezell, S.J. (2015). Kodak and Xerox: How high risk aversion kills companies. In *Innovating in a Service-Driven Economy* (pp. 166–179). London: Palgrave Macmillan.

Daft, R.L., & Weick, K.E. (1984). Toward a model of organizations as interpretation systems. *Academy of Management Review*, 9(2), 284–295.

Dai, L., Eden, L., & Beamish, P.W. (2013). Place, space, and geographical exposure: Foreign subsidiary survival in conflict zones. *Journal of International Business Studies*, 44(6), 554–578.

Damanpour, F. (1991). Organizational innovation: A meta-analysis of effects of determinants and moderators. *Academy of Management Journal*, 34(3), 555–590.

Darnhofer, I., Lamine, C., Strauss, A., & Navarrete, M. (2016). The resilience of family farms: Towards a relational approach. *Journal of Rural Studies*, 44, 111–122.

Deal, T.E., & Kennedy, A.A. (1982). *Corporate cultures: The rites and rituals of corporate life*. Reading, MA: Addison Wesley.

Dedoussis, V. (2001). Keiretsu and management practices in Japan: Resilience amid change. *Journal of Managerial Psychology*, 16(2), 1–16.

Delios, A., & Beamish, P.W. (2001). Survival and profitability: The roles of experience and intangible assets in foreign subsidiary performance. *Academy of Management Journal*, 44(5), 1028–1038.

Doorn, N. (2017). Resilience indicators: Opportunities for including distributive justice concerns in disaster management. *Journal of Risk Research*, 20(6), 711–731.

Driffield, N., Jones, C., & Crotty, J. (2013). International business research and risky investments: An analysis of FDI in conflict zones. *International Business Review*, 22(1), 140–155.

Dundas, K.N., & Richardson, P.R. (1980). Corporate strategy and the concept of market failure. *Strategic Management Journal*, 1(2), 177–188.

Eisenhardt, K.M. (1985). Control: Organizational and economic approaches. *Management Science*, 31(2), 134–149.

Encontre, P. (1999). The vulnerability and resilience of small island developing states in the context of globalization. *Natural Resources Forum*, 23(3), 261–270).

Everly, G.S. (2011). Building a resilient organizational culture. *Harvard Business Review*, 10(2), 109–138.

Fairholm, G.W. (1994). *Leadership and the culture of trust*. Westport, CT: Praeger.

Fiksel, J. (2006). Sustainability and resilience: Toward a systems approach. *Sustainability: Science, Practice and Policy*, 2(2), 14–21.

Fleming, J., & Ledogar, R.J. (2008). Resilience, an evolving concept: A review of literature relevant to Aboriginal research. *Pimatisiwin*, 6(2), 7–23.

Flint, S.W., Plumley, D., & Wilson, R. (2016). You're getting sacked in the morning: Managerial change in the English Premier League. *Marketing Intelligence & Planning*, 34(2), 223–235.

Funder, A. (2002). *Stasiland: Stories from behind the Berlin Wall*. New York: Harper.

Furniss, D., Back, J., Blandford, A., Hildebrandt, M., & Broberg, H. (2011). A resilience markers framework for small teams. *Reliability Engineering & System Safety*, 96(1), 2–10.

Garg, M., & Delios, A. (2007). Survival of the foreign subsidiaries of TMNCs: The influence of business group affiliation. *Journal of International Management*, 13(3), 278–295.

Garmestani, A.S., Allen, C.R., Mittelstaedt, J.D., Stow, C.A., & Ward, W.A. (2006). Firm size diversity, functional richness, and resilience. *Environment and Development Economics*, 11(4), 533–551.

Gaur, A.S., & Lu, J.W. (2007). Ownership strategies and survival of foreign subsidiaries: Impacts of institutional distance and experience. *Journal of Management*, 33(1), 84–110.

Ghemawat, P. (2001). Distance still matters. *Harvard Business Review*, 79(8), 137–147.

Gibbs, P.A. (1993). Determinants of corporate restructuring: The relative importance of corporate governance, takeover threat, and free cash flow. *Strategic Management Journal*, 14(S1), 51–68.

Gilly, J.P., Kechidi, M., & Talbot, D. (2014). Resilience of organisations and territories: The role of pivot firms. *European Management Journal*, 32(4), 596–602.

Gioia, D.A., Corley, K.G., & Hamilton, A.L. (2013). Seeking qualitative rigor in inductive research: Notes on the Gioia methodology. *Organizational Research Methods*, 16(1), 15–31.

Glover, J. (2012). Rural resilience through continued learning and innovation. *Local Economy*, 27(4), 355–372.

Golgeci, I., & Ponomarov, S.Y. (2013). Does firm innovativeness enable effective responses to supply chain disruptions? An empirical study. *Supply Chain Management: An International Journal*, 18(6), 604–617.

Grant, A.M., Curtayne, L., & Burton, G. (2009). Executive coaching enhances goal attainment, resilience and workplace well-being: A randomised controlled study. *Journal of Positive Psychology*, 4(5), 396–407.

Green, S., Grant, A., & Rynsaardt, J. (2007). Evidence-based life coaching for senior high school students: Building hardiness and hope. *International Coaching Psychology Review*, 2(1), 24–32.

Gunasekaran, A., Rai, B.K., & Griffin, M. (2011). Resilience and competitiveness of small and medium size enterprises: an empirical research. *International Journal of Production Research*, 49(18), 5489–5509.

Guridi, J.A., Pertuze, J.A., & Pfotenhauer, S.M. (2020). Natural laboratories as policy instruments for technological learning and institutional capacity building: The case of Chile's astronomy cluster. *Research Policy*, 49(2). https://doi.org/10.1016/j.respol.2019.103899.

Hall, R.I. (1976). A system pathology of an organization: The rise and fall of the old *Saturday Evening Post*. *Administrative Science Quarterly*, 21(2), 185–211.

Hambrick, D.C., & D'Aveni, R.A. (1988). Large corporate failures as downward spirals. *Administrative Science Quarterly*, 33(1), 1–23.

Hambrick, D.C., & D'Aveni, R.A. (1992). Top team deterioration as part of the downward spiral of large corporate bankruptcies. *Management Science*, 38(10), 1445–1466.

Hambrick, D.C., & Fredrickson, J.W. (2005). Are you sure you have a strategy?. *Academy of Management Perspectives*, 19(4), 51–62.

Hammond, W.R., & Yung, B.R. (1991). Preventing violence in at-risk African-American youth. *Journal of Health care for the Poor and Underserved*, 2(3), 359–373.

Hare, B.R. (1988). African American youth at risk. *Urban League Review*, 12(1/2), 25–28.

Hedner, T., Abouzeedan, A., & Klofsten, M. (2011). Entrepreneurial resilience. *Annals of Innovation and Entrepreneurship*, 2(1), 1–4.

Henri, J.F. (2006). Organizational culture and performance measurement systems. *Accounting, Organizations and Society*, 31(1), 77–103.

Herbane, B. (2010). Small business research: Time for a crisis-based view. *International Small Business Journal*, 28(1), 43–64.

Hill, E., Wial, H., & Wolman, H. (2008). Exploring regional economic resilience (No. 2008, 04). Working paper.

Hitt, M.A., Li, H., & Worthington, W.J. (2005). Emerging markets as learning laboratories: Learning behaviors of local firms and foreign entrants in different institutional contexts. *Management and Organization Review*, 1(3), 353–380.

Holian, R. (2002). Management decision making and ethics: Practices, skills and preferences. *Management Decision*, 40(9): 862–870.

Holling, C.S. (1973). Resilience and stability of ecological systems. *Annual Review of Ecology and Systematics*, 4(1), 1–23.

Jensen, M.C. (1993). The modern industrial revolution, exit, and the failure of internal control systems. *Journal of Finance*, 48(3), 831–880.

Jones, T.M., Harrison, J.S., & Felps, W. (2018). How applying instrumental stakeholder theory can provide sustainable competitive advantage. *Academy of Management Review*, 43(3), 371–391.

Kahn, W.A., Barton, M.A., Fisher, C.M., Heaphy, E.D., Reid, E.M., & Rouse, E.D. (2018). The geography of strain: Organizational resilience as a function of intergroup relations. *Academy of Management Review*, 43(3), 509–529.

Katz, D., & Kahn, R.L. (1966). Organizations and the system concept. *Social Psychology of Organizations*, 1, 14–29.

Kimhi, S. (2016). Levels of resilience: Associations among individual, community, and national resilience. *Journal of Health Psychology*, 21(2), 164–170.

King, D.D., Newman, A., & Luthans, F. (2016). Not if, but when we need resilience in the workplace. *Journal of Organizational Behavior*, 37(5), 782–786.

Kleinknecht, R.H. (2015). Employee participation in corporate governance: Implications for company resilience. *European Journal of Industrial Relations*, 21(1), 57–72.

Kogut, B., & Singh, H. (1988). The effect of national culture on the choice of entry mode. *Journal of International Business Studies*, 19(3), 411–432.

Kolar, T., & Toporišič, A. (2007). Marketing as warfare, revisited. *Marketing Intelligence & Planning*, 25(3), 203–216.

Kornbluh, P. (2016). *The Pinochet file: A declassified dossier on atrocity and accountability*. New York: New Press.

Lai, Y., Saridakis, G., Blackburn, R., & Johnstone, S. (2016). Are the HR responses of small firms different from large firms in times of recession?. *Journal of Business Venturing*, 31(1), 113–131.

Lakshan, A.M.I., & Wijekoon, W.M.H.N. (2012). Corporate governance and corporate failure. *Procedia Economics and Finance*, 2, 191–198.

Lamberg, J.A., & Parvinen, P. (2003). The river metaphor for strategic management. *European Management Journal*, 21(5), 549–557.

Lave, J., & Wenger, E. (1991). *Situated learning: Legitimate peripheral participation*. Cambridge: Cambridge University Press.

Lee, S.H., & Williams, C. (2007). Dispersed entrepreneurship within multinational corporations: A community perspective. *Journal of World Business*, 42(4), 505–519.

Lengnick-Hall, C.A., & Beck, T.E. (2005). Adaptive fit versus robust transformation: How organizations respond to environmental change. *Journal of Management*, 31(5), 738–757.

Lengnick-Hall, C.A., Beck, T.E., & Lengnick-Hall, M.L. (2011). Developing a capacity for organizational resilience through strategic human resource management. *Human Resource Management Review*, 21(3), 243–255.

Levinthal, D., & Rerup, C. (2006). Crossing an apparent chasm: Bridging mindful and less-mindful perspectives on organizational learning. *Organization Science*, 17(4), 502–513.

Li, J. (1995). Foreign entry and survival: Effects of strategic choices on performance in international markets. *Strategic Management Journal*, 16(5), 333–351.

Liao, J. (2004). Entrepreneurial failures: Key challenges and future directions. In H.P. Welsch (ed.), *Entrepreneurship: The way ahead*. London: Routledge.

Liao, J.J., Welsch, H., & Moutray, C. (2008). Start-up resources and entrepreneurial discontinuance: The case of nascent entrepreneurs. *Journal of Small Business Strategy*, 19(2), 1–16.

Lindbom, H., Tehler, H., Eriksson, K., & Aven, T. (2015). The capability concept: On how to define and describe capability in relation to risk, vulnerability and resilience. *Reliability Engineering & System Safety*, 135, 45–54.

Linnenluecke, M.K. (2017). Resilience in business and management research: A review of influential publications and a research agenda. *International Journal of Management Reviews*, 19(1), 4–30.

Liu, J.J., Reed, M., & Girard, T. A. (2017). Advancing resilience: An integrative, multi-system model of resilience. *Personality and Individual Differences*, 111, 111–118.

Lowe, S.R., Sampson, L., Gruebner, O., & Galea, S. (2015). Psychological resilience after Hurricane Sandy: The influence of individual-and community-level factors on mental health after a large-scale natural disaster. *PloS one*, 10(5).

Magis, K. (2010). Community resilience: An indicator of social sustainability. *Society and Natural Resources*, 23(5), 401–416.

Markman, G.M., & Venzin, M. (2014). Resilience: Lessons from banks that have braved the economic crisis—and from those that have not. *International Business Review*, 23(6), 1096–1107.

Marston, J.M. (2015). Modeling resilience and sustainability in ancient agricultural systems. *Journal of Ethnobiology*, 35(3), 585–605.

Maslach, C., Schaufeli, W.B., & Leiter, M.P. (2001). Job burnout. *Annual Review of Psychology*, 52(1), 397–422.

Masten, A.S. (2001). Ordinary magic: Resilience processes in development. *American Psychologist*, 56, 227–238.

McCann, L., Morris, J., & Hassard, J. (2008). Normalized intensity: The new labour process of middle management. *Journal of Management Studies*, 45(2), 343–371.

McFarlane, A., & Norris, F. (2006). Definitions and concepts in disaster research. In F. Norris, S. Galea, M. Friedman, & P. Waston (eds), *Methods for Disaster Mental Health Research*, 3–19. New York: Guilford Press.

Meister, A., Sinclair, A., & Jehn, K.A. (2017). Identities under scrutiny: How women leaders navigate feeling misidentified at work. *Leadership Quarterly, 28*(5), 672–690.

Meredith, L.S., Sherbourne, C.D., Gaillot, S J., Hansell, L., Ritschard, H.V., Parker, A.M., & Wrenn, G. (2011). Promoting psychological resilience in the US military. *Rand Health Quarterly*, 1(2), 2.

Meredith, M. (2013). *The state of Africa: A history of fifty years of independence.* London: Simon & Schuster.

Meyer, A.D., Brooks, G.R., & Goes, J.B. (1990). Environmental jolts and industry revolutions: Organizational responses to discontinuous change. *Strategic Management Journal*, 11(Summer), 93–110.

Moenkemeyer, G., Hoegl, M., & Weiss, M. (2012). Innovator resilience potential: A process perspective of individual resilience as influenced by innovation project termination. *Human Relations*, 65(5), 627–655.

Moore, S.B., & Manring, S.L. (2009). Strategy development in small and medium sized enterprises for sustainability and increased value creation. *Journal of Cleaner Production*, 17(2), 276–282.

Morgeson, F.P., Mitchell, T.R., & Liu, D. (2015). Event system theory: An event-oriented approach to the organizational sciences. *Academy of Management Review*, 40(4), 515–537.

National Research Council (2011). Building community disaster resilience through private-public collaboration: Highlight for community leaders. National Academy of Sciences, Washington, DC.

Nohara, H., & Verdier, E. (2001). Sources of resilience in the computer and software industries in France. *Industry and Innovation*, 8(2), 201–220.

Nohria, N., & Ghoshal, S. (1994). Differentiated fit and shared values: Alternatives for managing headquarters-subsidiary relations. *Strategic Management Journal*, 15(6), 491–502.

Nonaka, I., Toyama, R., & Konno, N. (2000). SECI, Ba and leadership: A unified model of dynamic knowledge creation. *Long Range Planning*, 33(1), 5–34.

Norris, F.H., Stevens, S.P., Pfefferbaum, B., Wyche, K.F., & Pfefferbaum, R.L. (2008). Community resilience as a metaphor, theory, set of capacities, and strategy for disaster readiness. *American Journal of Community Psychology*, 41(1/2), 127–150.

Norris, F.H., Tracy, M., & Galea, S. (2009). Looking for resilience: Understanding the longitudinal trajectories of responses to stress. *Social Science & Medicine*, 68(12), 2190–2198.

Obrist, B., Pfeiffer, C., & Henley, R. (2010). Multi-layered social resilience: A new approach in mitigation research. *Progress in Development Studies*, 10(4), 283–293.

Oe, A., & Mitsuhashi, H. (2013). Founders' experiences for startups' fast break-even. *Journal of Business Research*, 66(11), 2193–2201.

Olekalns, M., Caza, B.B., & Vogus, T.J. (2020). Gradual drifts, abrupt shocks: From relationship fractures to relational resilience. *Academy of Management Annals*, 14(1), 1–28.

Özesmi, U., & Özesmi, S.L. (2004). Ecological models based on people's knowledge: A multi-step fuzzy cognitive mapping approach. *Ecological Modelling*, 176(1/2), 43–64.

Palich, L.E., Cardinal, L.B., & Miller, C.C. (2000). Curvilinearity in the diversification–performance linkage: An examination of over three decades of research. *Strategic Management Journal*, 21(2), 155–174.

Park, Y.R., Yul Lee, J., & Hong, S. (2011). Effects of international entry-order strategies on foreign subsidiary exit: The case of Korean chaebols. *Management Decision*, 49(9), 1471–1488.

Parker, H., & Ameen, K. (2018). The role of resilience capabilities in shaping how firms respond to disruptions. *Journal of Business Research*, 88, 535–541.

Parker, S., Peters, G.F., & Turetsky, H.F. (2002). Corporate governance and corporate failure: A survival analysis. *Corporate Governance: The International Journal of Business in Society*, 2(2), 4–12.

Peek, L. (2008). Children and disasters: Understanding vulnerability, developing capacities, and promoting resilience—an introduction. *Children Youth and Environments*, 18(1), 1–29.

Perrow, C. (1984). *Normal accidents: Living with high-risk technologies*. New York: Basic Books.

Perry, P.J. (2007). *Myanmar (Burma) since 1962: The failure of development*. Farnham, UK: Ashgate.

Pietrantoni, L., & Prati, G. (2008). Resilience among first responders. *African Health Sciences*, 8(3), S14–20.

Ponomarov, S.Y. & Holcomb, M.C. (2009). Understanding the concept of supply chain resilience. *International Journal of Logistics Management*, 20(1), 124–143.

Poortinga, W. (2012). Community resilience and health: The role of bonding, bridging, and linking aspects of social capital. *Health & Place*, 18(2), 286–295.

Posnikoff, J.F. (1997). Disinvestment from South Africa: They did well by doing good. *Contemporary Economic Policy*, 15(1), 76–86.

Post, C., De Lia, E., DiTomaso, N., Tirpak, T.M., & Borwankar, R. (2009). Capitalizing on thought diversity for innovation. *Research-Technology Management*, 52(6), 14–25.

Quarantelli, E.L., Lagadec, P., & Boin, A. (2007). A heuristic approach to future disasters and crises: New, old, and in-between types. In H. Rodriguez, E.L. Quarantelli, & R.R. Dynes, *Handbook of Disaster Research* (pp. 16–41). New York: Springer.

Reinmoeller, P., & van Baardwijk, N. (2005). The link between diversity and resilience. *MIT Sloan Management Review*, 46(4), 61–65.

Richtnér, A., & Sœdergren, B. (2008). Innovation projects need resilience. *International Journal of Technology Intelligence and Planning*, 4(3), 257–275.

Roberts, K.H. (1990). Managing high reliability organizations. *California Management Review*, 32(4), 101–113.

Robins, J.A. (1993). Organization as strategy: Restructuring production in the film industry. *Strategic Management Journal*, 14(S1), 103–118.

Rockenbauch, T., & Sakdapolrak, P. (2017). Social networks and the resilience of rural communities in the Global South: A critical review and conceptual reflections. *Ecology and Society*, 22(1), 10.

Rodriguez, V.P., & Anderson, K.C. (2013). Terracing in the Mixteca Alta, Mexico: Cycles of resilience of an ancient land-use strategy. *Human Ecology*, 41(3), 335–349.

Rumelt, R.P. (1974). *Strategy, structure, and economic performance*. Cambridge, MA: Harvard University Press.

Rutter, M. (1987). Psychosocial resilience and protective mechanisms. *American Journal of Orthopsychiatry*, 37, 317–331.

Sachdev, J.C. (1976). Disinvestment: A corporate failure or a strategic success. *International Studies of Management & Organization*, 6(1/2), 112–130.

Sajko, M., Boone, C., & Buyl, T. (2020). CEO greed, corporate social responsibility, and organizational resilience to systemic shocks. *Journal of Management*, https://doi.org/10.1177/0149206320902528.

Schwarz, A.M., Béné, C., Bennett, G., Boso, D., Hilly, Z., Paul, C., Posala, R., Sibiti, S., & Andrew, N. (2011). Vulnerability and resilience of remote rural communities to shocks and global changes: Empirical analysis from Solomon Islands. *Global Environmental Change*, 21(3), 1128–1140.

SEDP (2012). Sustainable Economic Development Plan, 2012, St Helena Government. Retrieved from www.investinsthelena.com/wp-content/uploads/2015/01/sedp-final-draft.pdf.

Serdijn, M., Kolk, A., & Fransen, L. (2020). Uncovering missing links in global value chain research – and implications for corporate social responsibility and international business. *Critical Perspectives on International Business*, https://doi.org/10.1108/cpoib-01-2020-0002.

Shih, M. (2004). Positive stigma: Examining resilience and empowerment in overcoming stigma. *ANNALS of the American Academy of Political and Social Science*, 591(1), 175–185.

Sippel, L., Pietrzak, R., Charney, D., Mayes, L., & Southwick, S. (2015). How does social support enhance resilience in the trauma-exposed individual? *Ecology and Society*, 20(4), 10.

Smallbone, D., North, D., & Kalantaridis, C. (1999). Adapting to peripherality: A study of small rural manufacturing firms in northern England. *Entrepreneurship & Regional Development*, 11(2), 109–127.

Smallbone, D., Deakins, D., Battisti, M., & Kitching, J. (2012). Small business responses to a major economic downturn: Empirical perspectives from New Zealand and the United Kingdom. *International Small Business Journal*, 30(7), 754–777.

Sonn, C.C., & Fisher, A.T. (1998). Sense of community: Community resilient responses to oppression and change. *Journal of Community Psychology*, 26(5), 457–472.

Sousa, C.M., & Tan, Q. (2015). Exit from a foreign market: Do poor performance, strategic fit, cultural distance, and international experience matter? *Journal of International Marketing*, 23(4), 84–104.

Southwick, S.M., Bonanno, G.A., Masten, A.S., Panter-Brick, C., & Yehuda, R. (2014). Resilience definitions, theory, and challenges: Interdisciplinary perspectives. *European Journal of Psychotraumatology*, 5(1), 25338.

Southwick, S.M., Sippel, L., Krystal, J., Charney, D., Mayes, L., & Pietrzak, R. (2016). Why are some individuals more resilient than others: The role of social support. *World Psychiatry*, 15(1), 77–79.

Spielmann, N., & Williams, C. (2016). It goes with the territory: Communal leverage as a marketing resource among origin specific firms. *Journal of Business Research*, 69(12), 5636–5643.

Srivastava, A., & Lee, H. (2005). Predicting order and timing of new product moves: The role of top management in corporate entrepreneurship. *Journal of Business Venturing*, 20(4), 459–481.

Staw, B.M., Sandelands, L.E., & Dutton, J.E. (1981). Threat rigidity effects in organizational behavior: A multilevel analysis. *Administrative Science Quarterly*, 26(4), 501–524.

Stephens, J.P., Heaphy, E.D., Carmeli, A., Spreitzer, G.M., & Dutton, J.E. (2013). Relationship quality and virtuousness: Emotional carrying capacity as a source of individual and team resilience. *Journal of Applied Behavioral Science*, 49(1), 13–41.

Sullivan-Taylor, B., & Branicki, L. (2011). Creating resilient SMEs: Why one size might not fit all. *International Journal of Production Research*, 49(18), 5565–5579.

Szreter, S., & Woolcock, M. (2004). Health by association? Social capital, social theory, and the political economy of public health. *International Journal of Epidemiology*, 33(4), 650–667.

Thomas, D.E., Eden, L., Hitt, M. A., & Miller, S.R. (2007). Experience of emerging market firms: The role of cognitive bias in developed market entry and survival. *Management International Review*, 47(6), 845–867.

Thornley, L., Ball, J., Signal, L., Lawson-Te Aho, K., & Rawson, E. (2015). Building community resilience: Learning from the Canterbury earthquakes. *Kotuitui: New Zealand Journal of Social Sciences Online*, 10(1), 23–35.

Thrash, T.M., & Elliot, A.J. (2003). Inspiration as a psychological construct. *Journal of Personality and Social Psychology*, 84(4), 871.

Todt, G., Weiss, M., & Hoegl, M. (2018). Mitigating negative side-effects of innovation project terminations: The role of resilience and social support. *Journal of Product Innovation Management*, 35(4), 518–542.

Toland, J., & Carrigan, D. (2011). Educational psychology and resilience: New concept, new opportunities. *School Psychology International*, 32, 95–106.

Ungar, M. (2008). Resilience across cultures. *British Journal of Social Work*, 38, 218–235.

Ungar, M., Brown, M., Liebenberg, L., & Othman, R. (2007). Unique pathways to resilience across cultures. *Adolescence*, 42(166), 287–310.

van der Vegt, G.S., Essens, P., Wahlstrøm, M., & George, G. (2015). Managing risk and resilience. From the Editors. *Academy of Management Journal*, 58(4), 971–980.

von Bertalanffy, L. (1950). The theory of open systems in physics and biology. *Science*, 111(2872), 23–29.

Wedawatta, G., Ingirige, B., & Amaratunga, D. (2010). Building up resilience of construction sector SMEs and their supply chains to extreme weather events. *International Journal of Strategic Property Management*, 14(4), 362–375.

Weick, K.E., & Roberts, K.H. (1993). Collective mind in organizations: Heedful interrelating on flight decks. *Administrative Science Quarterly*, 38(3), 357–381.

Weick, K.E., & Sutcliffe, K.M. (2001). *Managing the unexpected* (vol. 9). San Francisco: Jossey-Bass.

Weick, K.E., & Sutcliffe, K.M. (2006). Mindfulness and the quality of organizational attention. *Organization Science*, 17(4), 514–524.

Welsh, M. (2014). Resilience and responsibility: governing uncertainty in a complex world. *Geographical Journal*, 180(1), 15–26.

Wieland, A., & Wallenburg, C.M. (2013). The influence of relational competencies on supply chain resilience: A relational view. *International Journal of Physical Distribution & Logistics Management*, 43(4), 300–320.

Williams, C. (2018). *Venturing in international firms: Contexts and cases in a high-tech world*. Abingdon, UK: Routledge.

Williams, C. (2019). *Management consultancy for innovation*. Abingdon, UK: Routledge.

Williams, C., & Du, J. (2014). The impact of trust and local learning on the innovative performance of MNE subsidiaries in China. *Asia Pacific Journal of Management*, 31(4): 973–996.

Williams, C. & Lee, S.H. (2009). International management, political arena, and dispersed entrepreneurship in the MNC. *Journal of World Business*, 44(3), 287–299.

Williams, C., & Lee, S.H. (2016). Knowledge flows in the emerging market MNC: The role of subsidiary HRM practices. *International Business Review*, 25(1), 233–243.

Williams, C., & Martinez, C.A. (2012). Government effectiveness, the global financial crisis, and multinational enterprise internationalization. *Journal of International Marketing*, 20(3), 65–78.

Williams, C., & Vrabie, A. (2018). Host country R&D determinants of MNE entry strategy: A study of ownership in the automobile industry. *Research Policy*, 47(2), 474–486.

Williams, C., & You, J. (2018). Building resilience in client organizations: The consultant's challenge. *Management Consulting Journal*, 2: 10–12.

Williams, C., Colovic, A., & Zhu, J. (2017). Integration-responsiveness, local hires and subsidiary performance amidst turbulence: Insights from a survey of Chinese subsidiaries. *Journal of World Business*, 52(6), 842–853.

Williams, C., Du, J., & Zhang, H. (2020). International orientation of Chinese internet SMEs: Direct and indirect effects of foreign and indigenous social networking site use. *Journal of World Business*, 55(3), https://doi.org/10.1016/j.jwb.2019.101051.

Williams, C., You, J.J., & Joshua, K. (2020). Small-business resilience in a remote tourist destination: Exploring close relationship capabilities on the island of St Helena. *Journal of Sustainable Tourism*, 28(7), 937–955.

Williams, T.A., Gruber, D.A., Sutcliffe, K.M., Shepherd, D.A., & Zhao, E.Y. (2017). Organizational response to adversity: Fusing crisis management and resilience research streams. *Academy of Management Annals*, 11(2), 733–769.

Winfield, L.F. (1991). Resilience, schooling, and development in African-American youth: A conceptual framework. *Education and Urban Society*, 24, 5–14.

You, J.J., Vu, M.C., & Williams, C. (2021). Building skillful resilience amid uncertainty. In S.H. Park, M.A. Gonzalez-Perez and D.E. Floriani (eds), *The Palgrave Handbook of Corporate Sustainability in the Digital Era*. London: Palgrave-MacMillan.

Young, K.L., & Park, S.H. (2013). Regulatory opportunism: Cross-national patterns in national banking regulatory responses following the global financial crisis. *Public Administration*, 91(3), 561–581.

Zajac, E.J., & Kraatz, M.S. (1993). A diametric forces model of strategic change: Assessing the antecedents and consequences of restructuring in the higher education industry. *Strategic Management Journal*, 14(S1), 83–102.

Zhu, J., & Ruth, M. (2013). Exploring the resilience of industrial ecosystems. *Journal of Environmental Management*, 122, 65–75.

INDEX

Numbers in *italics* refer to figures and numbers in **bold** refer to tables.

For Product Safety Concerns and Information please contact our EU
representative GPSR@taylorandfrancis.com
Taylor & Francis Verlag GmbH, Kaufingerstraße 24, 80331 München, Germany

www.ingramcontent.com/pod-product-compliance
Lightning Source LLC
LaVergne TN
LVHW021119300926
849160LV00010B/784
* 9 7 8 0 3 6 7 6 8 0 4 5 9 *